NORMA LEE

*Normally one wouldn't conquer life
in such an extraordinary way.*

DEBBIE DRAYTON

Scriptures taken from the Holy Bible, New International Version®, NIV®. Copyright © 1973, 1978, 1984, 2011 by Biblica, Inc.™ Used by permission of Zondervan. All rights reserved worldwide. www.zondervan.com The "NIV" and "New International Version" are trademarks registered in the United States Patent and Trademark Office by Biblica, Inc.™

LifeRich Publishing is a registered trademark of The Reader's Digest Association, Inc.

LifeRich Publishing books may be ordered through booksellers or by contacting:

LifeRich Publishing
1663 Liberty Drive
Bloomington, IN 47403
www.liferichpublishing.com
1 (888) 238-8637

Because of the dynamic nature of the Internet, any web addresses or links contained in this book may have changed since publication and may no longer be valid. The views expressed in this work are solely those of the author and do not necessarily reflect the views of the publisher, and the publisher hereby disclaims any responsibility for them.

Any people depicted in stock imagery provided by Getty Images are models, and such images are being used for illustrative purposes only. Certain stock imagery © Getty Images.

ISBN: 978-1-4897-1832-7 (sc)
ISBN: 978-1-4897-1831-0 (e)

Library of Congress Control Number: 2018950277

Print information available on the last page.

LifeRich Publishing rev. date: 09/06/2018

NORMA LEE

TABLE OF CONTENTS

DEDICATION

This book is dedicated to my husband, who supported me in taking a year off from teaching to focus on my brother, Larry, who had just been diagnosed with Alzheimer's. Little did I know a book would come out of that time. Larry passed away January, 31st 2010.

I also want to dedicate this book to my sister and brothers. The experiences in our growing years were rich, unique and creative, and God's hand was in it all the way. Thanks for the laughs, tears together and communication invested to allow me to handle the often-stressful circumstances surrounding our unusual family dynamics.

Acknowledgements

I want to thank the late Norma Combs who taught me what it meant to work hard, persevere and deal with the trials and blessings of life. The example she laid before me was powerful! Thank you mom that you wrote your thoughts down– day in and day out– over a span of numerous years. I felt your joys and pain as I read through the bountiful pages.

I'm grateful to God for changing me through circumstances and a learning environment that brought rich blessings even though they were not always appreciated at the time.

Thank you to friends and family who read this book when in its early stages, very raw. Not an easy task!

Thank you Becky Raabe for spending hours of your own time in editing and revising and out of the kindness of your heart, made sure you encouraged me to keep going with this endeavor.

Thank you to brother Dave for your persistence in making sure everyone living at the 5th Ave home truly understood what it meant to have a relationship with God.

Thank you to the Little family who provided an unbelievable friendship. The numerous refreshing and enjoyable gatherings were exactly what the Combs' family needed. I often thank God that YOU were the family who lived in that house down the street. We became better people because of you.

Thank you to all those compassionate and hard-working people who have contributed to Marc Community Resources throughout the years and who have made it the astounding organization it is today. You are true heros!

To Randy Gray who gives so much of his life to the cause. Your love, passion and understanding became obvious through your actions.

Laura,

May you be blessed and inspired as you read the pages of this book — realizing, as I did, the ultimate plan of God. I loved how so (especially) at Church of Redeemer) were friends of Harry. Thanks for being a part of that. I have great memories of our times together — Remember "Life?" So many laughs together!

May God Bless you (and heal you)

ENJOY DeAnn Drayton

INTRODUCTION

Norma Lee Harrold/Combs' unfolding of life wasn't what she planned or expected!

In the 1949 she married Allen Combs, the man of her dreams. They started a family and a life of many promises. What they didn't know until six months after the birth of their second-born, was that Larry had Mental Retardation and labeled, at the time, "Mongoloid."

In those days society's answer to providing for children like their son, was to place them in an institution and away from the mainstream of humanity: to let someone else take care of for this 'ill-finished' child while remaining inside the walls of a designated building.

"It is best for the child and for all involved to be away from the siblings and the flow of life," she was told over and over.

Norma was determined to change this way of thinking and to raise her child at home. As a result, and in collaboration with other families who felt the same way, 1957 Marc School was born. Marc Community Resources continues to thrive. Recently named 6th largest nonprofit human services provider in Arizona, Marc has over 80 sites in the state and serves an excess of 14,00 people each year and growing.

As you read the pages of this book you will experience and understand the fighter that Norma became. She was willing to research, read, ask questions, get to know the right people, have pertinent conversations and highlight needed change. She spent hours writing letters, journaling, making phone calls, contributed lots of ideas, attend numerous meetings and continually stirred the pot by making others aware and accountable. The true benefit was that Norma had lots of energy and could accomplish much in a day.

Still, both her and Allen didn't realize what an uphill battle this life would bring and at some points along the way, this reality nearly broke their marriage (as well as other stressful factors)

The family learned to invest in humor, creative activities and music to sustain the sometimes heartaches that came with the many and varied attention-getting behaviors of one family member. But it was the complete reliance on God, friends and even a church family that truly became their mainstay.

This book spans 6 decades of progress toward the disabled in the fast growing city of Mesa, Arizona.

It demonstrates and identifies the numerous struggles families with special needs encounter on a daily basis.

Circumstances may differ, disabilities vary greatly, reactions can change but the same story line runs throughout.

THE BIG MOVE -1955/
FLASHBACK TO 1953

The new tires of the dark green sedan screeched up along the concrete curb. Two black numbers had been carefully painted on top of the white cement that cornered up against the black asphalt. Norma Lee took a mirror out of her purse sitting on the car floor and checked the small amount of makeup near her eyes, carefully stroking her bottom lash and pressing her lips together, savoring what little lipstick she had left. Now clasping the compact, she turned her head toward the front of the small but quaint building. It would be their new temporary home, her heart filled up with mixed emotions. She looked at her husband sitting behind the steering wheel and watched him put the gearshift into park. He rested his hands on the large circle and exhaled.

"Well this is it!" he proclaimed with a half smile, "A place where it never snows! What do you think?" Glancing back at his little girl, her soft blond curls set carefully on her shoulders and her short legs sticking straight out.

"But I like snow, Daddy." She replied.

He looked back again, this time to catch her expression and hoping the worries were concealed behind his caring eyes.

"Oh, you'll get use to not having snow, I'm sure. It means you will be able to play outside more. Remember how long it takes to get ready, all those extra clothes you have to put on? Well, you don't have to worry about that anymore." Opening the driver's door and stepping out onto the street, he continued. "You won't even need snow pants." He swung the passenger door out, tugged on his daughter's small hand and gave her a boost off the seat. Speaking with confidence to his little girl, his mind was preoccupied with doubts. Will she make new friends? What are people like around here? Will they accept her and her brother? She is so far from her grandparents. What about schools? And ultimately, did they make the right decision by coming to a new state? He hoped for the best, but the many questions weighed heavy.

Linda let go of her daddy's hand and skipped toward the yard. Allen walked around the car and pulled the handle, opening the opposite door. Norma slowly cracked her door, pulling herself up and stretching her legs; she remained quiet. Allen's eyes then met the eyes of his one-year-old boy. Little "Poody's" finger was planted in the side of his mouth, chewing on it as he often did for contentment.

He rocked back and forth and made a humming noise even as his daddy picked him up. Allen couldn't help but give him a kiss on his chubby chapped cheek and whisper in his ear while reaching in his back pocket. He pulled out his handy white handkerchief, now for the fourth time today, and wiped Larry Allen's crusty nose.

It was 1955, a January day here in this new town where it was not cold, but chilly. A few small weeds pushed their way up through the cracks along the wide sidewalk; outlining the front yard of dry Bermuda grass. The small dwelling in this curious neighborhood stood out with yellow shutters around the large front window and a screen door trimmed in an even brighter yellow.

Norma and Allen looked down the street and stared at the massive and stately building dominating their view. The grounds were meticulously landscaped with a wrought iron fence maintaining the necessary privacy. Tall palm trees bent slightly toward the massive two stories of concrete. They couldn't see it from the outside; especially looking on from the back, but Norma knew from the pictures that it had been designed around a grand staircase leading to the Celestial Room. The eggshell-colored terracotta tiles and the front as well as side glass doors of the temple, overlooked a cactus garden and large reflection pool.[1]

First impressions told this young family that those in the neighborhood cared and took pride in their land. She knew that these ample streets around the popular building would give way to lots of traffic and she hoped the public would observe the residential speed limit signs.

"What a change this will be." Norma said under her breath, while peeling off the heavy rose-colored winter coat she "just had to" bring. Now beginning to stroll toward the front door, she was feeling a little hesitant to look inside their modest future living space. *The lives of everyone in this family will be changing,* she thought, as she turned to watch her light-haired daughter twirling in circles and falling to the soft, cushioned earth. Oh, how Norma longed for such a carefree life again. She was beginning to realize things just weren't the way they used to be and more challenges could be just around the corner.

Her mind raced back to the year before . . .

The labor pains were intense. It felt like it had been days not hours, lying in the narrow hospital bed with glossy white walls glaring at her. As the doctor pulled her baby boy from her body, she heard nothing but silence in what was only seconds frozen in time. Larry Allen's body was blue and he took his time catching his breath to scream that lung-filling cry every parent longs to hear. The two nurses scurried like rats measuring, cleaning and then wrapping Larry in a warm white flannel blanket to mimic the comfort of the womb. They said nothing but smiled the same smile they kept for all deliveries in the small town of Gillette, Wyoming. Norma closed her eyes and fell asleep with a prayer on her lips thanking God that all went well.

Hours later she slowly stretched and grinned at her husband who was sitting next to her bed. The wrinkled forehead on his clean and youthful face made it clear that he was concerned.

"When can I hold my baby?" she questioned.

"He's in the incubator," Allen replied.

"Can I hold him?" Norma repeated.

A stern voice answered from across the room. "He had a slow start. He has to be in the incubator until certain times."

Norma angled her head up to see an older stone-faced nurse making the bed a few feet away. She wore the required all-white attire. The cap pinned to the top of her gray hair accentuated her knee-length shift-type dress. She was focused and hardly looked at the couple, going about her business and pulling the sheet from the corners. Norma couldn't quite make out the lack of expression on the woman's face.

"So when can I hold my baby?" Norma was determined and hoped for a different answer.

"When the doctor gives the order!" the nurse barked while storming through the doorway.

Finally the moment had arrived. Sitting up in bed and fluffing the pillows under her arms, Norma opened her hands to cuddle her second born. Allen extended the tiny body toward her, this time wrapped tight in a boy-blue blanket. She looked into Allen's crystal eyes, his sandy straight hair combed back and full lips tightened as he handed little Larry to her. It scared her when he was more quiet than usual.

"He must be put back into the incubator very soon," it was a softer voice this time, of a nurse they knew well. Marie was a neighbor and happened to be working that day. She not only helped deliver Larry but was also now available to give Norma the best of care.

Any worry from Marie's statement disappeared while looking into her baby's eyes. She was excited to have a boy after the birth of their daughter four years earlier. She noticed his stubby little fingers, unlike Linda's newborn hands. And, while slowly tugging at the blanket, to look at all the perfect digits on his feet, her jaw dropped! The look of disappointment was apparent. His toes were not all lined up in their proper place; the one next to the pinky rode clear up in the middle of the foot. It was obvious they were deformed. She now understood Allen's concentrated look and couldn't wait to talk to the doctor about this concern.

"I'm sure something can be done. I'm definite of that! Some sort of surgery, perhaps." She spoke her thoughts out loud. Taking a deep breath she contemplated her husband's title. He was a different kind of doctor, though he still had the initials in front of his name. Surely he could have some influence in the medical profession, or maybe not- since he believes in a drugless system of treating bodily ailments.

She glanced up at Allen and knew he was disillusioned at the less-than-perfect child they had produced. Pulling tight and re-wrapping the soft blanket around Larry's legs, she said nothing, hoping all her confusion would go away soon. Maybe this was a dream; after all she was still groggy and needed more sleep.

Several days later Allen and Linda wheeled Norma holding Larry out the hospital doors and into the car. The doctor seemed to avoid Norma's questions about Larry's feet. Was I too forward or abrasive about the matter? Maybe I could address it later. She had too much to think about now. Her sore body reminded her of the desire of having enough help once they arrived home. Oh how Norma needed her Mother and wanted only her kind of assistance, but Freda was miles away from Wyoming.

She missed her old stomping grounds there in Kansas where she grew up and even attended college close by in Winfield. How her parents paid for her tuition was still a mystery. They always found a way to provide for her and her siblings, but she was sure it took some sort of grand sacrifice. Her mother was a praying woman and she couldn't wait to talk with her on the phone about Larry's physical condition.

Allen had assured her that between the neighbors and church ladies, meals would be provided. Linda would also be eager to help in her own way. Though no one could take the place of the very one who raised her, Norma had to seize whatever help was offered. Allen would need to work his long hours in order to continue building his chiropractic business and provide for what was now a family of four.

It was a few days later that Marie, her neighbor and delivery nurse told her about Larry's first night.

"It was a little scary and I didn't want you to know this right away, but Larry had an extreme case of asphyxia. They kept him on the artificial respirator for a long time to get him to breathe normally."

In hindsight this explained the quiet doctor and demanding nurse. Norma looked up while folding her hands. "Thank you God that Larry is healthy!" Reaching around Marie's shoulders for a quick squeeze, she smiled, grateful for her discernment . . .

Norma watched Allen swing his little "Poody" onto one hip while fumbling in his pocket to find the silver key and turned it to fit the jagged hole of the knob. As he pushed the door open, she noticed the number 22 on the doorframe and stepped into the square living room. It was furnished with a short, cream-colored couch against one wall and a dark platform rocker angled toward it, setting off the décor. For such a small and cozy area, it still had stairs leading to a basement and the extra space would be available for a college renter. Norma hoped her plans would happen soon for they needed the money to reduce their own monthly rental payment. Resting on the promise of some day owning their own place, she patted her husband's shoulder.

"Not bad, not bad at all," her eyes scanned the room.

Allen carefully placed Larry's wiggling body on the colorful rug that was extended over the linoleum floor and tucked under the furniture. The stale smell suggested a previous long vacancy and Norma resolved to open windows before the long task of unpacking.

Moving her hand across her forehead, she let out a sigh, " Whew! We made it!"

CONTINUATION OF FLASHBACK/ MEMORIES-1953

It hadn't been long ago since the newlyweds, Mr. and Mrs. Allen Combs, had looked inside a similar-looking living room in Cheyenne, Wyoming. Norma had been proud of her previous job working for the welfare department in Sedgwick County, Kansas; but then, shortly after their marriage, Allen had started his prestigious work a few states away. She was equally proud, if not more, of the day he and his brother opened the door to their chiropractic office; their names boldly displayed on the small signboard out front. Just months later, the partnership they thought would be a good idea, came to an end. The two doctors couldn't get along and Herbert bailed. They were forced to sell all but a few small pieces of office furniture and had invested hard-earned money to purchase the latest technical equipment. Now they were desperate to unload it. Norma's hidden feelings that the partnership would fail were validated the day she read the Cheyenne newspaper ad stating, "selling next to new equipment purchased for a doctor's office." Thankfully, Dr. Combs was able to buy a fully equipped office several hundred miles away in Gillette. Now another move was necessary . . .

Norma was still fighting the bitterness from the previous journey, and here it was, move number three. How is it that we keep traveling farther and farther away from family? She remembered the assurance Allen had given her of visiting relatives as often as possible and she hung on every word. This is the exact time when extended family should be close by: Two children and now another one on the way. Will our kids ever really know the aunts, uncles and grandparents the way they should? The future was now Norma's friend, but she couldn't help but ponder the past.

She felt assured they would be in Mesa, Arizona for a long time; they needed the stability. Meeting new people always intrigued her and she was ready to plant her feet in one place. She wanted to finally, "stay put!"

Although Mormonism wasn't their religion, she had heard what nice and giving people they were. Raising her children in a high-moral environment was appealing.

Realistically, she recognized that they were probably the only non-Mormons in the neighborhood, and was curious as to the true acceptance of her unbelieving family, especially living so close to the guarded building and knowing of the importance of the early Mormon settlers.

They had a glance at the nice Pioneer Park while pulling into their neighborhood. She was already anxious to take advantage of this sunny state and could picture the family strolling to the nearby playground. It would be a desired release of energy for the children.

Norma had read about Mesa's history and recalled that it wasn't that long ago when President Roosevelt ordered the Japanese Americans living in the Western states to leave their homes. Mesa's main drag had historical significance for it became the boundary line for the few Japanese who lived on the outskirts of the city and were considered safe in the "security zone." These lucky ones, however, were prohibited from crossing the famous Main Street.[2]

Norma motioned to Allen to get the crib from the trailer they had pulled from Wyoming to their new home in Arizona. Larry was heading towards crankiness and would need a nap after his bottle.

She, too, desired to lie down from the long trip. Traveling with a baby in her tummy, six months along, was nerve-racking. She had tightness in her neck and leftover tension from the winding roads of Jerome: a once thriving mining place, now a ghost town and tourist attraction located in a mountainous area. Maybe things won't be so bad after all. She could easily get used to this lovely weather and was already sensing numerous possibilities. It wasn't a choice now. They had made the "easier said than done" trip and there was no going back. The gap between here and her fond memories of home had just widened. The cherished pictures, letters, scrapbooks, phone calls and her own thoughts were all she had to keep the reminiscing fresh. Unpacking the new camera from the decorated box, she thought of the church people they left behind in Gillette . . .

The light snow didn't detour the friends from coming to the fellowship room that Sunday afternoon. It was Pastor Bill and Alice who planned the surprised going away party and they pulled it off nicely. The looks of adoration from those who benefited from Allen's line of work and had heard the announcement of his business from the "News of the World" on the KFBC radio program, made her feel special. They had received lots of practical gifts that day and undeniably the classic Kodak Brownie camera would be put to good use.

Norma adored the Baptist women in Wyoming and through she felt a momentary emptiness, couldn't wait to find something similar here in Mesa. It wouldn't be long before they would again be a fashionable couple, once Allen got things rolling, that is. She was sure he would become such an important part of the community; imagining, he would also go back to teaching an adult Sunday school class. His gift of public speaking was confirmed the day he gave the message called "The Foremost Commandment" at the First Baptist Church. She was filled with delight for the deep, spiritual insights of this quiet man she married.

Unfolding another large box, she found her treasured high school and college memorabilia of scrapbooks and yearbooks . . .

It was the laughs and friendships of those on the speech and debate team in high school that kept life so basic. She was a flirt and thought every guy was attractive, though she had a steady boyfriend with a swell car. Her free spirit led her to cheerleading, choir, and acting in plays from time to time. Opportunities were abundant and she was fearless!

In her college years she was named Moundbuilder queen and given a seat of honor along with a full page in the yearbook. Her heart burst with joy when the crown was placed on her head and roses were laid across her folded arms . . .

Closing the book and glaring into the distance, she contemplated how it was that life could spin out of control. This is not how it's supposed to be. Her responsibilities were more intense than she ever imaged and life had taken unforeseeable turns.

Now climbing onto the newly put together bed, she lay on her side, and rested her head on top of her extended arm. Slowly, she closed her eyes and rubbed her protruding belly. Although she was comfortable, her rigid face verified the thoughts of that ghastly windy Wyoming day, a year and a half ago .

CHAPTER 3

CONTINUATION OF FLASHBACK/ HUFFING AND PUFFING-1954

Norma stood to open the door. She shifted her baby to one side, squeezed the knob and pulled the door wide, inviting her neighbor in. She had lots to do that day, but could always take time for her friend.

Sipping the hot coffee just served to her, Marie hesitantly made a suggestion to have the doctor check Larry.

"What do you mean?"

Marie paused to wring her hands. "I don't know, Norma, it's just that there may be some problems."

"What kind of problems?" Norma's voice got louder.

Marie looked into Norma's eyes. "Don't you think something might be wrong?" She tried to say it as gently as possible, but apparently not gentle enough.

Norma jumped from her chair and told Marie she needed to get back to her ironing. Huffing, she stomped toward the door. "He is perfectly fine! Dr. Joe will confirm it soon, I take him for his six month check-up next week"

Marie slowly set the cup in the saucer and stood, giving Norma a sorrowful look. It was very clear this topic was too sensitive.

"Bye Marie!" Norma's harsh farewell and abrupt closing of the door confirmed the frustration she felt.

"Ahhhhh!!" she muttered. "The gall of that woman! Ahh!"

Norma considered Marie a good neighbor, but today was different! She began to pace the floor, anxious for Allen to arrive. Blowing off steam was always helpful for her and her husband was a good sounding board. When he arrived home, he quietly listened. It seemed this time his silence suggested that Marie might be right. She wanted him to tell her that maybe her friend didn't know what she was talking about and was just being a busybody. Don't listen to her, she wished he would say.

"Of course Marie is a nurse," Norma's voice softened.

"Yeah," Allen replied.

"She works closely with the doctor, maybe she knows something we don't."

"Yeah," he agreed again.

"But the nerve! I tell you! Who does she think she is," spewing her thoughts louder.

Taking a deep breath Allen tried to speak.

"I wish she'd mind her own business!" Norma kept going. "Why would she say such a thing? I can't believe it!" She continued and Allen patiently waited." I mean that takes a lot of nerve! Don't you think?"

Maintaining stillness, Allen watched her pace. "If there was anything wrong, I'm sure the doctor would have said something!" finally able to squeeze in his opinion. "Let's just wait and see," he continued using a soothing tone. "Talk to the doctor next week and don't worry about it till then."

"I certainly didn't need that today! The nerve! Ahhh!"

He realized she wasn't even listening and attempted again to calm her, "You may be getting all worked up over nothing, just wait and see."

Norma didn't respond but grumbled under her breath while cleaning the kitchen table, using wide strokes as she wiped the surface.

Hours later her bad mood softened, "I guess I do need to stop worrying, but the timing of all this, the timing . . ."

Only last week Norma had gotten word of her mother's breast cancer. "Don't worry, honey," her mother's voice confident, "The doctors are sure they can get it all by removing the left breast."

It scared her to think of her own mother under the knife. How will she cope? How long will it take to recover and could her dad take good care of her? Oh how she wanted to be there with her.

Norma stared at her husband as she sorted through her jumbled thoughts and possible solutions. "I think it's just too complicated to figure out any kind of babysitter situation."

"Besides, we don't have the money for you to go," he replied.

After talking with her brother Donny on the phone, she was reassured and relieved to know a family arrangement, was in place. "Well at least my sister and brothers will be available and ready to give support, especially for dad," she said as she hung up the phone.

Her request to God was not only to get her mother through this awful nightmare and heal her body quickly, but also to take care of her dad and lessen the concerns she knew he would hide. . . .

In 1933, eight-year-old Norma also lay in a hospital bed. The praying faces of her parents were etched in her memory. The one headlight on that model A Coupe was not in her vision that day as she ran across the dusty country road- the car struck her body and tossed her several feet away, both legs were broken. It would take months before she taught herself to walk again but she knew it was the prayers of her parents that got her through such a painful trial. Now it was her turn to do the praying.

As the sun set, Norma speculated on the morning conversation. She had finally concluded that Marie was not the villain and she understood those piercing words were just a result of a concerned friend. It would be only a matter of time before she could prove that her neighbor, friend and Larry's nurse was completely and utterly well, just plain wrong!

Continuation of Flashback/Revelation

There was absolutely no way on earth I would even consider putting my own flesh and blood in an institution. I don't care what's wrong with him! How can a person even suggest this, the spineless doctor who wouldn't tell me there was a problem in the first place? He knew it all along, what a wimp! I'll change doctors; that's what I'll do! Maybe he doesn't know what he's talking about, after all he's just a small town doctor. I could go somewhere else, to a bigger city perhaps.

She couldn't pay attention to the drive home and by the time she pulled into their parking spot, didn't remember turning the corners to get there. Using deliberate force she pushed the column shift lever into park and felt her stomach rise to her throat. Her body weakened. A quick turn of the knob for air, she frowned towards Larry still sleeping on the seat next to her. Her head felt heavy and she had to lay it against her arm, pressed across the steering wheel. It was nausea that was keeping her body still and the need to gain composure. The anguish was unbearable as she played those awful words again in her head.

"His expression is a great deal like that of a mentally retarded patient I had," he said. Everything suddenly moved in slow motion after that and all she could do was to stare at the doctor's mouth. "Mentally Retarded individuals are very difficult to raise without help from an institution." The words cut deep. She just needed to leave. She had to get out! With haste, she grabbed her things and scuttled out the office door.

Bursting into tears once again, this time she held nothing back. The pain welled up from her gut. This grave, ill feeling was all too familiar.

Before she met Allen she was so in love with Forest, a ministerial student in college. They were nineteen and engaged to be married. He was the typical tall, dark and handsome man. Her friends were so happy for the two and even a little jealous. He went in for a supposedly minor operation to make him draft-ready. . .the shock of his death was devastating. Within minutes her life was completely altered and it took weeks before she could or would talk to anyone. She had never felt such desperation and helplessness. Surely she could not endure the death of the man of her dreams.

The words of her good college friend, Ginny, brought some assurance. She displayed her steadfast friendship as she encouraged Norma to carrying on. They spent time praying and reading scripture together and many months later Norma picked herself up and tackled the life she once knew, only with trepidation; careful and always aware of not to taking any relationships for granted.

Ginny was right, God would once again bless her life. She fell face-down in love with Allen, thinking of the day she saw the dazzling innocent man in Navy uniform; thin, blond hair and a melting smile. A friend introduced them, and by no accident. God had blessed her with such a patient, soft-spoken and timid young man. He studied the Bible and assured her of his deep faith in God. Their strengths complimented each other and there was no doubt that he was to be her life long-partner but now... Supposedly, we have produced a retarded child together? How could this be? Well I'm not going to have it- no sir ree! I'll figure out what the true problem is and fight it to the end! God is just testing me! I know it.

Wiping the hot tears from her face, she needed more time before going inside the apartment. Unsure of how Allen would handle the news, she wanted to display at least some strength herself.

Inspecting her puffy eyes in the rear-view mirror, Norma settled her look. It happened again, she couldn't help herself, her eyes watered and her thoughts questioned this supposedly well-educated doctor she previously trusted. Did he tell me the right things to do during pregnancy? I ate lots of fruits and vegetables, tried to exercise. Why would this happen? Did I take something during pregnancy that I shouldn't have? How could this be? Maybe this is my fault. Who knows, maybe this is hereditary. Is this passed down from my family or even Allen's family? How dare Dr. Joe put me through this? Who does he think he is anyway I'll get another doctor to tell me everything is fine and then we'll see what he says about that! Besides such appalling news, he had the nerve to give me a list of what he called "good institutions." *Grabbing the paper from the beige dashboard she crumbled it into a tight ball and threw it to the back seat.* Let someone else raise my child? I can't believe he would say such a horrible thing! **It just hit her.** If he would have been up-front and honest from the beginning maybe I could have avoided all the funny looks! *Her chest tightened. Recent conversations with friends permeated her thoughts.* It is a mystery that no one ever said, Larry has your nose or he looks like Allen. Am I the only one that didn't know or didn' see it? He does have unique features. *Her head tilted towards Larry's sleeping body again. She glared at his peaceful look and opened mouth: small nose, small eyes, and wide tongue.* It's true, he may have a slightly different look about him but still friends' have oooed and awed over his pretty face.

Checking the side mirror, her glimpse of Allen walking up the breezeway toward the car, Linda skipping behind him, caused her to pull another tissue from the bag. She hurried to pat the wetness from her distended face.

Allen quickly glanced at his wife and opened the passenger door. He picked up his son and gently cradled him while his hands draped the blanket. Norma watched him kiss their baby's forehead and avoid eye contact with her.

Linda walked around to her mother's window. Norma slowly rolled it down and swallowed big.

"Hi Mommy!" Her smile suddenly straightened. "What's wrong mommy?"

"Oh nothing, honey," she opened the door, and pulled the diaper bag to carry.

Once inside, Allen put his sleeping boy in the crib and whooshed Linda onto the living room floor with a few toys. Norma loved Allen's compassion and strong interest in their children. He always knew how to comfort and redirect their daughter.

She understood he was aware of the bad news and horrible morning she experienced but they had to wait for the right time for discussion.

Entering the bedroom, she swiftly shut the door and flung herself on the bed with a pillow to her mouth, muffling the loud cry. This time she bargained with God.

Are we being punished? I will do anything. What do you want me to do? Please, God Help me! Feeling an urge to scream, she buried her face deeper.

Allen decided to put one of his clear, red records on the record player. He placed the needle at the edge of the large disc and gestured for Linda to sing along. "Cooool, clear, water, water," He looked at his daughter and sang, but Linda was not interested and walked towards the closed bedroom door.

"Let your mommy sleep, she's tired" Allen pried her tiny hands off the knob. Linda whined and squeezed tighter. Looking down at her pouting face, Allen immediately became attentive to his daughter's needs. After all Norma had been gone a long time and it seemed Linda was feeling the separation as well as the tension.

Suddenly, the door flung open and Norma quickly pulled her daughter towards her, gulping back her tears and using her sweet voice, "Isn't it about time for your nap, honey?" Linda tilted her head down while rubbing her eyes.

Norma put her arm around her daughter's shoulders and the two paced towards the pale green room across the hallway. Careful not to wake the baby, Norma reached for a couple of small books and pulled them off the shelf. They positioned their bodies on the bed pillows and opened the pages of Linda's favorite story. Norma heard the car pull away outside the window and knew Allen was leaving. What a strange way to handle bad news…take off? It was quite opposite of her reaction to tough situations. Oh how she needed to talk about it. How could he be so insensitive?

It was in learning of Allen's upbringing shortly after the wedding, that Norma better understood his suppression of emotions. Any information had to come from other family members and even then she couldn't quite get the full picture. She remembered Allen's sister allude to the instability of a constant back and forth separations of their parents. "Divorce was not even in ones' vocabulary in those days and counseling was unheard of, so they split for a while, back together, split again, several times" Mabelle revealed. "Mom and dad threatened each other of taking the kids; so it was back and forth for the four of us. We almost anticipated a kidnapping situation from the other parent and pretty much lived in fear for lots of years."

"What a terrible thing to do to your children!" Norma was disgusted.

Allen refused to talk about it when she tried to bring it up in previous conversations. He deliberately changed the subject. She wondered about the impact of his fears and if it would penetrate their marriage, but she would gladly counsel him through the process.

"What did the squirrel say mommy?" Linda pulled her mother's face towards her. Norma relaxed her body and continued reading.

CHAPTER 5

CONTINUATION OF FLASHBACK/IRONY

Did she ever know anyone with mental retardation? Of course not! They were locked inside institutions all over the country, Norma thought back to a short film she viewed in college. Her degree was in social work from Southwestern Methodist College in Kansas, and therefore the study of various societies required an overview.

She recollected one particular institution scene: the dirty faces, children in cribs and tied to their beds, crying out of desperation, no one to hug or hold, and older children sat in corners alone waiting for food. The ratio of staff to children was outrageously low and she remembered squirming in her chair while noticing others in her class doing the same. She was highly affected at the time by those oppressed children, but they were far removed from her . . . until now.

Norma and Allen spent the next several days in solitude, often staring at their son in deep thought. Allen sensed a problem all along, he concluded, but of what magnitude he wasn't sure.

"And you didn't say anything?" Norma picked Larry up from the crib.

"I don't know. Guess I thought it was my imagination." he replied.

She turned to study her husband's expression, realizing he often relied on her confidence. Carrying her son into the living room, Allen followed. The bounce was gone from her walk. She was exasperated. "What a week!" shaking her head. The two had dialoged frequently the last few days. She did most of the talking, and Allen considered her words. But now she just wanted to go about business as usual and rest her sleep-deprived body.

"Man cannot read another man's mind by the expression on his face." Allen suddenly blurted out of now where. He slid to the floor toward Larry and shook a rattle over his head. Larry kicked his feet and smiled.

"The irony. . . we are so sad and he is so happy." She replied. Norma looked at her husband's expression. She loved his square jaw and high cheekbones and viewed the love aimed at their son. Gently shaking Larry's tummy back and forth, she watched Allen arouse a playful boy. Larry giggled. He had an adorable look. Linda paused from her play and turned to watch. The three chuckled, realizing that it felt good to finally laugh.

Allen made an announcement that day! "He's a Poody! That's what he is, a Poody boy!"

Despite her mother's recent triumph over surgery, Freda wasn't out of the woods yet. Norma concluded not to bother her parents of her recent news. Her dad called to report the success of the removal of cancer and Norma was proud of herself, keeping control until she hung up. Often she broke into tears while locking the phone in place, but as far as her parents knew . . .things were great in the Combs household.

The couple was still determined to get a second opinion and now the goal was to take a recommended trip to Colorado. The Children's Hospital was well known for its professional staff. What a relief! She was desperate to talk with competent medical people who hopefully would give a more positive diagnosis, but this meant she would need to write her sister who lived close to their destination, requesting a few nights stay.

Her hand shook as she wrote the word "retarded" on paper, knowing her sister would be distraught reading such a dreadful label. She begged Marjory not to pass the information on to their parents. "I will contact mother's doctor and get his opinion concerning the right time to tell her, but for now please don't say a word."

Ginny also lived in Colorado and Norma desired to connect with her long time friend and college roommate. Since those memory-building days, the two made sure they kept in touch through letters, phone calls and occasional visit.

"Making this into a family vacation would at least shed some positive light on the trip." She announced while opening the calendar. Allen agreed and now another letter had to be written. "Could your husband take the time to baptize Larry while we are there? She was proud of Ginny having married a Methodist minister and thought this would be a favorable time to visibly dedicate their second born to God. The plans were in place and preparing brought a wave of much needed excitement.

They hardly had time, however, to process a new problem. What would they tell their friends? How would they pacify the inevitable questions about their son? Established relationships in a small town meant news traveled fast; and often exaggerated, if not incorrect. Norma had already been aware of the stares toward Larry while buying groceries or running errands at various places in the community. Church was not much better. No one knew how to react to a rare situation. New evils were intruding the mix; embarrassment, gossip, rumors, curious looks and standoffish people. Phone calls came and the couple began to uncover genuine friendships. Do they really care or do they possess an inward judgmental attitude, as if **I** did something wrong? *Norma wondered. She noticed the glaring was not only at Larry, but aimed at her as well. Sundays were the toughest, for church used to be a refuge place-not now.*

She was determined to talk to Dr. Joe when she saw him sitting in the pew several rows in front of her one Sunday morning. Before he disappeared after the service, she held Larry in her arms and mustered up the courage to corner him in confrontation. With boldness, she spoke her mind. He demonstrated embarrassment and yet compassion towards her situation. Though she really didn't listen to his response, it was liberating to get the anger off her chest. How many times had they seen each other at church during the past six months and he remained closed mouth? I certainly don't respect this man the way I used to, *Norma thought.*

Marie had pulled her aside in the restroom just minutes before and privately, with tears streaming down her face, asked Norma's forgiveness for not telling her sooner of Larry's full condition.

"Well, Marie, at least we had six months thinking our baby was normal and healthy. Those were happy days!"

"What's wrong?" Allen walked into the kitchen after work one day and focused on his wife sitting hunched over at the table. Norma straightened and looked at her husband: her heart pounding. She opened her mouth but couldn't get the words out. Her eyes were swollen and red. Allen stood behind her, squeezing her shoulder. He asked of Linda's whereabouts and watched his wife point toward the bedroom. He waited for her to catch her breath. Finally, doing her best to control herself, *"I just talked to Helen on the phone. She, (gulping) she said that Mr. and Mrs. Ryan at church said that we, that we, we should have never brought Larry home from the hospital."* She quickly unfolded the ball of tissue in her hand and blew her nose.

"What? We should have never brought him home! What's that supposed to mean?" Allen's face reddened as he slowly sat down. Now looking away and tightened his jaw, he became speechless and hung his head into his opened palm.

CHAPTER 6

BACK TO MESA/ GROWING-1955

Though Mesa wasn't a huge city, it was still large enough to maintain one's own privacy. The freshness of starting over was appealing. They could control the amount of information to tell acquaintances while adjusting into this new life. Neighbors were stopping by with a smile and a welcome over warm cookies. Linda had quickly befriended a few neighborhood girls and they kept entertained outside, allowing Norma to attend to Larry's needs inside. Allen's momentary job selling sewing machines at Singer would suffice for now. It wasn't his final occupation destination but the depletion of funds deemed it necessary. Comfort was setting in.

"I figured out where those chimes we hear everyday are coming from," Allen announced after spending the entire day at the store.

"Where?" Norma listened carefully.

"Downtown. It's large Methodist church"

"Oh, let's go this Sunday!"

"Yep, I stopped in to find out what time the services are." He handed Norma the paper. She studied it, calculating the child morning schedules in her head.

"Oh boy!" her face lifted.

Allen turned toward Linda. "Did you hear that, little girl? We are going to the big Methodist church." He grabbed her hands and swung her around, tossing her to the couch. She picked herself up, chuckled and began bouncing on the cushions, her dad's arms supporting her.

"Oh! Don't do that!" Norma groaned.

Oblivious to her command, Allen watched his daughter's energized body and kept going. Norma hated it when Allen ignored her; but after inspecting the laughter between the two, decided to say no more—this time.

The grandiose A-frame ceiling held the heavy black chains and the magnificent suspended lights. It was the large stained glass window at the front, which gave a holy sanctuary feel and the added balcony in the back made it all seem bigger than life. This massive room held more than 400 people dressed in their Sunday best. Blush blue pews extended in long rows and an intricate mesh of colors within the round stained glass windows along the sidewalls, demanded immediate attention.

Allen and Norma were not used to this kind of church atmosphere, but rather liked it. Just sitting and staring at this magnificent architecture was brilliant enough, however, the powerful words spoken from the minister, doubled the inspiration. Several people had introduced themselves, and although others kept their distance after seeing Larry, by the time they loaded the kids into car, they knew this would be their church home.

They couldn't wait to involve themselves and never missed a Sunday service—except on March 18th when Norma went into labor with their third child, David Harrold, a perfect second boy! They had already established ties with couples of the downtown church and meals were on the way.

Norma had spent time on her knees in prayer during this pregnancy; nervously asking for a physically and mentally healthy child and she felt God had answered her plea. Though she was known for her vigor, now daily washing numerous clothe diapers, chasing Larry's crawling body around the house, and the interrupted sleep attending to her crying newborn was beginning to wear her down. Allen tried to help as often as he could but it seemed the store was starting to own him. Of course big sister wanted to assist, and although it was a challenging task for a small child, Norma left her in charge of the "entertaining Larry" department.

When Norma read the words in her mother-in–law's letter, she exhaled a sigh of relieve. Stella would soon be traveling from Arkansas to visit with the family and lend a hand. Norma would take any kind of help at this point, even if it felt awkward.

Her relationship with her mother-in-law was, at first, uncomfortable but the temporary bonding became a nice surprise. They just focused on the kids. Conversations were only about the children, keeping things light and less "nerve-racking" for all. Though her stay was short, it was helpful.

When the store allowed days off, the couple walked through open houses and negotiated with realtors. The market was steady and there was no question as to needing more space for this growing clan. Now was the time! They had become familiar with Mesa neighborhoods and had already had several discussions with friends about appealing schools.

Norma often questioned her husband about his medical practice, but he appeared unmotivated concerning the subject.

"I don't think I want to pursue the practice. I just don't care for it. I guess it's the idea of being cooped up in an office all day." She overheard him tell a friend.

Lately, she had noticed a generous amount of humor and jokes at the end of a workday and imagined he took delight in selling. She hoped this was only a phase and that he would eventually go back to his first love. In the meantime, Norma was glad to see the humor that attracted her to her spouse in the first place. Becoming conscious of the needed male friendships evolving at his job, she was willing to join him for visits with the Singer families. And, now friendships with other Mesa people were expanding. Although the constant gazing toward Larry did not let up, the true interest of concerned friends at least lifted some humiliation. He was developing at a slow pace, but was happy and content for the most part. Norma entered Larry's accomplishments in his baby book:

"He loves to play peek-a-boo. His attention span was long with one toy and he could entertain himself in his crib for a decent amount of time. He doesn't show very many emotions such as fear, or anger, but seems happy most of the time. He loves to take baths and play in the water and he loves music. He likes his daddy to play his records. He crawls everywhere, always on the move and has lots of energy!"

They soon learned the new house was ready on the other side of town. The Combs family moved into the three bedrooms, one bath home on Fifth Avenue. Linda could have her very own room and decorate it with a frilly pink bedspread and curtains to match. The lush green front yard stretched into the neighbor's area, allowing for a long and spacious lawn while a few flimsy branches of a grand pepper tree slightly hung over the driveway. Two perfect Mulberry shade trees would keep a cool backyard breeze and a row of native oleanders lined the boundary on one side. Behind this tall row of poisonous bushes, spread a spacious dirt field, the size of an entire block. They were living on the outskirts of town and buildings were not yet jamming the view to the newly formed intersection of Stapley and Broadway (4th St.) just yards a way. Young families infiltrated this new and clean neighborhood leaving no lack of playmates for the kids.

Norma bettered herself on journaling every day. She found it became a tension release as well as good old-fashioned therapy. Some days more problematic than others: if she weren't careful, her worries would get the best of her. Upon the rare event of all three children napping at the same time, her desk, squared in the corner of her new bedroom, became the altar of Bible reading and writing. She opened her diary and struggled for the words to record the previous doctor trips from the Gillette home . . .

CHAPTER 7

FLASHBACK TO GILLETTE/
SECOND OPINION- 1954

Silence permeated the vehicle for most of the outing. The hope of a different diagnosis at the Children's Hospital sustained them. Allen couldn't concentrate on his driving and Norma the same on her reading. What came to mind was the memorized Apostles' Creed she knew from her early Methodist years and recited it over and over in her head while gaping at the moving road from the passenger window.

I believe in God the Father Almighty, maker of heaven and earth; And in Jesus Christ his only Son our Lord: who was conceived by the Holy Spirit, born of the Virgin Mary, suffered under Pontius Pilate, was crucified, dead, and buried; the third day he rose from the dead; he descended to the dead. On the third day he rose again; he ascended into heaven, and sitteth at the right hand of God the Father Almighty; from thence he shall come to judge the quick and the dead. I believe in the Holy Spirit, the holy Catholic Church, the communion of saints, the forgiveness of sins, the resurrection of the body, and the life everlasting.[3]Amen.

Nevertheless, their hopes were dashed. Dr. Roberts had confirmed the terrible news and was more brutal than the previous doctor.

"I wish I could tell you something good about your baby, but I can't!" his words severed.

The diagnosis was solidified when the doctor confirmed, "He had the slanted eyes, low bridge nose, slight deformity of the ears, feet and arms, short stubby fingers and toes, and the tongue beginning to protrude. All the characteristics were there. We call it Mongoloid" She looked at her son; Norma could now see Larry's disability more than ever. And so a new term was added to their future vocabulary of hated labels.

Dr. Roberts also said the despised "institution" word. "Once you visit some of these excellent places –namely Lander –250 miles away, your mind will be at ease. It is rated 3rd in the country. They actually have an open house, parent day they call it, coming up," he said.

"My mind will be at ease?! My mind will never be at ease!" She rudely spouted. How in the heck would HE know? Was her silent thought only from biting her tongue. Why, God, did you do this to us? Why us? What of the future? Could we possibly keep Larry with us? I just can't give my

own child to someone else to feed, hold. They probably won't have time to play with him. He won't get the real kind of attention that a child should have. No one can care for MY son the way I can!

Her thoughts went back to a horrific article she recently read about the true goings on inside the institution walls from years past. There just wasn't enough staff to truly care for these children and so they were left alone without toys to play with. The children had no true identity, the article continued. Emotional needs were certainly not met. It was if they could be treated like animals. If a child was sick, they could be left for hours before being attended to. It could mean sleeping in or rolling around in his/her own vomit. She had a difficult time sleeping several nights after reading those words and wondered how accurate it was or if things had truly improved since the article was published. How can he say this is an excellent institution? Does he really know that?

She wanted to break down but again had to maintain as Linda's curiosity was forming. Discussions and grueling decisions would have to be made after her bedtime. At least Allen was there to hear the piercing words himself and they could comfort each other.

"Mongoloid children seldom exceed a mental age of 2 or 3 years old. Life expectancy is from one to fifteen years. Many die within the first year of life. Most have breathing problems and/or a defective heart." He had so many horrible things to say she was glad the nurse in the front office gave to occupying Linda while they were behind closed doors. The doc's words sounded as if he had researched it in depth, but despite the cruel language he gave Norma a hug. Allen sustained a grave expression while staring at the floor and arms folded across his chest.

The only bit of good news came in rare form. "Although Larry got a slow start, he seems to be unusually well physically. Maybe he will live longer than we think. We don't know the cause of this. There are many theories. A wild gene mutation or nature has just made a mistake, but it almost never happens twice in the same family." She could now stop blaming herself and possibly release some guilt as to Larry's condition but 'nature's mistake? Really? Does he realize he is talking about a human being? Does God make mistakes?

The baptism ceremony and most of the socializing took place earlier that week. It worked out well for neither could sort out their thoughts, let alone talk to others about it.

Glancing to the back seat of the vehicle, Linda's Bugs Bunny coloring book sliding off her lap and eyes drooping, Norma broke the silence. "At least I did remember to ask about his constant chest wheezing and did you hear him suggest moving to a place where it's a drier climate? Arizona maybe?"

Allen nodded. "The wet and cold winters might be too much for the respiratory problems associated with Mongolism." He repeated the exact words and continued, "The move would be hard but I say let's do it! I don't like the long winters, anyway." He gazed at the road.

"And you would set up practice in Arizona?" Norma turned her head towards him. He nodded again. Glancing back out the window, Norma chewed over the doctor's words in her head. A sustained hush reentered the vehicle; just the hum of the motor was heard.

They had pressing future decisions to make, ones that could affect them forever. Her heart hurt! She pondered a Henry Ford quote that Allen often recited. "If I find something I cannot handle, I let it handle itself." Oh how I need to believe this! She thought.

CHAPTER 8

CONTINUATION OF FLASHBACK TO GILLETTE/CHURNING EMOTIONS

What really is retardation? Now a quest of feeding their lack of knowledge took place through the public library. She read before sleeping and often woke in the night with the ugly terms on her mind: Mongoloid, idiot, feebleminded, moron. She asked God why Larry couldn't have blindness or cerebral palsy, anything but mental retardation.

Allen read something that made him think there could be certain pressure on the brain, which could be helped by cranial molding. Hope became their mainstay and they had to check all avenues of recovery. In their readings they sought to find a different solution somewhere out there and because they both possessed a determination, giving up was not an option.

The next letter in the mail was from her mother's doctor, giving the okay of her good health. It was now time to unveil the news. Surely it will be troublesome to Norma's beloved parents. She wanted to procrastinate as long as possible but decided it just had to be done, and with pen in hand choose her words carefully.

After discussing the issue with her sister on the phone, they thought it best if her brother and sister-in-law tell their parents personally since they were close in proximity. The task was now in Lee and Laura's hands. They would verbally read the note Norma sent.

The frequent letters and phone calls from family didn't let up for several months. Freda assured her that Larry would be healed and to have faith. After all God had taken away her cancer. She even sent an "anointed" handkerchief through the mail. Lay this on Larry's head, she wrote, and pray for healing. Norma wanted to believe her but the nagging question of "What if?" was haunting. Oh how Norma wished she had her mother's faith.

*The institution subject was beyond her parent's comprehension and another letter from Freda offered a different solution. "Why don't you bring Larry to me and let **me** take care of him. We don't have other children at home and can dedicate our life to his well-being. I could give him just as good as care as anyone else." Norma wasn't sure if this made her feel better or worse, but either way it was beyond a mother and grandmother's duty and the request was a nice gesture.*

Getting used to numerous doctor visits became another piece to this growing complex life-puzzle and the next appointment was at the Crippled Children's Clinic. The subject of his feet wasn't much talked about. Now that the couple was well aware of ALL his other medical issues, it just seemed insignificant in comparison.

They also followed up and fit in the Landers open house. Though they regretted the day they had to step into an institution building, they would at least attend the "parent's day" to conciliate the advice of friends and doctors. The calendar was quickly filling up with Larry appointments. When Norma's parents begged for their daughter and family to visit and even sent prices of inexpensive airline tickets, she wrote back, "It's just out of the question right now, Mother. We have too many out of town engagements. I know it is probably not wise to travel so shortly after surgery but I think if you saw Larry, how sweet and happy he is, it would be a comfort to you. Please come here." Much to her delight, the returning letter announced a visit as soon as the doctor gave the okay for travel.

Norma stayed in close contact with three of her best friends. Conversing with her female companions helped her release the constant inward fretting, but when discussion leaned towards her needing the courage to institutionalize her son, she became angry. They had no idea what they were asking of her! She sometimes sought revenge in her heart; wishing they could feel her pain.

"Norma, even Dr. Spock suggests institutionalization . . .and he's the expert," Her friend then handed her a recent article. Another friend gave her a book by Roy and Dale Evans called "Angels Unaware". Though it was refreshing to read about a couple's relatable up and down life, their Mongoloid child passed in infancy. The thought of Larry dying sent a rush of depression through her blood. "I guess when comparing that situation to having Larry reside in one of those places, I would take the latter," she finally revealed. " It's just so painful to think about or to grasp either one!"

The trip to Crippled Children's Clinic was just slightly easier from previous visits. Dr. Wayman said Larry was only about 3 months behind the average baby but that it did not alter the fact that he is definitely mongloid. "There are varying degrees of mongolism but we know they can never take care of themselves and that early institutional care is recommended. You have to think of the welfare of the child as well as the welfare of the family, especially other normal children in the home. This happens one in every ten thousand births. The improper development of the ill-finished child begins somewhere in about the 16th week of pregnancy." Norma read her notes afterwards. This time she had the sense to write it down and reviewed later all the information thrown at them in such a short time.

The Landers visit was tolerable. "I couldn't believe all the other children who have it much worse than Larry." Norma said upon arriving home.

"Yeah." Allen replied.

She knew her husband couldn't move his thoughts towards Larry being gone, but felt he would possibly have a new perspective from this trip. "What did you think?" she inquired.

"Don't know, have to think about it" was his short answer.

"Well they have really improved the quality of institutions over the years. Don't you think?"

"I suppose."

"It was better than I thought" she kept talking.

"Humm.umm." She watched him gaze into the distance.

There was a brief conversation Norma had with one of the parents during the tour and she knew Allen was listening although he appeared disinterested. She too, didn't like what she was hearing at the time, but now fought to heed the words again. "We find this to be a great place for our child and our only regret is that we didn't place him here sooner." The statement from this sincere stranger confirmed an article she recently read in a magazine. The one they had subscribed to; a well-informed publication.

"I've read a lot about the importance of early institution, most of the material from the Children Limited magazine," breaking the silence again. "It seemed to make at least a little bit of sense." At this point she wasn't sure if she was trying to convince her husband or herself, possibly both.

Allen blinked a few times glimpsed into her eyes and then looked away. Though she was getting impatient and could easily demand his responses, it was evident her husband's grief needed time.

CHAPTER 9

CONTINUATION OF FLASHBACK/ DARKEST HOUR -1954

The couple spent many future nights tossing and turning in bed. Advise was coming from every direction; friends, family, co-workers, medical people. The conversations from the day magnified during sleep. 'Institution' was the buzzword in books and circles of professionals.

Freda's visit was welcomed but even **she** *didn't hold back her forceful opinion. Though not the exact words, Norma knew her mother was telling her she would be literately be giving up on her own child; still fixated on Larry's healing. Norma mounted enough nerve to tell her that often God does not answer our prayers the way we think he should. Throwing her arms in the air, Norma blinked back tears and declared, "I don't know what to believe anymore! It's just too* **overwhelming***!"*

The waiting list was a long one at Landers. They were told that it was okay to put Larry's name down and still have plenty of time, a year perhaps, before having to make the final decision. Norma embarked on the alternative. Sometimes it made her feel ill. She had to write her thoughts...

"This was better than death. Oh Lord if I have to deal with one of these, I'd rather deal with the institution right now. Please don't take my baby away from me completely! Oh God help me in that 11th hour if it is to come when I entrust others more trained in the care of my precious baby Larry. If he is to leave us, I will have to throw myself into much to keep busy. Yesterday I bargained with God although maybe it isn't right. God, I said if you will spare Larry for us I will try to make a better Christian home for him, maybe direct him toward the ministry if he has any desire for that service at all. This afternoon I felt a calmness, a full acceptance of what is to come. It will not be my will, but God's."

At least out of the entire United States, one of the top-notch institutions just happened to be in their home state. They joined the Wyoming Association of Retarded Children, a large and growing organization with other branches in almost all states made up of parents, for the most part, and social workers as well as teachers interested in retarded children all over the nation. They had the opportunity to connect with parents experiencing the same major obstacles and at the same time become educated as to their exclusive situation.

The dreaded task of drawing up the commitment papers was inevitable but knowing they could change their mind later, comforted them. Allen took the job that day and Norma understood that her husband's sorrow was overpowering. She felt his pain as she watched him wipe the wetness under his eye and move the pen along the paper.

Norma paused often throughout the day to observed her daughter engage with her little brother and in her head she questioned the allowance of frequent bonding playtimes between her children. How will Linda understand when her brother doesn't live in our home anymore? How will Allen and I answer her many questions? She too will feel the void and they will have to explain it again and again. A simple young mind will have to adjust without the knowledge and coping skills of an adult. It will surely leave an emotional scar.

"What do I say to her?" she asked Allen. "That babies are like puppies— first you have them and then you don't? I've already cut out the prayer times together before bed unless Linda specifically asks to have Larry in the room and then I say "We have to always pray for Larry no matter where he is."

Though Landers promised frequent visits from the family, some warned against it. "It could really make matters worse for all involved, In fact, the farther away the relatives, sometimes the better."

Norma wrote a solemn letter to her siblings . . ."It seems this to be a wise choice and the best for Larry, so they say. If we actually go through with it, it will surely be the darkest hour in our lives!"

CHAPTER 10

CONTINUATION OF FLASHBACK/
PREPARATIONS

While waiting they subscribed to the Phoenix paper. Studying the weather reports, classified and rental ads, helped switch gears to concentrate on a brighter future.

"We are pretty definite now about Phoenix," she told her mother. "A new chiropractor came to Gillette and the lease is up on our house the first of January, so there is nothing to keep us from going through with it."

"If Larry is going to be in an institution in Wyoming, why are you moving?" Friends and family questioned. It really didn't make sense to anyone, even to Norma and Allen, but the two resided in positive thinking and tried to hold onto a miracle mentality. They answered the curiosity by saying they would take Larry with them and if the dreaded phone call came before leaving they would have to make the decision at that time. It was one of those "cross that bridge when we come to it" answers. For now, it wasn't beyond them to search an Arizona institution as another possibility. After talking with a few doctors, Norma had an address for a place called the Children's Colony. She quickly wrote, requesting information.

At present, the thought of a new start brought a fresh perspective. Beginning again, either with Larry or without, they maintained their hidden dream that their life included the son they loved and were desperate to hold onto.

Reaping the blessings of both children in the back seat, the trailer loaded with a few favorite pieces of furniture, plenty of boxes and Allen's excellent driving skills, they could breath freely for the only institution they heard from before departure was the Colony in Arizona.

"You need to be a state resident for at least three years before we would consider putting Larry on our waiting list, which is 350 children long and is growing daily. I am sure, in the meantime, your Mongoloid child can improve by keeping him at home." Wow! Finally! Words harmonious to their desires! This counsel was welcomed with open arms and a huge sigh of relief, confirming their own convictions. "Your family physician can be a constant reference for questions as to his physical development," the letter continued. Yes! This was the glimmer of hope they urgently needed and the timing was perfect.

Allen had previously mailed the first month's rent for a place near downtown Mesa and was sent the key. It was just a matter of finding their humble abode once they entered their new city. But they didn't realize how close their new residence was to the highly respected and eye-catching building, known to many across the state as the great Mormon Temple.

They had spent several months, prior to moving, to research the origins of this interesting town. The Hohokam Indians were the first to build the original canal system that remained in use. Among the missionaries and explorers in the 1500 and 1600's were Father Kino and Marcos De Niza. In the early 1900's Kit Carson came through the Salt River Valley. And, the first Mormon polygamous settlers were Crismon, Pomeroy, Sirrine and Robson. It was Dr. Chandler who enlarged the Mesa Canal, built the first office complex and started an electric power plant.

Chinese and Japanese immigrants were farmers and business owners. More than 50 percent of residents earned their living either directly or indirectly from farming, mainly citrus and cotton. Falcon field airstrip and Williams air force base were built in l941 to provide training for World War II pilots. The current Population is seventeen thousand.[4]

As the family traveled across state lines to Arizona, Norma's emotions alternated between tearful moments of joy and gloom- but still excited anticipation for the unknown future. She had a strong desire to accomplish much and was thankful for the disciplined life her parents taught her in those early molding years. She knew how to strive for excellence and was even a little surprised at her own accomplishments thus far; yet she sensed a great deal of personal growth still in front of her. Being young and active was to her advantage not discounting the fact that she was full of life and stubborn as an ox! Maybe this is why God chose her! Though she didn't want to, she had to admit there was a bit of honor in it.

CHAPTER 11

BACK TO THE MESA HOME/ THE PHONE CALL

Several months in this warm state was now behind them, they were beginning to hang their hats. The voice on the other end sounded familiar when Norma answered the newly installed black phone located in the hallway cubby of their 5th Ave residence. The person initiating the conversation sounded apologetic concerning the waiting list at Landers in Wyoming. Norma stood feeble as she listened to the forthcoming words.

Larry's name was next for housing... but the organization had since learned the family had moved to Arizona. "It means he would no longer be eligible for care in our building until gaining legal residency in the state you chose to live in. At that time he would again be put on the bottom of the long list and who knows when you will hear from us again-- possibly years."

Though she didn't see this coming, she considered it the answer to their dilemma. Her legs locked as she slowly and deliberately put the receiver in place, tilted her head back, squeezed her eyes shut and proclaimed a thank-you towards the heavens. It was now out of their hands. God was listening and demonstrated His power over the situation. Larry's stay was extensive and open-ended, at least till she heard from the Colony, which also projected placement years down the road. It meant putting a halt to the uncertainties and, without looking back, pressing onward with the life they were handed. She marveled at this day, acknowledging the rhythm of the unfolding tasks of motherhood in the morning to a delightful surprise call that afternoon. Amidst the busyness, God demonstrated His love through a simple phone call.

"You're not going to believe what just happened!" she said nervously opening the door to the carport when Allen pulled the car forward slowly and carefully parked under the hanging tennis ball.

She was anxious and shouted the words she had just heard on the other end of the line. The two paused to hold each other. Allen smiled and acknowledged the great news!

"Let's celebrate! How about I take everyone to get a dilly bar at that new ice-cream place called Dairy Queen?" Two lively children verified their excitement with screams and Norma rushed around to get the youngest baby ready.

David was the only one not able to enjoy the lip-smacking taste of the cold soft treat against the 100-degree weather. Norma knew to get plenty of napkins for Larry but to no avail, for the messy eater gladly put on a public display. He wore the ice cream more than ate it but all that mattered was that he was their son and was in **their** care. They were a family of five; and for now, it would remain so.

The unknowns! Life teetering in silence for too long but today it broke. "Today we heard and can move on." Norma wrote in her journal. "Thank you God for a special answer to a special prayer!"

CHAPTER 12

MILESTONES AND DISCIPLINE 1955/56

Little wonders were taking place at the pleasant surprise of the family. So far, Larry's accomplishments defied the doctors' predictions. "He probably won't walk till he is 2 or 3," they said. She ran to the phone and dialed her parents of the good news. "Larry just took his first step and he is 18 months old, only a few months later from when his older sister walked."

The cutting words of the medical staff were at the forefront of her mind.

"I wish I could tell you something good about your child but I can't"!

"An ill-finished baby"

"Nature's mistake"

What gross and mistakable inaccuracies"! Oh, if they could see him now! She thought. There is no stopping him!

Larry had discovered this new-found mobility that brought additional problems and was now part of the daily routine. Near heart attacks while watching Larry meant family and friends had to always be on their toes. His every move had to be scrutinized. It became a learning process for all. Quickness of feet, viewing him from all angles of a room, following him about the house and yard, and a persistent red alert was in full force. "Larry must have his own guardian angels" Norma expressed to others to retain some needed humor. He climbed anywhere and everywhere. His interest in opening all doorknobs predetermined locks on every potential danger. They knew to arrange furniture to a childproof environment, but still, he could find unsecured situations. If he somehow finagled security to the outside world, he would see it as an open playground without limits. The lack of fear intertwined with the obstinate behavior meant everyone had to be aware of only one person… Poody boy!

Norma cherished the few times she could still sit to hold and rock him, and was thankful he continued to respond to the body contact, though less frequent and for shorter periods of time. He seemed to benefit from hearing his own voice through a flat maintained note, a finger to chew on and a rocking motion while sitting on the couch. It was a self-calming mechanism and became his inner world… an activity he would carry into future years.

The family came to appreciate the silly but entertaining Wallace and Ladmo show (a local Phoenix show for children) on their new Zenith black and white TV. Few things held Larry's attention but this won the prize. It not only kept him quiet for short intervals, but the family played on the humor for future jokes, amusing him. He knew when to laugh, even if he didn't fully understand the funny comebacks. Picking up on some social cues, when the family responded to something humorous, he let out a cutzie giggle for all to enjoy and just watching this perpetuated more laughter from anyone close by.

At least Larry was not in any pain. The doctor said that Mongoloid children are about the happiest people in the world. In fact Larry just didn't cry much. "Yes, he somewhat understands humor and that's wonderful but he sure pushes the limits of patience several times a day when he insists on his own way." Norma said to a close church friend. "Yesterday he climbed on top of our car in the carport. I pulled him down and gave him a swat on the rear-end, he wiggled from my arms and climbed on top of the vehicle again, another spanking. Five times this happened before he got it into that little blond head of his that he's not in charge. I often wonder if he even understands consequences."

The motive of breast-feeding tiny David was strong but unrealistic. Allen needed to help wherever possible and Norma had to let go of the guilt in order to maintain her sanity. It meant she held him less but hoped Allen would spend more time feeding and cuddling their third born. Even six-year old Linda could hold a bottle to a baby's mouth and rock him for short periods of time.

Larry insisted on his mother's attention and it was beginning to take on various forms. "Whew! I can't wait till the day the two boys will be able to occupy each other." Norma said to Allen. "I'm exhausted!" Her enlarged belly held baby number four. Hanging on to any extra dose of forbearance, she was unsure if she had it in her to handle the trials coupled with the blessings of motherhood. This pregnancy was not planned but Linda and Allen put in their request of a baby girl. Frequent comments about a live baby doll became wishful thinking for Linda. Big sister would certainly keep another female busy with girly things and so it was Norma, too, yearned for this to come to pass.

"No more children after this," she made it clear to Allen. The red in his face affirmed awkwardness of such sensitive topics like permanent birth control but she insisted he had to be the one to make sure it happened. "The constant juggling of taking care of three children, one child with great needs and demands requires a super mom some days, in fact most days." She uttered to Allen. She fought to balance her attention with the other two and now with the fourth child on its way, "No more is an absolute must!" She made sure her husband understood her strong opinion. "Sometimes I think Larry is like having two toddlers into one!" Norma vented. "Just when I think I'm making headway around the house, Larry finds something to get into or open. I have to follow him everywhere. Saying the word NO means absolutely nothing to him. He just looks at me with a smile and keeps going. Poody is already learning how to use that little face to his advantage. He can be a real pistol, that boy!"

Allen tried to support her the best way he knew how, but there were certain areas he just wouldn't touch no matter the fuss his wife made.

"You have to help me with the spankings! She demanded. "I can't do it by myself!" Discussions were turning into disagreements concerning the topic of discipline.

Though she wouldn't acknowledge it, Norma secretly recollected the words of another doctor and even friends. "Think of the other children in the home and their needs! Larry will require lots of your time and you are robbing the other children because of it." This judgment became the overbearing reason for suggesting Larry be placed in an institution, but her determination relinquished any weakness and she was more focused than ever to make it work, especially when Debra Sue was born.

FLASHBACK/ SKELETON IN THE CLOSET

It was a Saturday morning, Norma had returned from Southside hospital with the infant baby girl Linda hoped for. A rare moment of solitude was taking place in the house. Her seven-year-old daughter was occupied with a toy tea set and three babies were napping. Norma's to-do list included unpacking the last few boxes still taking up residence on the closet floor of her bedroom. Her goal was to hang the framed wedding photos on the wall once her body healed from childbirth.

Linda walked in the room to "help" her mommy. Putting her index finger to her own lips, Norma motioned for her daughter to whisper for she was basking in the quietness she knew would be short lived.

"Where did you get the buutiful dress?" Linda's toothless mouth distorted her whispered words as she pulled out the first picture from the opened box and carefully handed the glass frame to her mother. The photograph displayed a strikingly beautiful woman in a fitted, floor length ivory-colored gown. Norma reached out both hands to place the large rectangle on her lap and pulling the hand towel off her shoulder, she wiped the dust from the glass. Now clearing the view of this youthful woman she hardly recognized she finally answered her curious little girl.

"I ordered it from a catalog," beginning to enjoy their time together. The netted veil draped around her shoulders and hung below the tiny waist she once possessed. A flowered headcrown kept the flowing piece in place. Norma stared at her mother's string of rich pearls lying in a perfect oval shape against her fair neckline. The liberal amount of white contrasted her black hair and chocolate eyes. She was so proud of the puffy and stylish shoulder length hair and broke a smile remembering the laborious task of setting those numerous pin curls the night before. What a joyful day—May 25, 1947.

Linda watched her mommy draw the photograph closer toward her face, examining the details. Little did her first-born know she was checking to see if the thick make-up concealed her black eye . . .

Just two more days and her name was to be Mrs. Allen Combs. Norma received an urgent notice in the mail. She was to sign for a letter waiting at the only post office in Wichita, Kansas. Very puzzled her curiosity immediately sent her there. Her stomach churned while sliding a finger to unlatch the tightly sealed envelope handed to her by the postmaster. Who could be sending me a letter, one I have to sign for? Good grief. Scanning the words of a distraught and confrontational note, bold letters screamed at her: "DON'T MARRY ALLEN COMBS!" Her eyes widened as she kept reading. "Allen and I were boyfriend and girlfriend not long ago and now I am with child. I'm carrying his baby. I have told him this but he refused to believe it so now I'm telling you. He IS the father and if you marry him you will be making a grave mistake!"

Tucking the folded letter into her pocket, she managed her emotions but her insides began to pulsate. The few people standing near her were taking care of their own business of the day and hardly noticed her shaking body. *Surely this is a nightmare and I'll wake up soon.* It was the only outrageous thought she could conclude.

Heading toward the exit door she whispered under her breath, *Please, I hope I don't see anyone I know.* Tears of sorrow and anger were fast erupting and blurring her vision as her hand wrapped around the door handle. A man on the other side forced the door inward and the sharp edge smacked her smooth face. The impact jerked her head back and caught her right eye. A loud groan burst from her lungs and a pleading elderly man begged for an answer. "Are you all right? I'm so sorry! Are you all right?"

Norma cupped both hands over the affected eye; the aftershock of the impact shot pangs of intense pain to the area and caused a pounding sensation to the tender skin. She lied with a sketchy "Yes" to the man while gaining her balance. He intently watched her anxious body go through the doorway and race toward the car, still holding a hand to her face and focused downward to avoid tripping.

Slamming the car door to shut out the world, her thoughts overpowered her. *Should I call off the wedding? What am I going to tell mother and dad?* She began to cry while her jumbled thoughts continued. *What am I going to tell my friends? Maybe I should call off the wedding! But how can I? Out of town people coming, money spent on my dress and cake. My family will be so upset. It's a small wedding but still not easy to undo. I love this man and he loves me! Does he have hidden secrets he hasn't told me? Apparently he does! Maybe more than one!* The more she thought about it, the louder the sobbing became. *I've got to drive over right now and talk to him* she thought. *I'm sure there is a perfectly good explanation, no use me sitting here stewing over it. He couldn't have kept something like this from me! That's just not like him. Maybe this woman is obsessed with the man I'm going to marry. Great! What a way to start a marriage! I've got to talk to him now!*

Looking at her watch she figured he was getting his hair cut about now. She found a tissue in her purse, wiped her cheeks and started the car. It was only a few blocks away and as she turned the corner and navigated the car toward the curb, the swirling candy cane pole outside of Wally's barbershop was now in full view. She sat a moment and took a deep breath. The emotional pain was overriding any physical pain but Norma could feel the affected skin was beginning to tighten. The aches around her entire head were setting in.

As soon as she saw Allen's lean military-looking body saunter out of the barbershop door with his hands in his pockets and a whistle on his lips, she exited the car and swiftly walked toward him. He looked up and tried to focus on her scrunched face and discolored spot. The whistling suddenly stopped.

She approached her fiancé and without words shoved the crumpled letter toward his face. He caught it, straightened the crinkles and moved his eyes along the dreaded words. Then he pulled her tightly into *his arms, allowing her to sob into his shoulder. His consoling voice and soothing words began to explain that she had nothing to worry about.*

"This woman was with many men! She's crazy! Yes, I went out with her a few times before I realized she was a Jezebel and I needed to get away quickly. Believe me, it is not my baby. I know this for a fact. She just needs someone to blame and needs a father for her child. I'm sure there are many possibilities out there, but certainly not me! You have nothing to concern yourself with, and we need to go on with our lives."

He stepped back ripping the letter several times and squishing the pieces into the pocket of his Navy car jacket. These words were the sweet honey she needed to hear. They were the exact words necessary to revive the life-long commitment they would soon embark on. The consummation of this couple would now move forward. He said everything she hoped for and more. "I trust you", she said. "After all, isn't that was marriage is all about . . . trust?" She then explained the goose egg forming on her eye. Allen tugged on her hand as the two moved swiftly to the car. Ice for the injured area was way overdue.

As a result of this day, two new concerns were added to the already stressful wedding day: coping with a black eye and hoping that this woman would not suddenly decide to show up at the ceremony. One of the two . . . did happen!

CHAPTER 14

PUBLIC STARES

The spin of time seemed out of control. Norma couldn't believe how fast the days were rocketing past. When she and Allen were finally able to crank the window open above the headboard for cool night spring air, lay their heads on the pillow and settle into a crucial slumber, it felt as though they had just woken up and made their double bed for the day. She didn't have time to spotlight on the fact that washing diapers for two children was a piece of cake in comparison to now, three little ones. Larry's stubbornness was certainly playing into the challenges of potty training or was it that he just didn't understand? This was to become the lifelong question, which led the way to a constant awareness of a very fine line. Is he playing games with us? Does he understand? Should I discipline him? Or, is he pulling the wool over our eyes? Is it willful spirit or a lack of mental processing? And thus the inconsistency of controlling Larry's behaviors began. Norma remembered when a doctor had told her that he would make progress for some time and then there would be a period of regression. Maybe he was declining or maybe it was plain laziness. Perhaps it was just the attention he demanded in strange ways.

The couple was eager to seek advice from others when it came to Larry's behaviors. The many friendships now forming in their lives could not relate, however. They talked about the behaviors of their own children as if it were the same thing. Those who attempted to offer opinions for her situation were "building walls" as far as Norma was concerned. "They have not walked a mile in my shoes," was her rebuttal as she discussed the topic with Allen.

Resources were few. Resorting to written words in articles and books seemed so impersonal now that the difficulty level of managing Larry was heightening. It was not the type of communication they needed or even desired.

An arduous problem inhabited an issue not written in the books about Mongoloidism-the people they **didn't** know stared at Larry and the people they **did** know stared at Larry. Now that the family was spending more time in the community, anyone encountering him in some fashion had an enormous amount of curiosity, causing un-comfortableness for all. That, added to the frustration of not having all the answers increased heaps of more irritations in trying to respond to the ongoing questions from inquisitive friends.

Larry was losing his baby look and his unique personality was now surfacing. While his walking, talking and the emerging lack of ability to keep his tongue inside his mouth, caused heads to turn, even from afar. Larry was now putting together 3-4 word sentences; but usually a mimic of what he had heard, occasionally in correct context, but most of the time, not. His scratchy sounding voice, interesting speech and unusual look felt as though he was some kind of freak-show available to entertain the public's rudeness.

In spite of his distinctive traits, Larry still possessed an adorable countenance. The family became experts at reading body language from those watching and if they stuck around him long enough, onlookers usually broke into smiles and amusement observing Larry's charm. It was his dad's humor trickling down and playing into the fun character their son was becoming. Larry quickly learned how to use this adorable poise to his favor.

"What a funny boy!" was a widespread comment from the public.

"Yes, he is "ha-Larry-ious" Allen's comic relief kicked in. Either way, Larry had an audience to keep him going and the attention, positive or negative, transpired a cold hard fact for the family: educating society as to the behavior of a mongoloid child. This was to be their lot in the crazy life the family now possessed.

Norma was glad she found first-rate doctors in their town. Dr. Kerr and Dr. Brown were the pediatricians of all four kids but, like others, were highly interested in Larry's particular handicap. This patient was like no other. They, however, were willing to encourage where they could; even giving Norma and Allen extra time for questions during a visit and if they didn't know the answer, were willing to research it themselves. They had true and sincere motives. The added benefit was the fun persona they both owned and it wasn't a rare occasion for Norma to walk out of the office, after an appointment, laughing at Dr. Kerr's jokes. He helped her see the lighter side of life and the two young aspiring men added a sparkle to this unique family.

It was certainly no joke, however, the day Norma ran into the building holding David's bleeding head; a screaming two year old in her arms. Once the doctors quickly cleaned up the oozing wound, closed it with eight stitches and wrapped a white turban-looking gauze around his soft brown hair, Norma explained that Larry had picked up a two-by-four piece of wood in the backyard and just for fun, pounded it on top of his brother's head—all the while David nonchalantly played in the dirt.

"Never a dull moment" became common verbiage from Norma's mouth. It contained an enormous amount of truth and often was the only thing to say when there were no other words. In this case there WERE no other words.

CHAPTER 15

FORMATION AND FORWARD-1957

The desire to connect with anyone out there sympathetic to this same kind of existence, forced Norma to call a lady named Mrs. West. A friend she hardly knew had written her name and number down on a small piece of paper and slipped it inside Norma's dress pocket at church. Larry was extra fussy during the Sunday school class and it was her turn to take him outside the room so he could wiggle away from her arms, squirm and scream to his desire, without interrupting; a ritual common to Sunday mornings. Heaven knew he surely couldn't be in the same Sunday school class as his siblings!

Norma talked a long time to Mrs. West about HER young mentally retarded child, also living at home—not in an institution. Though Norma couldn't see her face, an unexplainable power infiltrated the phone lines that day. Mrs. West knew other parents who had made the decision of keeping their special child out of "those awful establishments" and what do you know . . . they all lived in Mesa! Future meetings with these people introduced Norma and Allen into a welcomed arena of relationships.

"Finally, people who could relate. What a relief!" She often expressed. It not only became a strong link no one else could understand or penetrate, but a continued dialog among them, concerned of the future for their children, set things in motion. They wanted a school to be specific to their children's needs. Despite the rollercoaster hills and valleys now beginning to intrude the lives of the Combs' members, the couple was about to embark on something new and exciting and they could feel it.

Three things were added to Norma's prayer list...first, thankfulness for this unique circle of friends, now part of their growing list of Mesa relationships. Second, she was asking God to help them find a building to begin this endeavor and using the name the group agreed upon; Mesa Association for Retarded Children- MARC school, and third, they needed the first teacher willing to take on this delicate commission. Although the parents agreed to take turns with assistance, they wanted one person to carry the name of Marc preschool's first volunteer teacher.

Norma and Emma Jean West talked it around and found they could use the first Methodist church building to start with, until funds were provided otherwise. The first preschool opened its doors because of nine motivated families.[5] Mrs. Freda Wills was Larry's founding teacher at age four. The class was small and not only was Poody-boy able to get his attention-getting behaviors satisfied from someone other than his parents, the preschool curriculum included some basic self-help skills to be learned. Though not able to attend the same school as his sister and neighbor friends, his school was at least in the same community and best of all, he didn't have to live away from his own flesh and blood.

Beyond their wishes coming to pass, they were beginning to expand on something big and outside of their own little corner of the world. Progress was taking place in society.

There was a write-up in the paper as to the opening of this school and although slow, interest was growing. It was not only a different option but also a better one to "society's backward thinking," Norma opinionated towards others. She spoke of history time-lines concerning people like her son. "To begin with, Mentally Illness is not the same as mental retardation and further more, the mentally retarded should not live in closets, hospitals and yes, especially Institutions."

The fire in her was growing everyday and beginning to push her towards the role of spokeswoman, not only for her son, but also on behalf of other families who were in the same situation. She read all she could get her hands on and conversed with others in the field to increase the knowledge that was now necessary. She even wrote an article about her experience and published it in the popular Mesa Tribune.

"Only those who have experienced it know the silent miseries, the repressed hope and the buried agony that we knew when we were given the news of Larry's mental state."

She ended the lengthy message by saying,

"Of course we do not know what the future has in store for our retarded child, but right now we will to live in the present, and will pledge ourselves to make the most of every day."

It was a pleasure to drive to the school location several times a week to assist where needed. The added benefit was taking her two younger children along and seeing the interface of play between the handicap and non-handicap. It pleased her to watch this integration and it reminded her of another one happening across this great Nation. . .

Only three years ago the popular Brown vs. Board of education headlines sprayed the newspapers. The hot news revealed a major landmark of the United States Supreme Court in the history of segregated schools. Separate public schools for black and white students denied black children equal educational opportunities. As a result, segregation was ruled a violation of the equal protection clause of the fourteenth amendment of the United States constitution".[6]

CHAPTER 16

CLOSE CALL

The developing subdivisions around their new home were swarming with neighbors made up of young families, hence lots of playmates. The hot and hotter weather didn't seem to faze the kids. Linda rode her bike around the streets with friends her own age and the three youngest played "house" in the cool breeze of the covered carport.

It was the day Norma walked outside to ensure all was well with her children when Larry slithered inside the house behind her and locked the door. He laughed and thought it funny to hear his mommy at her mercy, pounding on the other side. The true seriousness was the poisoned bottles of cleaning supplies she stored under the kitchen sink. It happened to be, the exact place he was headed. Norma saw this when she ran around the corner of the house to peer through the window. Her son's interest moved in the direction of the opened eye-level cupboard where she had just finished scouring the sinks with Ajax! Earlier that day she had turned the handle on the bottom of a kitchen window and cranked it slightly open, exposing the screen and bringing in fresh air. It was now to be the negotiating place for her communication headquarters. Reasoning with a "Curious George" type was not easy!

"Larry, look at me!" she said. "I want you to open the door right now!" She knew he could hear her but didn't bother to look up.

Watching him pick up an easily accessible white bleach bottle, he began his endeavor to open it. "Larry, Larry... LARRY!" Each plea louder! Again, no response. She screamed. "Larry, don't open that! No! NO Larry, don't!"

He was set on twisting the cap in his favor turning it one way and then the other. Norma's emergency reactions took on an extreme keenness and she tried a different approach. "Larry. Hi, Larry! Oh look Poody. Look at Felix." She picked up the black cat circling her legs. Larry adored the new kitty that recently joined their family. Responding to her high-pitched voice and the word "Felix", he turned his attention away from the Clorox and gawked at the kitty's honey face behind the screen. As if it was planned and right on cue, Felix let out a meow and Larry put down the container, stood and walked towards the pet he loved to hold, usually with an inescapable squeeze. Tilting his head back, he looked up at the window, stood still for seconds to focus. His arms extended upward as if his mother had the ability to hand him the tiny ball of black fur.

She spoke slowly and deliberately. "Open. . .the. . . door . . . and. . . you. . . can. . . hold. . . Felix," bribing with voice intonation.

He stood in a stupor and she repeated the same words this time pointing her finger towards the doorknob across his path. His face broke into the common ornery expression and he turned towards the door, giving way to the necessary steps for her command.

She ran around the outside corner, halted at the door and listened to the cracking back and forth of the knob. Her hand enclosed the round gold ball ready to pull it toward her. Seconds felt like minutes and a panicked thought came over her. What if he can't open it? It became obvious that he was having a difficult time twisting the lock into position. She wasn't sure how long he would stick with it before giving up. As a last resort, she gave it a hard twist to the right and to her surprise the latch released and the door opened!

Larry flashed a jovial smile and spread his broad fingers apart in position to grab the Felix kitty Norma no longer held. Now running past him, she quickly pulled out the cleaning supplies and banged the cupboard door shut. Her body doubled over on the kitchen counter, opened palms held her face, and taking in a slow deep breath she prevented her own melt down.

Similar close calls were on the rise. They were happening too frequently and Norma didn't know what to do! This woman, who seemed to always have answers, now didn't; and, her list of questions was getting longer.

When Allen came home—he wrestled with both sons on the living room floor. Larry's sizeable strength and endless energy wore the two out but it was the day that Allen discovered an unplanned cat and mouse chasing game, using wadded-up wet washrags; rubber bands keeping it tight, as ammunition, which brought a new aspiration for the these three cave men.

"That's not funny, Norma shrieked as she attempted to shoo them out the door. "You're going to break a lamp! Go outside!"

Allen laughed and snuck around the bedroom corner, arm extended and in position to plow David hiding in the closet.

"Someone's going to get hurt! Get out! This is just horseplay, Now shoo!" She circled her arms in motion toward the door. It was as if she was invisible to these three lively males; they were unstoppable.

"You're full of beans!" Allen flung the washcloth towards Larry's stomach. Weakened with laughter and barely able to mold the cloth tighter, he readied himself for revenge. Larry's strong arms sent the rag flying toward his dad. "No, uhh you fulla beans!" he said.

"Well you're full of prunes!" Allen caught the rag in mid air and returned fire attaching a revved up motor sound from his throat and a hardy "whoop."

"No, you fulla grunes." The amused girls watched and burst into delight at Larry's garbled imitated words. Even Norma's mad face softened. Who was really having the most fun? She thought, the kids or the adult?

"Why do I always have to be the heavy?" Norma suddenly straightened. Allen watched her annoyance grow. "You play with the kids and I have to be the disciplinarian!"

"I'm getting them out of your hair, I thought you'd be happy," was his instant reply.

"Well for Pete's sake, at least take it outside! I don't want anyone coming to me crying. Heavens to Betsy!" the lines on her forehead deepened.

Angry, Allen dropped the wet rag in the kitchen sink and opened the icebox. Carefully pulling the cold watermelon ready for cutting, he spotted the knife handle sticking up between the counters, grabbed it and stabbed it into the melon. With a big exhale, he opened the back door and all four children followed their daddy in single file toward the back yard

"Don't forget the salt," Allen turned to remind David who was bringing up the rear.

CHAPTER 17

GOD'S LITTLE GIFT-1959/1960

Among the many benefits of living on 5th Avenue Street was meeting the Little family. The two four-year-old Davids began playing together outside. An "on the spot" attachment happened between them. David Combs brought his new friend, David Little, to meet his family. What the boys didn't know was that their mommies had already met at the Methodist church earlier that day.

Norma motioned for the two boys to sit at the small picnic table placed in the shade of the pepper tree. She poured lemonade for all the neighborhood kids gathered round. The extended front yard was becoming a mutual meeting place for long hours of play, including kids on this street and even a few streets up. Norma was flattered they picked her house.

"Where do you live, David?" She kept pouring and hardly noticed a new face in the crowd.

"Down there," he pointed in the direction of the house with the flat roof.

Just for conversation Norma asked about his family but wasn't getting much information. She dropped it realizing this David attested some shyness and she was moving too fast.

Looking up she noticed another new face of a little girl with dark hair, dark eyes, protruding lips and an uneasy look. Unsure of what to think of this neighborhood crowd, the little girl kept her distance.

"Hi" Norma greeted and was ready to include her.

"That's my sister" David Little announced.

"Are you Linda?" Norma tried to be mild.

"Yes, her name is Linda" her brother was proud to volunteer the information again.

With no answer, the shy girl stared at Larry and continued to maintain her space.

David Combs had already warned the other David about his brother in hopes of alleviating some fear ahead of time. When David L watched the other neighborhood children able to handle the situation he relaxed; however, his sister was not quite bold enough for this endeavor.

"Why don't you go ask her to come over here?" Norma questioned her youngest. Debbie stood and slowly walked over to the timid girl. Using few words, Debbie's sensitivity moved her hand toward the folded arms across Linda's chest. She slightly pulled as a gesture to join the others. Finally, Linda gave way to the gentle tug, and although she was noticeably embarrassed that the crowd was watching, with puppy eyes, she looked up and dropped her arms.

When Larry approached the other children too closely David and Debbie took on a different role —a response Norma hated to see. They became his parents and demanded that he sit down and leave the other kids alone, guarding their many friendships. He didn't quite get the whole personal space concept but Larry tried to buck the system reminding them, "I oder, I'm oder (older) brother, uhh, you no, you not my boss!" Arguments among these three usually started in the presence of other children and Larry's up-and-down moods supplied inconsistencies of how to handle the frequent encounters. Larry was to learn social skills under the commands of his siblings and depending on his frame of mind at the time he resisted or accepted. It concerned Norma, wondering if her children were taking on too much beyond their years.

Previously Norma and Nancy Little had noticed each other in the adult Sunday school class. Allen was teaching that day and upon his conclusion the two greeted each other with introductions, quickly exchanging information.

"Funny, we live on the same street and our children so close in age," they laughed together.

Now acquaintances were turning to kindred spirits. It was as if God set this other family straight from heaven and placed them smack onto Fifth Avenue Street specifically for the Combs crew. David Combs and David Little both had birthdays in March, Debbie and Linda Little were the same age and had birthdays in November. And wouldn't you know, they even had an older daughter, Shari, younger than Linda Combs but the same age as Larry.

All six children began bonding, especially the youngest four; it was if they were joined at the hip. Even Shari and Linda Combs shared the same humor and laughed frequently together using goofy faces. Larry certainly wanted to be included but he had no preference as to whom he interacted with. He just wanted to socialize! It was if he was demanding acceptance in all ways and in any area. It didn't matter the age of his playmates. He was a true extrovert with no social rules.

Beyond the children, Norma and Allen were aware of a growing commonality when communicating with Bill and Nancy. Norma smiled at God's humor. "An entire family's immediate linking with another entire family. They lived five houses down— the one with the flat roof— and attended First Methodist Church, no less. What were the odds?"

Frequently planned outings were now proposed: picnics, river trips and Arboretum hikes made all eleven people happy. The best part was that the Little family was willing to share the burden of gawking outsiders. Acceptance of Larry, with all his issues, was in place. And then there was the great surprise that this family not only understood the Combs' humor but even added more of their own. The repeated gatherings were bestowed with laughter. Oh how the Combs' family needed these friendships and in turn the Little's were benefiting from this exceptional situation. Bill and Nancy even had unspoken permission to assist with the discipline of their complex child. But best of all, the children, all six of them, could occupy Larry's time and keep him amused at least for a while. Finally, some relief and enjoyable adult conversation!

Norma was preparing for yet another organized Combs/Little picnic. She folded mayo into the potato salad while standing at the kitchen table. Wiping her hands on the sheer white apron tightly tied around her waist, she walked toward the desk in her bedroom to check her list of picnic items one last time. At the exact moment she passed the phone in the hallway, it rang. Quickly picked it up before the first ring completed, she knew Nancy was calling for last minute preps.

"Your Mother's cancer is back" her dad's voice shook out the words…

CHAPTER 18

HOT AND COLD-1961

Over the next several months the children viewed deep worry lines creasing Norma's young forehead. Listening to their mother conduct numerous conversations with her parents on the phone, the same scenario played out each time. Saying goodbye she placed the receiver in the cradle while clutching a tissue, slowly wiping the tears finding their way down her smooth cheeks. Her four children weren't sure how to take this sad countenance of their strong and vibrant mother and lacked the understanding of the emotion of mourning, especially not really knowing the person she was mourning over. Freda's doctor was not so hopeful this time and an aggressive cancer was taking over her body. The overwhelming grief was shared by another emotion . . . that of bitterness. The long discussions Norma had with her husband as to how to travel to Kansas to be with her family turned into full-fledged arguments. Not only had Allen's paychecks been slim lately, but the reality of Larry's surprising behaviors limited their babysitting options. Norma was reacting to an overwhelming feeling of being STUCK! Her times in prayer increased, for her own control of life was beyond her.

Mulling over the thought of possibly going back to work, Norma recognized the budget just couldn't get any slimmer. She was already buying the kids clothes at second hand stores, purchasing toys at Good Will, making cheap bean and hamburger meals for supper and even limiting snack time with the kids. She frequently lectured Larry and David for opening the icebox throughout the day, just from boredom, and threatened to cut off access to it. "You kids are going to eat us out of house and home." she nagged at her boys. "I'm not going grocery shopping for another week and that's all we have so stay out of that icebox! Gooood night! You kids are going to put me into the poor house! Someday I'm going to put a lock on that icebox and then we'll see how you feel. I bet you'll change your tune then. Now go outside and play, quit hanging around the kitchen!"

The need to purchase another couch was also in the future. Due to Larry's uncontrollable rocking, the springs behind the fabric were worn and some even broken. "I can yell at him till I'm blue in the face but it won't make a difference, he just won't stop," she complained, "it goes in one ear and out the other." But, she was proud of the good deals she could find and confident she could grab another piece of furniture at a garage sale for a reasonable price. Yet, she still had to save for it.

Allen showed no interest in his profession as doctor and even a dying desire in sewing machine sales.

The previously bright balloons in Norma's life were slowly deflating one by one but new ones were rising to the top, just not as conspicuous.

Marc School had moved to a rented location. Funding was promised by Mesa Public schools: thus the hiring of a stellar director — Mrs. Virginia Opincar, a child development specialist/teacher.[7] Norma and Allen could see the powerful influence this amazing woman had while in the presence of the children. She possessed an enormous amount of patience balanced with the firmness they needed. They were lucky to have her and the hopes of her sticking around for this great undertaking were in the minds of all involved. Norma kept tabs on the goings-on of this new location and growing school. Because she was so determined to write letters to anyone in authority asking for any kind of assistance, she became the designated unofficial secretary. The summer program provided numerous opportunities for Larry's love of the water and Mrs. Opincar taught him and others to swim. The increased support of backing for the school was coming around and Norma rested her head on the pillow at night finally feeling some long-awaited peace.

Because Larry was constantly "on the go" and swimming at the local pool, the blue eyed, adorable growing boy, came home tired and ready to rest. He persistently watched Tom and Jerry and Yogi Bear cartoons on TV, which gave everyone a short break. Linda was now able to help with the chores around the house and possibly control the younger ones a few hours a day. If the children were not playing outside with neighbors, Linda spent most of her day with her little sister, dressing up, putting on make-up and creating stories with the favorite bride doll that possessed the heavy purple eye shadow.

David spent his time out doors, building forts. He was obsessed and had no preference what they looked like on the outside, just as long as you could crawl inside his masterpiece and call it "cool!" He and David L's vision of conjuring a way to make a new fort each day meant scanning the area, especially the dirt road (really a dirt field) behind the oleanders, for raw material; wood, tumbleweeds, or even pieces of cardboard were prized construction supplies. Larry followed the two boys around and when he got bored, or was forced to leave, sought out the girls for a change of pace. He had someone to play with most of the time but trying to understand the rules of the made-up games strained the staying power of his siblings. The heated discussions circled round and round. He made no sense with the lack of rationale; in Larry's brain, it all made perfect sense and he couldn't understand why his siblings didn't get what he was so desperately trying to explain. This forced his playmates into total frustration when struggling to justify their case to the parents.

"Just try to include him the best you can- cut him some slack," was often the response.

The "ahhhh" sound frequently forced out of Norma's mouth, happened again the day Debbie and Larry had walked to the public pool just blocks away and returned shortly after. Debbie's obvious enduring embarrassment came through the words she spoke. "Larry was kicked out of the pool by Mr. Green" (the head life guard everyone knew and loved). Her frail voice came through as her lip quivered.

"What happened?"

"Mr. Green told him to get out of the pool and he wouldn't so the other life guards had to pull him out and drag him by the leg . . . clear across to the gate. He made a big scene! Everybody was staring and laughing!"

"Why did they do that?" Norma was now annoyed.

"Cause Larry wouldn't listen!"

"What did Larry do this time?

"I don't know I think he almost drowned someone. He held a boy under the water!" Debbie walked into her bedroom and shut the door. The conversation was over as far as she was concerned and Norma decided to let her be. Her little girl had already been through enough trauma because of her older, yet developmentally younger, brother who couldn't control himself in the water.

Turning to Larry, Norma demanded an answer! "Larry, what did you do?"

"I no do nothing!"

She stood glaring at his face remembering other encounters of watching children pool-play with him in the past; while splashing and grappling in the water, Larry often didn't comprehend when enough was enough! The teasing from others magnified as Larry's laughter kept it going but he had no comprehension of his own strength; situations quickly turned into danger and Larry, with a smile on his face, held a child's head under the water. Norma had spent numerous times talking to him about it and his response made her think he understood. Now she realized she was just blowing hot air.

"Well you are grounded from the pool!" she said at last. "You hear me?" As soon as the words came forth she knew this meant punishment for her as well for he would need full supervision. "Now go to your bed. You can't play outside!"

With head hung, he slowly paced inside the door of his room; using full upper body strength he slammed it shut, vibrating the other doors in the house. Jumping on his bed and pounding the mattress with both fists, he began screaming words. "I no do nothing. That man hurt me. That boy hurt me. I don't like that man! He mean to me!" The complaining continued for 10 minutes and when Larry paused long enough to slowly open the door and sneak out, Norma swished him right back on his bed. This time he remained quiet and listened through the door to his parent's conversing, perking up every time he heard his name.

"That boy makes me so mad, I could just spit! Ahhh" Norma yelled at Allen as if it was his fault. "I bet you the kids in the pool teased him to no end and he just reacted. I can't even send him to the swimming pool without some kind of problem!" Norma stood next to the door and watched it slowly creak open. Looking down she saw a snotty nose make its way around the door's edge. "Your working up to a spanking Mr." Bending down she grabbed his hand and turned his escaping body toward the bed, slamming the door again. "We certainly can't expect the kids to control him", she continued. "Lord knows they have enough to contend with. AHHH!"

Stone silence filled the house for a few seconds. The children watched yet another 'Larry scene' and all with the same thoughts: What do we do with Larry? Why doesn't he understand? Why does he act this way? He just doesn't get it!!

In the quietness, Larry slowly spoke out. "Ha, Ha, mom, I yissen!!"(I listen) He cracked the door again, stuck out his tongue and sassed at her. This feisty attitude portrayed retribution as if HIS listening to the dialog of the family was supposed to be hurting THEIR feelings.

Norma walked to the door, closed it after pushing him back into his room for the third time, repeating the same depiction. A fleeting look at Allen and the other three broke into smiles, all faces doing the same. Shoulders up and hands over their mouths, they snickered at each other and controlled the whispered giggles, vigilant to keep Larry from knowing the joy he was now providing. "I yissen?" they mocked quietly.

Hot and cold!! Cold and hot!! When Larry was the cause of his family's angry red faces, it was within the same minute something hilarious came out of this boy's mouth — whether he planned it or not and it dissolved the hearts around him causing a reoccurring thought…it's just too hard to stay mad at him! Especially looking at that adorable, yet rebellious face.

For now the Combs folks had another "Larryism" to add to their repertoire of Larry humor. It was becoming the glue to hold this family together: "Ha, ha, mom, I yissen! Now that Marc School published a monthly bulletin, Norma wanted to, from time to time, include articles written by siblings. "I got the idea from a piece called *The Retarded Child at Home*. We need the view point of others living in the house." Norma had tucked away a paper Linda had written a few years back and now used it as the first sibling publication.

My Brother
as told by Linda Combs, 9 years old.

My mother and daddy have told me that my brother is "mentally retarded." I don't know exactly what that means but I know that sometimes other children will say when they see my brother that he is "ugly" and that he is "dumb." I try to forgive them, though, when they say these things because I am sure that they do not understand my brother and they do not know how much I love him. They do not know how much happiness and sunshine he brings every day to me and my family.

First of all, my brother is a very good wrestler. He is always ready to wrestle with everyone, my littlest brother, my playmates, Danny (a neighbor) with my mother, my daddy, or me.

He loves to romp and giggle and fight. He is ticklish and happy and fun. Sometimes we call him our little "sharing boy" because he quickly shares with other kids. My mother says that all of us kids could learn a lot about sharing from him.

My brother and I like to play school and he is very patient to keep doing all the things I tell him, like going to recess, and to sit at his desk, to go sharpen his pencil and things like that. He is usually very sweet and patient even when mother says I'm being very bossy.

Our family has a lot of fun laughing at my brother and sometimes we call him a clown because he is always so full of tricks that he knows will make us laugh. Yes, I'm sure my family and me would not laugh so much if my brother had not been born.

CHAPTER 19

ENLIGHTENED

Freda M. Harrold was laid to rest July 25, 1961. Norma reflected fondly on her childhood.

The recollection of playing in the huge snow banks, shelling corn in the granary with the whole family around a large wash tub, scampering, rolling, and burying each other in the piles of leaves after long summer days, and playing along the edge of a sandy creek bed at the bottom of the hill near their house, brought comfort. What a great legacy one can give to their children: a solid beginning with loving parents in a farm setting.

Then in the mid-1930's came the drought and the realization that she had contacted dust pneumonia. The crops were lost and farm machinery lay rusting and idle in piles of dust drifts. They had to move and ended up living in a number of rented farmhouses. The family even moved in with a relative and Norma and her sister, Marjory, spent hours playing with their cousin, Donna. Times were unstable and she remembered her dad earning $1.00 per day in those desperate depression years. He only had an eighth grade education but as far as Norma was concerned had a Ph.D. in his knowledge of the Bible—that's what really counted!

She thought of the impact of her favorite teacher, Ms. Dixon, in her school years; now acknowledging this young, unique individual was truly a master instructor. The one-room building housed seven students of various ages. Ms. Dixon not only made learning fun, but organized meals so that the children had soup to snack on and the aroma to smell during instruction. The corn chowder was Norma's favorite and she could still smell it, even now.

Then there was the scary day she and her sister and brother stood terrified seeing their mother in pain and their dad running for the doctor. Baby brother Donny was born in their modest apartment. Excited about her role once again as big sister, Norma was faced with responsibilities related to taking care of much younger sibling. She was grateful for those life lessons.

While listening to the Methodist minister, Norma embraced her dad and realized this mighty man had shrunk with age. It brought an unfathomable thought about the day both parents would no longer be on this earth. The piercing pain in her chest wouldn't go away. The loss of such a godly woman who believed in her and whose example gave her strength, was devastating. She was really gone! Norma couldn't stand to think of her dad living alone. Freda cooked and cleaned for him all their married life. She embodied the Proverbs 31 woman and her legacy would forever live in the hearts of those who knew her. Donny and his wife, Marilyn, along with two delightful daughters, lived only blocks from their dad, Roy, and knowing this fine family would always be quickly available to keep him company provided some serenity for the rest of the family.

Norma was able to piece together childcare for her children while she was far away from home. Although Allen wouldn't give up his once a week Toastmasters meeting, he was home most of the time relying on Linda's irreplaceable help. The Little family was also willing to help. If it weren't for Norma's generous brother-in-law, Howard, speedily wiring the money, she wouldn't have been able to travel to Kansas. She was able to converse with her mother and speak of her love before watching her take her last breath. The memories would be a comforting friend, and the departing words between them were exactly what Norma needed for closure; besides the time away was extremely welcomed.

The sweet part of the bittersweet hometown visit was seeing the old friends she thought so much about. She had forgotten how close-knit this small town was and now was listening to the latest news from the people she adored. Visiting the familiar surroundings of her young years made her think about the ultimate plan of God in her life. She was ashamed of the doubts, which crept up each day, and she had hours to reflect upon them without small hands tugging on her blouse. It was if life stood still and she watched herself through a clear window: suddenly a new perspective of the brevity on this earth.

Attention from hurting friends was manifested through meals, gifts, and cards. The rejuvenation came at the right time for it was necessary, in support of her dad, to sift through mom's things as a family. Norma stumbled on a letter written by her dad to his future bride.

It was one December day,
And the air was cold and balmy,
That I came down to Funston and enlisted in the army.
How hard it was to leave you
Dear one,
I can't explain. But I was called to service.
How needless to complain.
Well do I remember when last
I saw you dear
Standing in the doorway, brave and full of cheer. My heart was
filled with sadness, sadness I couldn't control.
As my thoughts went out to the future,
No one to console; And as I took your hand dear we said our last good-byes
Your face is still before me,
And the expression of your eyes.

She hung her head and closed her eyes. Her thoughts of the love her parents had for each other, even to the end, filled her thoughts. This letter was the beginning of a beautiful love story and she was privileged to watch it play out while growing from child to young woman.

Sitting next to the window seat on the plane ride home, she hoped nobody would sit next to her. Faking a smile for the sake of meaningless chatter did not interest her. Tears never flowed so frequently as they did the past week and she couldn't guarantee that she could stop them now. Her old friend, anxiety, welled up inside her as the tires of the Boeing 707 touched ground in the sunny state. She thought back to the phone conversation with Allen a day ago and hoped he was feeling guilty about the tension between them before she left. Finding help for Larry and for an extended length of time was almost impossible. Oh sure, friends say they could help but they really didn't understand Larry and all his needs. They were willingly to volunteer for something about which they had no clue. The thought of any future getaways for her and Allen would be unheard of, she feared. This was her reality! She knew her husband was, himself, managing a few troubles in her absence but not from hearing his calm voice on the phone. It was the reading between the lines. He often held back information, protecting her from the inner turmoil. He knew her too well.

She struggled to play the words again and remembered him divulging Larry had chased a fire truck down the street again, this time without shoes. They guessed it was the sound of the sirens that triggered an adrenalin rush inside that little Poody head and though the emergency vehicles didn't turn the corner onto their street too often, when it did happen, Larry stopped his playtime and dangerously ran after the screaming trucks or ambulance wagon. It was impossible to catch up with him and so they conceded to taking turns walking down the street, ready to bring him home once he became weary and quit.

Exiting the plane and entering the Sky Harbor airport, she viewed in front of her an astonishing looking family. Everyone dressed up, clean and slick hairdos. She suddenly became ashamed of the jealousy concealed in her heart while watching those "normal" Mormon families in her community. Standing before her now was exactly what she wanted; needed and just realizing she wouldn't have it any other way.

PROTECTION THROUGH DISCIPLINE 1961-62

Marc had moved again and though the structure was a fixer-upper, this time the school was able to purchase the building. It was the true property of Marc school. Enrollment was growing.[8]

Mrs. Pippin, Mrs. Samples, Mrs. Jetter, and Mrs. Cox were all certified special education teachers. Larry was once again in capable hands. She hoped he would learn to read like other children and possibly alleviate one of the many disappointments in his life. He observed his siblings enter into the world of words. Kids all around him were reading and discussions about favorite books where entering conversations. Now the gap widened between his accomplishments and those of the other children his age. The frequent outbursts were probably a result of not being able to keep up. He tried in every way to imitate his brother and sisters, desiring to be exactly like them, but upon the constant awakening of lagging behind, frustrations erupted.

Norma poured the noodles into the skillet of hamburger and kidney beans steaming on the stove. She gave it a few swirls with the spoon, tapped it on the side of the pan, laid it down and walked to the screen front door.

"Kids, come in for dinner!" She paused a few minutes before realizing the loud talking and laughter behind the hedges outside had probably muffled her command.

"Kids! Time to eat!" This time she made sure she was heard.

"Dinner! Kids, now!" Still nothing.

"Ahhhh, Okay, that's it!" she marched toward the fly swatter hanging on the kitchen wall and jerked it down. "This is the third night in a row they have done this to me! This meal is getting cold! I slave over this hot stove and for what? Nothing! Well, I'm not going to have it!"

Allen watched her slap the screen door open. When the children saw her coming, they quickly noticed the alarming "stinger on the legs" weapon. She held the fly swatter up high and hit the ground running. The children almost laughed at the absurd woman chasing them. Was it some sort of game? Each child ran a different direction but it was the slow runner that got eaten by the bear and so it was Debbie's legs that felt the sting that evening…right in front of her siblings and even some neighborhood friends.

All four children sat around the table chewing on the bread and butter sandwiches and hot slumgullion. Debbie's head hung while she ate. Her stringy blond bangs dangled into her hazel eyes. The demonstration of her injured self-esteem and the realization she took the pain on everyone's behalf, was conveying a pouting self-pity until the deafening sound of a metal and glass clashing immediately put everyone on their feet!

All six members jumped from their chairs and ran towards the sound outside. A car had plowed down the brown picket fence across the street and landed only feet away from the front door of the Boatman's house. A man slowly exited the dented vehicle and stumbled around the yard. Instantly neighbors exited their homes to see the commotion and sirens were screaming towards Fifth Ave. Norma grabbed Larry's hand and squeezed it tight. Neighbors were coming from everywhere and were assessing the situation, scrambling towards the house and checking to see if the Boatman family members were okay. Men in uniform soon arrived. Police pushed the public back but not before questioning witnesses. Minutes turned into hours of evaluation and discussion, once the on-lookers and police knew everyone was miraculously intact. The circled crowd had moved to stare at the flattened grass and swerved tire marks on the front yard and sidewalk of the Combs residence, the very place where the children played just minutes before. The drunk driver had been handcuffed and placed in the back of the marked car. Everyone stood frozen as they watched the vehicle pull away.

Now realizing the magnitude of what just took place, bodies were shaking and weaken knees barely held them up, especially for the two families involved. The rest of the evening was somber and as darkness fell, sleep for all was embraced.

Weeks passed by before the shock wore off. Norma thought of the timing of her demands that day and was grateful to God for <u>His</u> perfect timing! She was finally able to resume status quo but woke up each day thanking God for protecting her children. Her acute awareness of God's goodness pushed her to thank God everyday for safety and protection.

CHAPTER 21

CRAZY LADY

Norma had already put in a few hours at the nearby Dog and Suds fast food restaurant. Her children skipped across Stapley Street to watch their mom serve up hamburgers as a carhop. The place had just opened its doors and it was perfect, for she didn't need a vehicle to get there. Such pure joy for the children to see their mother in this unusual environment and they snickered over the paper hat pinned to the top of her bulky dark hair. It was now a privilege for the family to be able to sit at the counter and sip on an iced mug root beer float from time to time, relishing an agreeable refreshment when the three-digit temperatures were unbearable . . . all while viewing their mother taking orders.

The extra money would help pay off the stacking bills mounting on the desk. Norma really didn't mind working outside the home as long as she was back in time for her only indulgence of the day—The Secret Storm and The Edge of Night soap operas.

It was the one and only hour she could exit her own wild life and enter the dysfunctional lives of her close friends inside the black box. The perspective of **her** life situations turned placid in comparison, at least for a short time.

The phone rang and Allen answered it. He paused and pulled the base of the phone toward him, unwound the long black cord and slipped into the bedroom. His voice instantly lowered. Norma watched his strange actions and a bewildered look punctured her dark eyes. Opening the door, she inquired. "Who is that?'

No answer.

"Who is on the phone?" she remained firm.

Allen paused for a long while. "Just a minute" he spoke into the bottom of the receiver, covered it with his hand and turned toward Norma. "I'll tell you later!" He unwrapped the phone cord from his hand, walked past her and slipped into another room. Gently pushing the door closed, he shut her out.

Norma stood by the wood barrier and listened with her ear pressed tight. She could only hear garbled sounds.

Finally hanging up He opened the door, Norma stood in his way without a budge.

"Who was that?'

"It was her"

"Who?"

"Lilly!" Allen wilted with the word.

"What!!" The rage started to erupt.

"She's been following us. She came in the store the other day" Allen confessed.

"She came here, all the way from Kansas to Arizona?" Norma jerked her finger down.

"She still insists that boy is mine. He's thirteen years old now."

"Is this woman crazy or what?" The anger lines deepened above her eyebrows and she screamed into Allen's face. "I want her out of our lives. Now! The gall! How did she find us anyway?" Yanking her body around, she marched into the bedroom, beginning to undress.

"I'm not sure." Allen followed behind her.

Norma wiggled her way into her girdle and forced the hanging clips onto her nylon. In staccato motion she slipped her dress over her head. "Well you tell her to back off and stop pestering us or she'll have ME to answer to!" She slapped on her shoes and jerked her back toward Allen. He routinely zipped her dress up and Norma stomped into the living room searching for her keys. She was never late for the Marc meetings and was determined to keep it a habit. Allen rummaged around for the keys himself. Dropping them in her hand, he watched her exit, slamming the front door behind her.

The engine to the Toyota revved up and squealing tires backed onto the street. The children stopped their play and slowly waved in wonderment at their mother from across the yard. The red in her face confirmed determination and as she pulled out onto busy Stapley Street, she spoke with no one.

"Is this lady crazy or what? The nerve, calling Allen at OUR home! The nerve! Ahhhh!" she reeled her window up in case she had to scream. The punishing thought of this phone call not being the first since their wedding, entered her mind. She remembered a period of time when they lived in Wyoming. Allen's behavior seemed a bit strange over a few weeks. She had suspicions at that time but blew them off as paranoia. After all, her young heart wanted to trust this enduring man. Now connecting the dots, she prayed those thoughts were just her imagination getting the best of her.

"I'm appalled!" she heard herself say. "I'm absolutely appalled!" Her eyes began to water but she wouldn't allow it. Now quickly turning the vehicle into her usual parking spot, she exiting the car, straightened her dress, cleared the wrinkled nylons across her knees, brushed lint off her sleeves, and stood with good posture before entering the building.

The need to tackle a busy night with the Marc clique was too important. They had lots on the agenda. Hugging her notebook, she took her place at the table and kept her head down in the name of writing. There was little contribution that night from Mrs. Combs and it was a surprise to all, especially when she didn't bother to stick around for chatting afterwards.

When she arrived home, Allen was already in bed sleeping. Avoidance! She hated that about him—his avoidance! He wanted to drop the subject completely every time she prodded him for more information in the coming days. He did what he could to steer clear of the topic. Recognizing she wasn't giving up, Allen finally confessed. Lilly needed money! This mystery woman has the gall and the madness to prey upon Allen's sensitive heart, she thought, and knowing him, he ultimately would give her the funds she "supposedly" had to have.

"If that's what it takes to get her out of our lives than so be it; but, how do we know that's all she wants and will leave us alone? Besides, when you give her money you are saying in a sense that boy is yours!" An aching pain packed her forehead as she squeezed between her eyes.

"I don't know," Allen replied. "I just don't know what to do."

"I'll tell you what to do. Tell her to take a hike! I mean it! Ahhhhh!"

The tension between the couple was thick for the next couple of weeks. Norma vented to a friend that she was "sickened by the whole thing." Every time the phone rang it sent a chill up her spine. She frequently answered with an angry voice in expectation. "She better not ever call here again! I'm going to lower the boom on THAT woman!"

CHAPTER 22

ADJUSTMENTS-1962

"Teasing! Teasing! That's all this family does anymore!" Norma waved her hand in the air as if swatting flies.

Debbie had just asked her mom if it was really true that a boy in the school cafeteria ate so much that he blew up! AND, that there was food and body parts everywhere.

"Oh for heaven's sakes. No!" Norma looked at her oldest daughter whose laughter penetrated the house. Linda was lying on the double bed she and Debbie shared and was hiding behind the worn pages of Teen magazine. "Look, your sister is curling her toes again. That's a sure sign she's playing with you." Norma conceded to join the fun.

"Yeah, check-out those hot dog bun-shaped feet." David delivered lines like a TV comedian. Linda gave another loud cackle. It was a family joke . . . Linda curled her long toes every time she joked, adding to the hilarity. Being older and the less gullible child in the family brought on way too much pleasure for her first born. She took advantage of numerous occasions to have such amusement by telling the most outlandish stories to young ears, especially Debbie. She believed anything! But it wasn't just the brothers and sister she teased; she made it a point to draw attention to her daddy's 'white chicken legs' every time he walked around the house in his underwear. Laughter became the exact medicine needed for this family and everyone participated. Larry quickly picked up on the joy it brought, but didn't grasp the idea of family jokes staying within the house walls. He delighted in telling everyone, even casual acquaintances, that his daddy had white chicken legs. Embarrassment was an emotion they would experience much more than others: often over things that came out of Larry's mouth, especially in public. It was a surprise as to what he would say or do. He was always looking for new ways to get attention and the way he went about it, usually caught his family off guard.

The flip side, however, was the child wonderment Linda instilled into these three believing minds. Norma watched the toothless and beaming smiles as her oldest talked about Santa and his reindeer prancing around on the roof shortly after the three little ones fell asleep Christmas Eve. This was after all four put on a short Christmas show under the direction of Linda: the audience—Norma and Allen. It included dance, stand-up comedy and lip-syncing holiday songs. Linda had a way of constructing their imagination and allowing them to bask in their childhood. She planned Debbie's Halloween costumes months in advance and readied her for birthday parties and dance recitals—even her hair and makeup! And although Larry's chronological age was only four years behind Linda, mentally he was the youngest. She kept watch over his actions and often intervened when necessary. Linda was a second mom to these three endearing children and Norma delighted in seeing it evolve. So proud that her daughter could clean the house while the kids played outside, make a simple lunch for everyone and best of all . . . she was happy to help. It was now time for Norma to focus on how she was going to make more money.

Allen said he wasn't going to stick with his new job at the Fuller Brush business, even though it had been only a few months since he had quit Baird's bread company. Previous to that he had decided he didn't want to work for Singer any longer. And, now he was going to pick up a Circle K store application.

"You're going to work at Circle K!" David acted so proud.

"Maybe you'll see your daddy-ee-o working at Circle K-ee-o. Doesn't everyone want to work there?" Allen chuckled and tapped the kitchen window pointing to the Circle K sign lit up above the oleanders.

The frequently used convenience store was located at the southwest corner of the intersection. They didn't know how they had possibly got along without it before. The bottles of milk were no longer placed at the door each week so Norma was pleased that she could send one of the children, before or after school, with a quarter and a dime to pick up milk only a short distance away. David often volunteered to be the runner but his hidden agenda was to view the newest and latest candy available; red and pink waxed lips, candy cigarettes, and the new 16 ounce sodas were his prime choices. If he walked slow enough, looking down and keeping his "eyes peeled" across the dirt field, he could find a penny or two for his own purchase to satisfy his sweet tooth.

Larry always begged to go along.

"You better hold your brother's hand, Larry, when you walk across that busy street," Norma threatened. "Or, you won't go next time. You hear me?"

"I know, you tode me mom!" Larry cocked his head.

"Don't get sassy with me young man. I mean it. You obey, Buster!"

"I know! I know! I know! Uhhh, you tode me once aready!" The talking back was on the rise. It seemed he enjoyed arguing way too much these days, and yet the family was figuring out that Larry knew what to say in order to appease his listeners. He responded with a "yeah, I know" but his actions showed that he really didn't know. His words were confusing at times and so much of his conversations were merely a tape recording of what he had heard from others—especially his siblings. When it came to his mother, however, he always wanted the upper hand and certainly didn't like her telling him what to do! The continued fight for independence became more concerning for all.

This added to the piled-up worries Norma had over Allen's dissatisfaction of jobs was leading her to more disappointments. He just couldn't figure out what he wanted and so it was time for her to find a REAL job, perhaps a career. Wondering if she would have to be the one to ultimately "bring home the bacon", she began a search related to her field of expertise.

CHAPTER 23

DEEP AND WIDE–1963/64

"What's wrong, mommy?" Debbie was worried.

Norma sat on the edge of the couch and frowned at the television. Her hand covered her mouth. It was just another day of walking home from school for David and Debbie and upon entering the house they usually found their mom busy with ironing. This time they noticed her watery eyes and concentrated look toward the TV and immediately realized her sadness was beyond the Combs clan.

"President Kennedy was shot!"

The children turned toward the man on the news, listening to his sad account of the details. They watched their mother wipe her tears holding a tissue in each fist. This was an unusual type of sorrow; one of the unknown and beyond their family, neighborhood, church and school. She continued to stare at the TV and paid little attention to the children.

A quick knock at the door, a voice shouted out, "Norma!" Ida opened the door and walked in. "Did you hear?" her next-door neighbor asked.

"I am watching it now!" Norma grabbed another Kleenex from the box, placing it under her small nose.

"What is this world coming to?" Ida exclaimed and the two shook their heads conversing about the events of the nation while still focused toward the small screen.

For days the children heard the adults speak about the terrible incident and observed those around them view the commentaries on television as well as reading the newspaper. The kids tried to make sense of it from bits and pieces and they knew it was serious, but didn't pause too long. They had too much playing, pretending, schooling and child relationships to content with, and more importantly bigger and better forts to build.

Allen had recently erected a tetherball on a poll cemented inside an old tire. Debbie and Linda Little played by the hour. That added to the makeshift Ping-Pong table, as well as the large tractor tire lying flat on the ground, full of sand and toys, became the many choices of outside actions. The ingenuity of Allen constructing toys for his children pulled out the creativity Norma knew he possessed. The prize winner was the day he searched for and found an used sewing machine peddle, fashioned to accelerate an actual go-cart with an extra long extension cord. An on-hand Kirby vacuum motor powered the thing and attached were wheels from an old wagon. The boys could drive it within the entire carport area. Norma had to stop what she was doing and take a picture of her delighted kids. Allen out did himself on this one.

The belief of not spending money pressed Allen into finding parts: sometimes in trashcans, but often just here and there. He assembled child-friendly action toys; better than ones found in stores. It was an anticipated surprise as to what he would come up with next. From the time the children came home from school, they dropped their stuff and turned right around to the backyard, front yard, carport or even the dirt road. There was way too much to do before the sun set. Not even going inside for drinking water, they pulled the cooler hose lying on the grass and gulped big to continue hard play. It didn't stop there, once darkness hit, the inside list of activities was just as long. A different type of make believe had to be accomplished.

The favorite was 'garbage men' using the bunk beds to be the garbage truck and the plastic toy dashboard/steering wheel for driving. To set up the real-life scenario, the youngest three first had to search the house for all the small trashcans and line them up in a row next to the truck. When David gave the exact whistle, Debbie jumped off the bed, grabbed one of the small containers and threw it to the top bed to be emptied by Larry, and then another whistle was the signal for the driver. Norma was impressed that the three had truly created this imitation only from observing the precise routine of the weekly sanitation engineers. It became evident that the daily lives of adults in their environment were fabricated play procedures for her children. Watching Larry was encouraging. He too understood how to participate in the creative games and could use his imagination nearly as well as his siblings. Norma smiled while watching her special son blend in.

On Linda's watch, she brought all the neighborhood kids inside the house and they searched for items to serve as desks and chairs for the classroom. Linda was the teacher and her school was full! Children who lived in this subdivision wanted to be at this particular address. And so word spread that the Combs house was the place to go for fun and activities. Allen included any child to be a part of his new inventions. He became the dad for those whose dad's were absent. The children crowned him emperor of their lives and Linda was a close runner-up. But hidden in this blend was the benefit of playing with a type of child not seen at school, church, parks and even stores. Larry's handicap and unusual behavior educated these lucky ones. It happened through daily exposure of child's play. They asked the Combs kids many why questions: Why doesn't Larry understand? Why does he act that way? Why does his tongue hang out like that?" And the most frequent, "What is he trying to say?" Because Debbie now spent the most time interacting with him, she understood 'Larryneese' and thus became the official 'Larry interpreter.' There were words even Norma and Allen couldn't get and had to call their youngest daughter into the room.

"Help us out, Debbie. We can't figure out what Larry is trying to say." Once, Debbie cleared it up, Larry nodded his head and said "Yea, um that what I mean." and then skipped off to finish whatever important task was at hand.

Allen was also the king at Toastmasters club for he had recently won a couple of speech trophies. His desire for public speaking vented itself in this club and Norma remembered that she, some day, had to frame that Dale Carnegie course completion certificate he had earned in the late 50's. He never spoke about his own accomplishments and the kids relied on their mom for that information.

Norma finally relented to the fact that Allen would never go back to his chiropractic business, and although the Circle K company provided the best Christmas party the family had ever experienced, it wasn't bringing enough weekly money to pay those heaping bills. So it was that he was re-hired at Singer, now Sears. The bills were going to get paid if Norma had anything to do with it. Even if it didn't bother Allen, it wasn't the way she was raised. It just wasn't right! She often followed him around the house complaining about the finances, waving the bills in his face. Over time he learned to ignore her fits, but it only enhanced her determination.

Allen was dedicated to another group called the Odd Fellows. She mocked him about the secretive once-a-week meetings. "You guys are really 'odd fellows' she said, pleased with her play on words.

"Keep it up," he teased, but still making sure he revealed nothing.

"Speaking of odd. . . kids, look at your dad." Norma smirked.

"What are you doing?" The kids questioned while staring at their dad and sustaining puzzled looks. They watched him pull the receiver of the phone across the hallway and into the bathroom. He hung it over the toilet bowl—then flushed. Allen quickly put his finger to his lips and gave a quiet shhh sound toward his kids. With a slight smile, he put the phone to his ear.

"Good that did the trick." He handed the phone to his wife. "There. . . now you can use it." He chuckled.

Norma reached out her hand, grabbed the phone and listened for a second to hear the dial tone. "Those yakking ladies on the party line talk way too much! I get so sick of waiting for them to get off. Don't they know other people need to use the phone? Yep that'll show them." She put her finger in the dial hole number nine on the base, spun it around and giggled. All four kids doubled over with laughter.

During the down times in Norma's day she thought of how much she missed her mother. After hearing her dad's voice on the phone, she tearfully wrote in her journal.

"It's a wonderful heritage to have an honest father. Thank you, Lord, for Roy Harrold's many qualities; integrity, humility, gentleness, bravery, faithful, honesty, devotion to his wife and children, hard working, consistent, devoted to God and the Bible, good values and spoke well of others. He always looked on the bright side of life."

She scanned the list and it suddenly hit her—The man she married possessed some of these same qualities and so those difficult days, in which she wallowed in self-pity and even anger toward Allen, she pulled out the list and counted her blessings for both of these great men in her life.

It didn't take long for Norma to land an interesting job working with children in the Mesa Public Schools. Head Start was a new early childhood education concept implemented by President Lyndon B. Johnson for helping financially challenged families and teaching proper parenting skills.[9] Her volunteer experience with the Red Cross in her younger years was a definite benefit on her resume as well as her previous schooling. Using her educational knowledge obtained from her social work degree reminded her of the passion she still had in her heart toward those in need, especially young ones.

Everyone at home had to get used to their mom's long absences from time to time. Adjustments were not liked but required. Yet, most days her presence was available by the time her children got home from school.

CHAPTER 24

HISTORY IN THE MAKING-1964

"Mom! Mom! Mom!" Linda shouted as she ran in the house on a Sunday afternoon.

"What! What! What is it? Who's hurt? Who's bleeding?"

Linda straightened and took a deep breath!

"What's wrong?" Norma implored for an immediate answer.

"We gotta watch the Ed Sullivan show tonight!"

"Oh, Linda! You scared me for Pete's sake!" Her hand slapped her chest.

"No really, mom. The Beatles are going to be on the Ed Sullivan show tonight!"

"What are you ranting and raving about? What? Insects? Who?"

"The Beatles!" she tilted her head and turned her hands out.

"Who in the world are the Beetles?"

Linda's two friends were running behind her and finally caught up slipping inside the front doorway in time to answer.

"A rock and roll group!"

"Yeah, mom, they have hair like this?' Linda circled her fingers around her head.

"They are so boss!"

"And soooo cute."

Norma looked into the eyes of these lovesick girls and chuckled at the urgency of such baloney.

"Oh Linda! You girls are something else!"

"Mom, call me Carol!"

"Why do you keep telling me that? What is this Carol bit?"

Sue, Linda's close friend from two-doors down, quickly reacted "We are all calling her by her middle name. That's what she wants."

"Well, fiddlesticks! Your name is Linda."

"Yeah, Linda Carol and I've decided I want to be called Carol so I'm telling everyone to call me Carol. Now back to the Beatles, we've got to watch them, okay?"

"Well, don't we watch the Ed Sullivan show every Sunday night? Yes, I suppose we can watch these Beetles, as you call them!"

"But this time, it's going to be a really big show!" her daughter's eyebrows raised up and waving her hands.

"No a really big shoooo." Lifting their shoulders, the girls imitated Mr. Sullivan himself. "Yeah, a really big shooo!" Giggling together, they ran out the door. Within the faded female chatter, Norma could hear Linda making promises to her run-around friends.

"Hey, maybe I can get my dad to make his delicious popcorn balls for everyone! They are really good and he has to wear rubber gloves on his hands to mix it and everything. It's really cool!"

"Okay, CAROL!" She heard the girls emphasize her new name.

"We named her Linda!" Norma whispered to herself.

The girls ran down the street laughing and returned within the hour. Her dad had already started the popcorn and the girls plopped their bodies in front of the boob tube. No one could see or hear once the faces of the four mop top singers covered the 12-inch screen. High pitched screaming of three infatuated girls drowned out the words "She loves you, Yeah, Yeah, Yeah!" The blond heads blocked the view, practically kissing the screen. In between shaking heads, the rest of the family slightly viewed weeping and fainting teenagers as the camera's panned the audience. The love was instant! These young lives would never be the same after tonight, as would the entire world!

A widespread Beatle madness enveloped the four kids in the weeks and months and even years to come. At just about any given moment you could hear a Beatle song being sung somewhere in the house or nearby outside and as the purchase of Beatle albums replaced forty fives, it became a fixation. New songs were entered into the Beatle memory repertoire. Linda and David plastered their walls with Beatle posters and Linda had dreams about Paul, or was it George?

"Let's be a band!" David pulled out the stand-up vacuum cleaner for a microphone and gave into Larry's strong desire. "I wan be Paul," he demanded. Debbie used a tennis racket as a guitar and sang while David pounded the top of the charcoal grill lid for the Ringo drums. If they could find another person in the vicinity to be George, than so be it. They shook their heads over and over to make the hair fly in all directions. "Oooooh, Oooohh I wanta hold your hand!" Even Larry could sing each word of every song. Though the words came out somewhat garbled and a little delayed. He was the biggest fanatical Beatle addict and knew every word of every song. When the world became his enemy, he slammed the door to his room, put the needle on the album, turned up the small record player as loud as it would go and sang at the top of his lungs. It was liberation of rebellion and a short, sure way, to forget his troubles. Music was becoming a high priority and on the same level as humor and child-play in this house, according to the Beatle-wannabees.

While imitating the dark-haired foursome from Liverpool, alongside millions of fans across the nation, Shari, David and Linda Little came over to be apart of the rock and roll concerts. They hardly noticed that Linda and Norma were actually babysitting them after school. Nancy Little's new job at Mesa Pediatrics put her "in a pickle." She needed childcare. That's why she and Norma planned a job-share of babysitting between the two families. Linda (Carol) helped too. It was this particular day that would forever be remembered . . .

CHAPTER 25

PERFECT TIMING

"I'm going with Linda and David Little to drop off their school stuff, be right back." Debbie declared to her sister. The girls had just finished another day in third grade. Homework can be done later, they thought. "Let's play."

The three ran down the street and opened the door to the Little's habitat. Shortly after stepping inside and closing the door, they heard a knock. David L. turned to open it slightly and viewed a large man standing behind it.

"Hi." The stranger said as he took the liberty to widen the space and make his way inside. "My name is Dr. Eddie. Are your Mom and Dad home?"

"No." David said hoping he'd turn around and go away but suddenly realizing the error of his response.

"Well, we have a very serious illness at a house down the street and I'm just checking door to door on the health of families. How old are you?" he looked at David.

The girls' curiosity forced them to turn and walk toward the kitchen, now glaring at this large person who claimed to be important.

"Hi girls. What are your names?" The man looked straight into their eyes and began inching his way further inside the kitchen.

All three exhibited an extreme nervousness and a strong feeling of something terribly wrong! Their eyes widened as long as the stranger kept talking, becoming more shocked at his forcefulness. He was a drill sergeant in his questioning and already knew way too much about this family.

"Where's your older sister? Where do your parents work? What time do they get home? Are there any other children in the family?"

The constant questions were producing a high level of anxiety, so they maintained their distance. They were still trying to believe what they were hearing. Would a doctor actually come to their home? Something, just didn't sit right and uneasiness was taking over the room. This unknown person, doctor or not, was asking very personal questions. Was this real? The two girls moved close together and held hands.

David stepped back when he heard the phone. The interrupting ring was highly welcomed! He quickly moved toward the phone hanging on the wall and grabbed it with a deep sigh. "Hello, hello mom!" he said with a quivering voice. Before she said a word, he told on the doctor. "Mom, there is a man here asking us all kinds of questions!"

The volume of Nancy's voice could be heard in the room. "Let me talk to him right now!"

David pulled the phone away from his ear and held it out toward the odd visitor. "My mom wants to talk to you," he said with confidence.

"Well, um, listen, um, I have to go! I can't talk right now, um, and um. I have lots to do today. So, bye!" He moved with haste and exited the house.

David intently frowned toward the girls. They stood gazing at each other, mouths open, in disbelief at the rapid departure of this peculiar person. David's face grimaced as he turned his head back and put the receiver to his ear.

"Mom, he's gone!"

"David, this is a friend of your mom's at work. She has left to come home and the police are on their way. Lock the doors," her voice reassuring.

"Okay," he moved in slow motion, placing the receiver inside the wall cradle. His hands trembled as he turned toward the girls, eyes widened. Swiftly walking to the door, he locked it, bolt and all, but not before Debbie darted out. She said she just wanted to be home and no one would convince her otherwise. Running down the street she looked up to see Shari strolling toward the house, her black violin case in one hand and a cold glass bottle of soda pop in the other. Shari's head tilted to focus on Debbie's frightened expression, now anxiously listened to the Dr. Eddie account.

Within minutes Norma, Shari, Nancy and Debbie entered the flat roofed house. The police, as well as two men wearing white shirts and ties, followed behind. They all sat down on the living room furniture; it was obvious an intense discussion was about to begin. **Now,** the questioning really came forth! These detectives had a concerned and concentrated look about them as the children told their side of the story. Listening to the outrageous tale this man told these innocent children for the sake of questioning, Norma couldn't believe it. Whoever he was, how could he get away with such gibberish? The detectives wanted all three children involved to look through a notebook of mug shots. Two children were instructed to go out of the room while one picked the correct picture, not having the influence of the others. Debbie, Linda L and David L. pointed to the same face. It was confirmed! The adults looked at each other across the room as they excused the children from the living room.

Walking out of the house and toward the Combs' place, the kids noticed a police car circling the streets and began conversing…

"This was big!"

"That man must have been a bad man."

"He definitely wasn't a doctor!"

"He lied to us."

"Do you think he made the whole thing up?"

"Yes"

"I knew something was wrong!"

"Me too!"

"Me too!"

"Who was he?"

"I don't know."

"Me neither."

They were in deep conversation and didn't notice Allen walking toward them.

"I'm going to your house." Allen paused long enough to look into the eyes of the children. "You kids stay in the house with Linda."

"You mean Carol."

"Linda, Carol…whatever her name is. Now, go!"

"Where's Larry, daddy?" Debbie turned her head.

"He's with your sister and they are playing the Felix the Cat game." Debbie sensed that her daddy was forcing himself to remain calm.

Walking into the house, Carol locked the door behind them. The adults were gone a long time and soon she got out another board game to ease curious minds. "So who was this person?" Carol looked up at her mom as she finally opened the back door.

Norma shook her head and paused before saying the right words— still trying to process it all. "He is a very bad person and is wanted by the police."

The kids looked up as if needing more information.

"The police have been looking for this man for a while." She faced the three involved, "You did a good job picking out his picture from the notebook, but you might have to do it again, this time out of a lineup down at the police station."

"What's that mean?" Debbie asked.

Norma explained in simple terms to the children and privately hoped they wouldn't have to go through with it. It will give surely give them nightmares, she thought.

As the children were tucked into bed that night, Norma and Allen closed their door and spent time lying on their backs, staring at the ceiling and rehashing the day's events.

"I can't believe he was wanted out of Michigan for child molestation and attempted murder!" Norma just had to say it out loud. Allen didn't want to hear it again. "According to some of the questions, he could have been planning this for days," she continued.

"Oh, it was obvious he had been watching their house." Allen spoke. "He knew the parents weren't going to be home."

"And somehow knew there was an older sister and that she came home from school later. Can you image what might have happened if Nancy hadn't called?"

"I don't want to think about it." Allen's glaring eyes still faced up.

"We will be forever indebted to her for calling when she did." Norma replied.

"It certainly wasn't a coincident." His wisdom came forth.

An invisible weight pushed on their bodies; neither could close their eyes for the night. The 'could haves' were now an acute, clearing thought and weighed heavily on their hearts. Norma swung her legs around the bed and stood, she walked toward the bedrooms, checking on the kids for the third time since tucking them in. Now looking at the sweet sleeping faces, she contemplated a contrast of complete innocence verses the darkness of Satan scathing a human being's deranged thoughts.

Her prayer was humble and filled with profound gratitude. "How great thou art! How great thou art!" she whispered and fell on her knees next to Debbie, watching her nine-year-old daughter's breathing pattern and thanking God for His unlimited protection that day!

"Thank you, God, for allowing my dear friend to call at exactly the right time.

Thank you, God . . . for you demonstrated your perfect timing!"

CHAPTER 26

RE-FOCUS

"I want to be a detective when I grow-up." Carol announced when the Dr. Eddie subject matter surfaced.

"Mom, why didn't we have to do that line-up thing?" Debbie asked.

"Because the police knew it was him. He's in jail now." She calmly responded and grateful it was all over.

"They get to solve murder mysteries." Carol continued.

"Oh, my stars, you read too many Nancy Drew books!" Norma told her oldest.

"I don't like that scary stuff." Debbie replied. "And, I don't like watching Alfred Hitchcock. It gave me nightmares last night."

Carol laughed, "It's just a show, kid!"

"You mean Debbie watched Alfred Hitchcock with you?" Norma was aggravated.

"Yeah, Mom, she rolled the TV into our room after you guys went to bed and I had to watch somebody being stabbed in the shower. I never want to take a shower again."

"What? Linda Carol!! Norma scolded.

"Whaaat?" She cocked her head and studied her mom's look.

"She's too young for that stuff!"

Carol gave her sister a defiant look, detesting that she told.

"Okay, Ms. Priss!" She squinted her eyes toward Debbie. It was a name commonly used by the siblings when their mother once again favored the "spoiled" youngest. Norma lectured her oldest about the matter and Carol made her usual here-we-go-again face.

Her curiosity about the world of the unknown moved her to organize something else her parents didn't know about, and she hoped her sister wouldn't rat on her again. It was the intriguing weekly séances. Any of the kids were invited and they could bring neighborhood friends inside the house once she prepared: drawing the drapes to a darkened living room. The more kids, the better to call upon the dead through the use of a Quiji board. Larry somehow knew to keep his body completely still when Carol dominated the circle around the table and entered the world of the deceased. It was all in fun—or so she said.

What WAS truly fun was the church couples and families coming over for backyard picnics. They reputed a strong foundation of building memories, especially around the Ping-Pong table in the backyard. Allen had hung floodlights to the edge of the roof aiming at the backyard toys. Larry's inability to connect the paddle with the ball allowed assistance from others. Everyone made sure he had some sort of involvement even if it was way beyond his abilities. Some friends had more patience than others. Norma took mental notes. The late night outside games, food and fellowship resounded with loud talking and laughter and echoed well into the summer nights. Neighbors were gracious not to complain about the noise.

The relationships of these First Methodist families were broadening because of the weeklong Mingus Mountain church camps. It became an annual, inexpensive vacation away from the heat and the rat race of the city. The Combs and Little families were getting to know new people. Norma thrived on surrounding herself with others and talking with new acquaintances from other Methodist churches.

Larry occupied himself with volleyball, horseshoes and chasing girls around the spacious land of wildflowers, pine needles, and large boulders, while relishing the cool breeze and pine aroma. He had such a unique way of drawing others to himself; more and more families were willing to assist, even if it was during his most rebellious moments. Norma and Allen could finally loosen the reigns on their first-born son to allow the freedom he wanted and often demanded. It also made way for stimulating and enjoyable adult conversation without interruption. The side benefit was that there was always someone around to help keep Larry in view, but it wasn't until someone bellowed "Where's Larry?" in which friends got a glimpse of his quick escape techniques and lack of self-adjusted boundaries. Once this question was heard, it alerted all for an organized search in the area. Because so many eyes were seeking, he was found within minutes but with the massive forest surrounding the camp of carefully positioned cabins around a large dinning hall, one thought of the worst, a mentally retarded child lost in the woods.

For once, their friends got a realistic picture of how the Combs family handled a child now labeled "trainable." (Which meant his IQ demonstrated that he could handle personal hygiene, self-help skills, as well as learning basic chores, and had the ability to remember the order of each simple step).

Each trip to these mountains brought a special memory; but it was one particular summer that the children giggled upon reflection . . .

The usual packing of suitcases, Norma's body brisk with action and commands to her children were on the rise. "Don't dawdle kids! Let's get into the car! Up and at 'em!"

"Are you kidding, Dad?" all the kids questioned when they saw the uniquely extended dark green vehicle pull into the driveway for loading.

"About what?" he responded with a half smile.

"About taking that thing to Mingus Mountain?"

"Yeah. Don't you want to ride in a hearse?" He laughed looking at the stunned expressions on each of the four faces.

It belonged to the Bucholtz family. Mr. Bucholtz, a work buddy, recently purchased it from a funeral home and talked Allen into taking it on vacation to the mountains. He convinced him of all the extra space holding several "bodies."

"Oh you'll have fun! It's comfortable and there's plenty of room for those suitcases plus it's a blast watching the reaction of people. Everyone's "dying" to ride in it! Uuuuuh!"

The uuuuuh sound (kind of a grunt) became the common noise toward the dry jokes, the groaners! Those closely involved picked up on the sound to use in place of a full laughter. It was to become a Combs/Little trademark. The funeral gags also became Allen's delight this particular summer and upon arriving at the mountaintop, the traveling hearse was the talk among the camp folk for the entire week.

David and his friends' latest fort was now an underground tunnel behind the Oleanders. Norma thought it strange that he was taking the shovel back there and by the time she walked out to the dirt field to spy several days later, they had already lost interest. The "novelty wore off." Finding assorted materials for a better one, this time above ground. These forts were looking more and more interesting and even somewhat sophisticated. They were improving with practice. Larry tagged along, craving to be included in the men's club. He was accepted as long as he could cooperate and his attention span allowed it. If the boys wanted to talk about something Larry was not to hear, spelling the word became secret code. Larry was clueless.

Norma and Allen watched their growing children enter into new stages of childhood (pre-adolescence) and Larry was once again falling further behind. Alienation would become a common feeling for this growing child and it pierced the heart of his parents viewing more frequent spaces of loneliness. Though his siblings were sensitive enough to include him as much as possible, they desired some independence themselves and were moving away from their own blood and toward friends. The revelation, however, came in watching them protect their brother, "who doesn't understand" from the criticism of others. All three siblings became the cat who arched his back ready to bounce on their prey as if to say: "I can correct my brother, but don't **you** dare!"

"Hey, Poody! Do you see those people over there staring at us?" Debbie said as the two walked side-by-side across the Pioneer Park grass, barefoot, on a Sunday afternoon.

"Where? Or, there?" he pointed in their direction.

Debbie quickly pulled his arm down: "Don't point! Don't even look. I say if they are going to stare, let's give them something to stare about. Here, grab my hand and let's be boyfriend and girlfriend."

"What? I you bofiend?" Larry looked at her.

"Just pretend. Here, take my hand. No, I mean lock fingers, like this!" she demonstrated.

"Okay, we, umm, be bofiend and gilfiend." He giggled and glared at the spectators. Larry instantly became aware of his protruding tongue and pulled it inside his mouth pressing his lips together and giving himself a handsome look. He stuck his nose in the air and jerked his hips as they strolled past the gossipers. Debbie turned and scowled, her bottom lip jutted and her buttocks projected. "Take a picture, it might last longer!" She yelled at the gawkers and continued her deliberate step. With a jerk she pulled her shoulders back and her blond ponytail swayed back and forth with each angry steps.

"Yeah, take a piture." Larry copied the same jesters and attitude with precision.

"I get so tired of being a freak show!" Debbie whispered under her breath.

"Wha you say?"

"Nothing, Larry. Keep walking and don't look back!"

"Okay!" Larry held his chin up, his head erect.

Once out of view they turned to face each other, splitting into laughter and high fiving their accomplishments.

"Anyway I already have a gilfiend." Larry declared, still stuck on the girlfriend bit.

"I know, Larry, besides I'm your sister, I can't be your girlfriend too! Sisters aren't girlfriends."

"I love Sheeri, anyway!"

"That's what I hear. You wrote her a love note and put it in her mailbox."

"Well she same age with me and, umm, well, she buetiful. I love her anyway." Larry took pride in the few words he could now write and spell. His favorite was "love." It would come in very handy for all the future affectionate notes. Shari Little was the recipient of most.

CHAPTER 27

LAUGHTER AND TEARS -1965

Noticing Carol's greater desire to spend her days with friends and very little time with family sent an adolescent blinking light to the family. If she wasn't hanging out with her girl friends, she was depleting most of her days in the one and only bathroom they owned. She kept up on the newest looks and moved away from the Haley Mills fashion, aspiring to look like the famous model, Twiggy. Her make-up and hair had to be just right before exiting the necessary room; it didn't matter how many times Norma yelled at her. The false eyelashes were to be perfectly split apart with a straight pin and every ratted hair, sprayed and positioned the correct way on her head. Finally giving up, David and Larry often walked to the backyard and watered the trees with urine. They just couldn't hold it for such a length of time.

"Hurry, I burp my hynee." Larry's hand held his buttocks and he screamed at his sister. (burb my hynee was the only allowable way to say fart without saying fart; otherwise, a very dirty look came from Norma to her children).

"Where were you, David?" Norma asked the two boys walking in the door after noticing their disappearance.

"This time we couldn't pee in the backyard, we had to go potty big so I took Larry and we walked to the gas station to use their bathroom." (In addition to Circle K and Dog and Suds, the Stapley and Broadway intersection now held a Gulf gas station.)

"Yeah, I had to go potty big real bad. I burp my hynee," Larry told his mom.

"Well, I hope you washed your hands." She scowled, trying not to encourage the potty talk.

Carol still behind a locked door of the room she considered her own, it just happened to be the only room with a toilet, a slight necessity for the other family members. In Norma's opinion, outward appearance was way too important for this girl… She was determined to buck this system her oldest had going. "I'm going to lay down the law!" She said while bent over the doorknob and picking the lock with a bobby pin. It was the only way to get her out of the very room everyone in the house HAD to use . . .sometimes without warning.

Added to the record of regulations were the evening sit-down dinners. The family was required to be present and ready to appreciate the hot meal that was "slaved over."

"Take the phone off the hook before you come, would ya?" Norma told Carol who was slowly easing toward the undersized dining room.

Carol pulled off the receiver and placed it next to the base. "But, I'm not hungry. Besides, stuffed peppers are David's favorite, not mine." She walked to the table and pulled her chair out with a frown.

"Well then you can just sit there, but you have to be with the family." Norma took Carol's hand and then grabbed Larry's chapped fingers on her right side. Bending her body into the chair, she scooched herself up to the table. This was code for all in preparation of sitting, holding hands and mouths in position for the daily prayer song—"For health and strength and daily bread, we give these thanks of Lord. Ahhhhhmeeeeen." The children had sung it so much they were now adding their own off-key harmony.

As soon as the last maintained note was butchered by the children's voices, Carol spouted, "Pass the butter!" She had her knife ready for the lonely piece of white Sunbeam bread that she quickly threw on her plate.

David cocked his head and with a bratty look, poked fun at her. "What do you say?" Impersonating his mom's frequent statement to stress good manners.

"Pass the butter before I belt you across the mouth?" Carol barely got out the last word and choked with an entertaining laugh, proud of her quick wit.

The kids busted into hilarity at Carol's surprise extremeness and encouraged the rebellious humor. Allen snickered under his breath.

"Oh, stop that!" Norma commanded.

"Please, pass the butter PLEASE!" Carol said the necessary words, this time with sarcasm and still laughing at the previous remark.

A weak knock at the back door immediately stopped the giggles. Norma turned her head toward the kitchen door and yelled out," We're eating!"

"Mawawawm!" Debbie whined.

"Why does Annie have to come over every evening at the same time? Right during supper! I'm sick and tired of it!" Norma grumbled. They watched the shadow cross over the window and heard the footsteps weaken towards the street.

"Mawawm, that hurts her feelings!" Debbie's eyebrows turned down.

"I don't care, she needs to learn that you can't play till we're done eating."

"I'm Annie's best friend, besides her mom is really ill and her daddy's mean!"

Knowing her daughter's compassion towards this skinny, freckled face, across-the-street friend was admired, but it didn't justify breaking the supper rules. "You can play with her after you eat!"

"Oh, boy!" Debbie's face lit up.

"**And,** after the dishes are done!" Norma hurried to finish her statement.

"Oh man!" Her arm swung around clicking her fingers. Like any other child, she often tried to finagle out of their nightly chores.

"It's your turn to wash!" David reminded his sister.

"No, I did it two nights ago. It's Larry's turn."

"No sirree, I did aready. Not my turn! Umm, I, uhh, I winse (rinse)."

"No, I rinse tonight." David had it planned.

Larry actually enjoyed taking his turn with the sibling arguments; often his sequence was out of whack. Yet, today he seemed to know what he was talking about and could hold his own debate. It was a surprise to all.

"Oh good grief, we go through this every night!" Norma shook her head and stood to pull the dessert of cherry Jell-O and bananas from the icebox. Larry smiled big and got everyone to look at him behind his mother's back. That familiar devious expression and crooked smile made it explicable that he was up to something. He slipped his fist under the table and turned it toward the underside of the pressed wood, copying the same exact knock heard minutes before.

"We're eating!!" Norma now angry, she quickly turned to pull the curtain back from the small window above the kitchen sink. No Annie this time. She watched her family bust into a hardy laugh and immediately realized she'd been "had"! Everyone seated at the table was proud of Larry's trickery. Norma was also amused and laughed with her family about her own foolishness. Larry pulled it off!

"Rats," she was now clicking HER fingers. "You were pulling my leg."

Larry giggled and acted so proud of himself! Of course seeing the ruckus he caused, he had to keep his hand stretched under the table and knocked over and over.

"It was only funny the first time, Larry!" everyone spoke at the same time. "You tricked her once, you can't do it again! Stop that!" they all demanded. Ignoring their advice, he tried several more times before he understood that it wasn't getting the same results.

"I need to go anyway!" Carol changed the subject and stared up at the gold-star clock on the wall.

"What about dessert?" her mother questioned.

"I don't want dessert"

"What about dishes?"

"It's my turn to dry, so I can do it later."

"Oh, let her go!" Allen interrupted.

Norma knew he was right. She had to remember to cut this pre-adult a little slack.

"Where are you off to?" She supposed it was with her friends for the third time today.

"Just outside" Carol pointed out the window to the front yard.

"What do you say?" Norma turned towards her juvenile daughter.

"May I be excused?" Finally she got it right.

"Yes, you may."

Carol jumped up, holding the last bite of her bread and walked out the front door. The remaining family members began to converse and passed the whipped cream, taking turns spraying it on top of the bright red Jell-O. Allen had the most white and his children teased him about the cream mountain in his bowl. "Where's the Jell-O, daddy-o? We don't see it" They snickered.

The jangling of plastic dishes in the sink, mumbled laughter, joke telling and Larry's goofy faces stopped in an instant. A piercing and high-pitched chilling scream broke the barrier. All eyes looked toward the sound coming from the pepper tree that was straight ahead outside the front window. The utter helplessness and terrified faces watched Carol's flopping body hit branches on her way down from the very top. Each extended branch breaking the speed against her petite back. The sound of cracking twigs and the screams of horror re-sounded the area. Within seconds she slammed the earth. Running feet and screaming children halted in the front yard and stared at her contorted face looking up at the sky. Bits of branches surrounded her broken body and instant pain-filled moaning ignited. All family members fell to their knees around her motionless legs and arms. Allen squeezed his daughter's hand while his wife jumped up and ran back into the house. Norma was limp, her fingers trembling to get control over the spin of the dial.

"Emergency!" the voice didn't come quick enough.

"My daughter just fell from a 25-foot tree! Hurry! 1224 Fifth Ave. Hurry!" She screamed into the receiver. Within seconds, the sirens blared in the distance.

"Someone, grab Larry's hand and hold it tight!" Allen yelled at the neighbors who were now circling and staring down at Carol.

Curious passengers in the cars slowly driving by asked questions, and as people from further away heard the closeness of the ear-piercing sirens, they exited their houses and ran toward the commotion.

"What happened? What happened?" Voices erupted and the scolding paramedics repeated their commands. "Step back! Move way back! Stand over there! Let us through!" The reality of what just took place was piercing and the tears of siblings and friends found hugs from adults standing near. Sniffling sounds quieted as the bystanders carefully gazed at the concentrated paramedics checking vitals; her moaning had now turned to blood-curdled screams. They carefully eased her body onto the stretcher and in unison lifted the narrow gurney up and onto the wagon. Norma and Allen conversed as to who would go with Carol and Allen helped his wife step inside the back of the vehicle. It pulled away as all eyes watched the Red Cross image fade down the street. Neighbors were silent as they slowly paced back into their homes.

Norma walked the hospital hall and quickly found a phone to call Allen of the news. "Her back is broken." Norma remained composed until she heard the horrid words come from her own mouth. Pause, "Her head is fine," her voice faltered. No answer, she gave Allen time to process and he gave her time to regain control. He finally asked a few questions and hung up to tell the children. They had gone to their rooms, laid on their beds and were weeping into their pillows.

"Thank you so much, Ida." Allen's troubled eyes hoped Larry would behave himself during the one hour he would be gone. This is when knowing and trusting neighbors came in very handy and he was grateful for their willingness. He hugged his children and assured them of being home soon. Oh, how he desperately wanted to get to the hospital and somehow take the pain of his first-born.

An all-family hospital visit anxiously came a few days later, Carol, now comfortable due to the drugs warding off her agony. The doctor had just come in to show a back brace she would wear for months ahead, even while sleeping.

"For heaven's sake, why in the world did you climb to the top?" Norma asked when the doctor left the room. She had seen many children climb the first few branches, but no one had the nerve to go higher.

"I wanted to see Mike"

"Mike! Mike, who?" Norma had no idea what she was talking about but looking toward the children realized a secret existed between them.

"Mike, from down the street. He drives a motorcycle and rides by our house the same time everyday." Linda revealed.

"The one you said has a big Adam's apple?" Debbie snickered.

"Yeah." Carol tried to laugh but it hurt too much. She expressed some embarrassment at her little sister's revelation of too much information, once again.

"What? How old is he?' Norma asked.

"Eighteen, he's so cute!"

"Was he worth a broken back?" Allen inquired.

"Did you know that he pulled up on his motorcycle when the ambulance came? He wanted to know what was going on." David was more than willing to publicize the news.

"Oh… if he only knew all of that was for him!" Allen chuckled.

"Maybe he can pay the medical bills!" Norma said.

"Funny, Mom!" Carol rolled her eyes.

"Well, that's the most ridiculous thing I've ever heard. You need your head examined!"

"Doctor already did!" Allen and David said it at the same time. Everyone but Norma laughed.

"Well… What were you thinking for crying out loud?" the volume of her voice increased. What in Sam Hill were you thinking?"

David's eyes widened while glaring at his mom. "Mom, don't cuss like that!" He had never heard such words come from his mom's mouth.

Allen laughed. That's not cussing . . . David.

Norma was not amused! She couldn't believe what her daughter just told her! "Phooey!" This naïve sixteen year-old child who thought she was a twenty-one year old adult, was infatuated, and foolishly climbed a 25-foot tree just to see a guy with a cute Adams apple!

A nurse swiftly walked in and stood at the end of the bed. She bent down and started to turn the crank. "Stop, stop! What are doing? Read the clipboard! She has a broken back! Don't you people know what to do?" Norma was now on her feet and yelling into her face. "She has to have a flat bed! Goooood niiiight!"

The person in white uniform looked at the clipboard again, checked it and quickly apologized. Her face flushed a deep red as she spun around and exited the room. The family members felt sorry for the poor lady.

"That could of cause her a lot of pain and this is why I'm staying right here." Norma's finger jerked down. She frowned at her family.

"I have to train these people! Criminy! If they think I'm leaving, well they have another thing coming! You guys can go on but I'm not going to budge! Ridiculous!" she baulked.

"Yeah, reduculous!" Larry wore his mother's anger and kept it until hospital visiting hours brought departure for the family members: everyone except for Norma, that is.

CHAPTER 28

RE-VISITING A CRUCIAL DECISION

Mabel stopped by just to "shoot the breeze." Her Down syndrome boy was only a few years older than Larry. While the two silly clowns scampered through the bedrooms chasing David and Debbie, the women known for their iron wills, sat talking in the living room.

Mabel was also a Marc parent but had recently decided to move Russell to the Children's Colony in the town of Coolidge. When she picked her son up for a weekend visit, they often dropped in at the Combs' house unannounced. Her and Norma had a unique connection and often she just needed to talk. Mabel had so many of the same personality traits as Norma but more powerful in magnitude; Norma almost wilted in comparisons to Mabel's forceful opinions. The conversations resounded throughout the house. As passionate loud voices talked on how to change the world, no one could interrupt.

"The Colony is a good place for Russell and it gives me a break. Most the time he gets along well with his roommates. I pick him on up on weekends and he's usually ready to go back after a couple of days. You need to call them and see if you can get Larry a spot as soon as possible!"

It was a response to Norma's recent complaining about the mounting taxing circumstances involving her boy. The newest concern was his wandering. It seemed for the expansion of family outings and even in the neighborhood, Larry wandered away and sometimes didn't know how to find his way back. Now safety was more of a concern than it had ever been. His body was growing in strength and no longer could the children keep him under control when playing outside. If he got mad, he walked away and often just, well, "wandered off."

Then there was the trust element for anyone in his path. He was known for long confusing discussions and even hugging an unfamiliar person. If someone was walking down the street, Larry said "Hi!" and then just started talking. Who knows exactly what he was saying. Any topic was fine with him.

Sometimes the kids would ask, "Larry do you know him?" Their brother would answer, "Yeah, he my friend." But they knew it was only the first or second time he laid eyes on the guy or girl. It didn't matter, however. Everyone was a long time buddy in Larry's mind.

"Someone pulled up in a car just a few days ago." She told Mabel. "I thought Larry was playing with the neighbor kids. I had no idea who it was but I looked up again and noticed Larry sitting in the back seat of this strange vehicle. The guy was dropping Larry off in front of the house. I went out to thank the man and he said he saw my son strolling around busy Broadway Street—was worried he might get hit by a car." Norma continued. "I thought, at least Larry had the know-how to show this Mr., whoever he was, where he lived."

"But Larry could have been kidnapped, the guy could have been a criminal, you never know." Mabel spouted. "You know how trusting both our boys are when it comes to strangers."

"Yeah, I guess you're right," Norma answered and quieted herself for thought. "I just can't figure out how much independence to give him; he wants to do the same things that his brother and sisters do." She finally spoke, "I mean I can't keep him inside the house all day. When he looks out the window and sees children playing outside with his siblings, he wants so much to be a part of the party and games, but the kids can no longer be the Larry-police, especially when he gets mad. It's frustrating for everyone when he doesn't know how to participate in a game and things get heated when they don't include him. He runs away or sometimes just walks away . . . down the street. The fit-throwing episodes have been escalating lately and I feel sorry for the others when that happens. They just don't know how to handle the situation anymore, so they just ignore him and I don't blame them. To be honest, I don't know how to handle it either. I'm running out of ideas."

"That's why you need help. The staff have been trained and know how to manage those difficult situations." Mabel replied.

"I suppose the Colony doesn't sound so bad." She hadn't heard from them since the initial phone call, but until now considered it a good sign. Recently a friend had told her of another place in Phoenix called The Valley of the Sun. The origins stemmed from Mrs. Bernice Krussell's desires to make a better life for the mentally retarded. Her passion brought some Phoenix hospital, developmental disabled residents to her home and as a result, a school began with a live-in component.[10]

The following days turned into months as her and Allen's frequent dialoging stirred up new possibilities. The air was finally cooling down and the kids were spending numerous hours out of the house. It was refreshing and permitted "parent-time" essential for long discussions and difficult decision-making. Until, that is, someone came in to complain about Larry: his rough play or anger once again creating havoc.

Social dysfunction was not only on the home front, but it was also happening at his school. Norma had recently become more aware of her son's obvious dislike for his classmates. She spent nights thinking about what might be going on in that brain of his and often had to make her own conclusions since Larry couldn't express his feelings in that way. Getting her husband's opinion helped put things in perspective. It appeared Larry was more in tune with his disability when surrounded by more severe and unusual handicaps. But really they could draw the same conclusion while watching interactions with his siblings and friends. He was caught between two worlds of discontent. How could they help him?

"It's always a guessing game with that boy." Norma uttered. "I never know what he's feeling or thinking and why he does what he does."

Yeah, and just when we think we have it figured out, he changes his behavior and completely throws us for a loop," Allen agreed.

The inner uproar within the couple began over the topic of Larry living away from home, yet again. "But what about Marc school? We can't cut our ties there!" Allen voiced.

"Oh, believe me, I'll still be involved and help wherever possible, but Marc doesn't have residential services yet and it will be way down the road for that undertaking. Besides, Larry's been having issues at school lately and maybe he does require close monitoring; you know, twenty-four-seven."

Allen and Norma decided to make it a family field trip to visit the Valley of the Sun. The younger children went along but stayed close to their parents as fear gripped their bodies. Seeing so many children with disabilities (physical and mental) and other various types of handicaps unfamiliar to them was frightening. Their brother was exceedingly normal in comparison.

The place had small houses, or cottages they called them, with a homey and comfortable atmosphere. Larry would live in one with other males and a set of cottage parents would supervise round the clock. During the week he would attend school in another building. The class size was small, allowing for tight control while learning the basics of reading and writing.

As society was educated about the handicap, improvements in these types of surroundings were penetrating the country. Forward thinking and positive attitudes toward the disabled was moving along. Still, there were always those close-minded folks who didn't see the need for children like Larry to be away from the institution setting. Educating others was on-going and keeping patience toward their ignorance. . . draining!

The benefits of having Valley of the Sun only 30-40 minutes away from Mesa lessened the guilt; Larry could come home frequently. They would make sure those days would be set aside for the much loved picnics, Sunday drives and hikes in the desert—especially with the Little family. He would desperately need the extra family bonding since he would be living with outsiders during the week.

"The other children will be gone during the day once school starts. Debbie and Carol have their dance lessons and gymnastics after school, and David his Boy Scouts. I'll be working. We are all busy weekdays and so weekends can be our connecting time."

It all sounded reasonable, but as Norma looked at her husband's droopy eyes, she knew he wasn't convinced.

CHAPTER 29

UTTER SHOCK AND CHOCOLATE MILK -1966

Saturday morning the children woke to hear the humming voice of their mother as she dusted the end tables and TV. Mornings were her favorite part of the day and her energy was at its peak. The kids slowly stretched and took their time climbing out of bed for they knew what was coming up.

"Come on…let's get up and go! Up and at em! The day is young! Lickety split! You're sleeping the best part of the day away. Get on the stick. This house looks like a pig pen!"

Oh, the dreaded Saturday morning routine! No one was to go anywhere with anybody until the house was clean. It was one of those set-in stone rules instilled in her young offspring from a very early age. All rooms were to be cleaned, sheets to be washed, furniture dusted, floors vacuumed, and even yard work. It was expected and demanded; therefore, everyone complied even if it was with attitude.

Allen was away canvassing for his new job of selling Electrolux vacuum cleaners door-to-door. He finally got his wish of having an outside job and being his own boss; however, it took him away on weekends.

Hearing the high-pitch of sirens screaming nearby, Norma looked at the clock and realized it was much too early for the usual emergency air-raid alarm that routinely penetrated the city. Making sure Larry was close to her, she kept the cleaning crew going and figured the ambulance was stopping at another car accident near the intersection. The steady flow of traffic was increasing as the town grew and sirens were now becoming a familiar sound.

"Carol! You guys! Everyone! Something terrible has happened at the Rosemar beauty school." Norma came out of the back room and watched Carol's friend bound through the kitchen door. Sue was barely able to move, as she held her stomach and breathed hard, her face wrought with horror. "There's been a murder, lots of them! " She stammered. No one spoke and stood staring at their neighbor, anxiously waiting for more information: "Some guy went inside the building and shot some people."

Now contemplated the look on Sue's face and taking in her words, all froze for a moment. Was this real? Was she exaggerating? How could this be?

All walked out the doorway and saw what seemed like masses of people walking down Stapley Street. Norma picked up and squeezed Larry's hand, cautiously following the crowds around the corner toward Broadway and beyond. Larry planted his index finger in the side of his mouth and began to chew on it for comfort. (The finger often went immediately in his mouth, especially if he was scared, bored or nervous).

The sight of the crowds infiltrated a surreal feeling among the family. It seemed like a horror movie. Debbie hung onto their mother's waist, as she kept silent. David was on his bike somewhere and Norma's eyes scanned the street, fretfully looking for her other son. Many stayed quiet in anticipation.

Several ambulances were parked outside the building and as the family got closer to the scene they noticed the crowds kept a wide distance. The low hum of whispered voices covered the street. Although some people knew more information than others, the news began to spread like wild fire.

Norma kept the kids back to protect them from any unsightly views. They stood for a long time and heard more descriptive reports.

"He walked in and demanded that the girls lie down. He just shot them all in the head."

"How many?"

"Don't know. Think six."

"Who? What? Why?" Frustrations began to rise as specifics for more information went unanswered; but what they had already heard was still too much information for these young innocent ears. Norma immediately knew she needed to leave. She turned and began walking home holding the hands of her children and wishing to cover their ears as they weaved in and out of the murmuring spectators.

Carol and her friends stayed. They were still curious and shaken over something so horrid and yet so close to their neighborhood. This felt like the six o'clock news with reporters arriving on the scene.

With two of her children inside the house, Norma tried to get their minds on something else. It was impossible! A full-body chill came over her when she gave into the horrible thought of the numerous Saturday hair appointments she and Carol had over the last several years at this now infamous place. She couldn't push back the mind-boggling thought that they could have easily been there when it all came down.

When Carol opened the door—her friends behind her she ran to her room and rummaged around for her high school annual. Thumbing through it, she opened it to a designated page.

"There, there he is! That's him." Carol pointed to the picture and turned the book around to show all who were standing near her. He was the murderer, Robert Smith, A fellow classmate!

"What a very disturbed young kid! " Norma said as she shook her head and clicked her tongue.

"I heard he used to tell people that someday he'd be famous." Carol said. "And to think we probably passed him everyday in the hallways at school." She looked wide-eyed at her friends. Now. . . that was spooky!

Talk about this ungodly incident went on for weeks. It WAS on the six o'clock news and the family viewed the pictures of the front of the building, still stunned that such an incident had taken place only blocks away from their home. Though Norma didn't know the families of the victims personally, she prayed every chance she got, her heart burdened with the complete devastations of friends and families. The paper stated how a baby survived because the mother kept her under her body. Another girl lived by pretending to be dead until police arrived. But this evil person still managed to kill 5 people, all females.[11] The entire city was in bereavement for months and years to come over the horrific account.

"I need you to go get some milk from circle K." Norma told Debbie a few days later. Her daughter hadn't left the house since the heinous crime.

"Why can't someone else go?"

"Because it's just you and Larry here. David and Carol are visiting friends. Why don't you want to go?"

"I don't know. Just don't. I'm still afraid." Debbie yelled through the bedroom door.

"Oh my stars, you have no reason to be."

"But what if I see Robert Smith?"

Norma chuckled. "Debbie, he is in jail."

"How do you know?"

"Because they arrested him the day it happened."

"How do you know?"

"It's been in the paper and on the news. Everybody knows that. He confessed."

"Okaaay", she sighed. "Give me the money!" She reluctantly stood up from her bed and slowly slid the coins off the top of the dresser.

Norma watched out the back window as her little girl's unenthusiastic body strolled between the opening of the oleanders and the corner of the neighbor's fence.

"She is being ridiculous!" Norma said as she handed Allen the weekly pile of clothes that needed mending. He was sitting at the new shinny Singer sewing machine they had recently purchased.

Within minutes she heard the back door slam. Debbie came running in, threw the quarters on the table and hurried to her room. The two glanced at each other and opened the bedroom door viewing their daughter curled up in a ball under the covers.

"What's wrong!" they both asked.

"I saw him! I saw him! She shouted.

"Who?"

"I saw Robert Smith. He's at Circle K!"

"Oh, that's absurd! I told you the police have him and he's in jail."

"Let her be." Allen said as he closed the door. "This is how your mind can play games when you're steeped in terror."

"I suppose." Norma answered.

"I go to Circle K." Larry put his hand up in the air as if he was in school.

"Do you think you can buy milk, Larry?"

"Yeah, I can!" he put his hand up again, this time jumping up and down. He cherished any independence and for once had a chance to prove himself.

Norma looked at Allen. He shrugged his shoulders and replied, "Why not! He's practically fourteen."

"Okay, here's the money. Make sure you go to the cross walk." She handed him the change. "Check for cars, look both ways. Cross at the light!"

"I know, I know, you, you tode me." Larry's responded sharply.

She followed him to the edge of the backyard, stopped and let go of his hand. Wringing her sweaty palms, she watched him cross the busy street and turn the corner. Staying in position and waiting for a long five minutes, she squinted her eyes and viewed in the distance Poody boy's short stature holding a brown bag.

"He did it!" she thought. "All by himself."

"What a big boy you are, Larry!" she proclaimed when he approached the tall bushes. She grabbed the bag and opened it with a big exhale, "Chocolate milk! Chocolate?" Norma yelled.

"Yeah, umm it good!" Larry smiled at his mom.

"Laaarrrry! You can't put chocolate milk on cereal for breakfast!"

"Yeah, it good, it really good!"

Norma looked at Allen and the two let out a big sigh.

CHAPTER 30

UPROAR-1967

"It's best for our son. It's best for our son. It's best for our son!" Norma had to circle the words in her head or the remorse would take over.

Larry's stout fourteen-year-old body stood outside the door of his new home. He titled his head in wonderment toward the back of the moving vehicle and dropped his jaw wide, tongue protruding. Lifting his chubby fingers he waved a half-held goodbye destined in the direction of his parents. They had just gotten Larry squared away and unpacked the suitcase. Norma knew Allen's insides were bursting while pulling away and he couldn't look back. He didn't often show emotion but this one was gut wrenching. Before exiting onto the freeway ramp, Allen pulled out his handkerchief, wiped under his eyes and blew his nose. Only the sound of sniffles was heard inside the vehicle while driving across Phoenix. A nagging question pestered their thoughts: Are we doing the right thing?

"I'm thankful that at least I was able to get Jack Bergman to administer the required developmental evaluation before admission." She looked at her husband as her thoughts wandered back to all the previous steps it took to get to this point. Jack was another very active participant in forming the Marc school and a psychiatric social worker. She was grateful for his friendship and willingness to help. Now they actually made the final and very difficult decision but was it truly the right one? Only the future will tell the tale.

When just three children settled into bed that night, David pulled the covers off his body and slowly walked into his parent's room. "I can't go to sleep without my brother!" he rubbed his eyes.

"Only seven more days and we can bring him back for a visit." She hoped this would be enough to send her third born to bed.

Each day the sadness deepened. It was the longest seven days they had ever experienced.

The following Saturday — Larry's first weekend home —was spent at Pioneer Park with the Little family. After nibbling on fried chicken, baked beans and Norma's famous potato salad, the children couldn't focus on their food and so the antsy kids were finally excused from the picnic table to play. The old locomotive train and a retired warplane had been brought to the park for the enjoyment of children everywhere; it put an instant smile on the faces of Carol, Larry, David, Debbie, Shari, Linda and David. For children of all ages, it was like Disneyland but the real deal! Wires still in place, smell of metal and movement of the gadgets took on a nostalgia era. David stood tall in the belly of the plane and once the line of kids tamed down at the cockpit, he sat in the pilot seat imagining he was flying over mountains and gunning down the enemy. The excitement moved the children back and forth between the massive climbing giants. The siblings learned to ignore the apprehensions of other park kids around their brother and Larry tried to do the same. Some children stood still and from a distance to watch Larry play, he kept going, however, as if he didn't care. If his brother and sisters could ignore the obtrusive faces, so could he.

Poody Boy's fearless demeanor scared the moms to the point of consistent peripheral vision while they talked. Larry climbed higher and higher, trying to reach tallest point of the train. Falling was never a concern for him. He was fearless!

As the female conversing between Nancy and Norma intensified, Norma told the story of her and her sister's first jobs working as riveters on warplanes after Pearl Harbor. Talking about it out loud took her there. She and Nancy spoke of the entire country's devastating affects during the war and now watching the carefree spirits of the next generation encompassed in activity, Norma silently said a prayer to God, *Please Lord, keep our children from the ugliness of future wars. Peace on Earth, I pray!*

Bill and Allen traipsed off to another section of the park: on a mission to play their favorite game—shuffleboard. Though the women couldn't see them, they could hear Bill's loud laughter and Allen's frequent sneezing, both echoed across the area. Windy days stirred-up Allen's hay fever, but the sun was bright and the temperature a perfect 80 degrees.

"Mom, where's Larry?" Debbie looked up, pulling at her shirt.

"What?" She ran toward the place she saw him last. "David, where's Larry?"

"Don't know." Enthralled with movement, he kept climbing.

Nancy and Norma split in separate ways and searched frantically. Carol ran for her dad. Within minutes even strangers at the park were looking for Larry.

"Here we go again!" Norma couldn't understand how he could slip away so quickly.

People ran in all directions.

"Here he is!" Bill spotted him running toward the teeter-totter clear across to the other side of the park. He ran over and scooped him up quickly, holding him up in the air using the belt loops of his shorts. Larry was flinging his arms and legs and screaming to get down. Bill carried him toward the car where Norma was pointing. She cracked the car windows and told him he had to sit inside for his playtime was over. Now everyone could hear the garbled remarks about his mother.

"I don't like you! You mean!" he screamed.

"David, look at Larry" Debbie said. They both viewed Larry's middle finger stand straight and tall out the car window and aimed at their mom. The two children looked at each other and giggled.

"He's giving mom the finger." Debbie said. "He's going to get in so much trouble."

"No, I don't think mom knows what it means." David answered, "Neither does Larry."

The two snickered again.

"Yeah, he probably just saw someone do it, huh?" Debbie asked.

"Not me!" David looked at Debbie's accusing face.

"I bet he learned it from those guys he lives with at the Valley of the Sun."

"Yeah, right!"

"It's time to go home anyway!" Norma said while gathering the food from the picnic table and calling everyone to help load the trunk.

"Ahhh, we always have to leave because of Larry!" the others grumbled.

That night they all flopped their bodies down into their beds and fell into a deep slumber. Though he knew how to ruin a picnic, it was still good to Larry back home at least for a few days. He completed the family unit and days without him felt strange.

Sunday evening Norma began packing a small black suitcase. Larry focused his attention toward her, trying to figure out what she was doing and why. But it was early Monday morning when the proclamation was made for Larry to get into the car in which he instantly put the pieces together. Throwing his body on the floor and screaming at the top of his lungs, Larry made it very clear that he hated his new home and didn't want to go back. Trying to reason or even bribe him was not going to work, not this time. The parents bent over him at the same time in an attempt to pick him up but his arms and legs moved so quickly that the scene was taking on the form of a wrestling match. His siblings stood wide-eyed listening to the loudest cries they had ever heard come from their brother's mouth. This was torture! After several minutes of viewing a "fit" at its peak and desperately hoping the neighbors wouldn't come out of their homes inquiring about the pandemonium, they were able to maneuver his body around enough to get him between the doorframe of the house and then inside the back seat of the yellow Toyota Corona. The trick was the ability to close the car door quick enough before he darted out for the second time. The adults hated this awful sight for the children to watch but the onset was a surprise to everyone. The siblings, however, couldn't comprehend the necessity of it all.

It was the scariest and most dangerous ride. Larry's trantrum did not subside for several miles into the trip. Those witnesses at the destination viewed the same nightmare. As soon as Larry could see the Valley of the Sun building, the scene was played out again.

This same spectacle continued each time Larry came home for a visit, but over time slowly produced less dramatic behavior. Norma and Allen had been warned about the difficulty of the first couple of weeks; but, Larry's strong will pushed it into several months. They never imagined it would be so intense, not like this!

CHAPTER 31

CHANGES

Norma signed her name to the contract of her new job and grinned with a self-importance beam. She looked at the six, nine, six, three number above her signature. Proud that she would contribute such an amount to the family income. It would almost be seven thousand in one year working for two public schools and she couldn't imagine the benefits on the horizon. Skiff and Wilson schools located in South Phoenix were in need of a social worker; her final career choice had been made. Having her own office, desk, phone and personal finishing touches to this comfortable but small square room made her feel like life was on the move. Things were finally looking up, especially in the financial department. The Valley of the Sun payment was pulling a lot from their monthly income but now they not only could keep the bills paid, but also had extra for a few indulgences. She knew this wasn't going to be an easy career path she chose but it would be where the "rubber meets the road" from years of education and some experience in this field. She was ready to tackle the many home visits, act as truant officer, manage an enormous amount of paper work, communicate closely with school nurses, teachers, principals and child protective services. She recognized the variety would ignite her love of social work in these poverty stricken sections of south Phoenix. Learning to be thick-skinned toward people and their excuses would mesh with her balance of kindheartedness in the direction of the victims— innocent children. With anticipation of learning all the ins and outs of this demanding job, she realized the hardest part would be the ability to "turn it off" once she got home. The rewards would keep the fire in her heart, however, and equip her for the jagged edges. It was those certain days of threats on her life by parents while entering apartments, mobile homes or simple shacks that she learned to take a police officer along.

Though the Phoenix schools held a slightly different calendar year from the Mesa schools, she would still have most of the same holidays, and summer days, with her children. The real bonus, however, was that she was just minutes from Larry's Monday through Friday residence. She wanted to stop in frequently and check on him. Every Friday afternoon she pulled into the parking lot viewing her boy waiting on the street corner, suitcase in hand and pacing while checking his watch. Funny how he picked up on the whole time concept and could basically read a watch, but didn't comprehend the reading of most words.

Routinely the two stopped at the bargain Food City store on the way home to buy the weekly family groceries, drive 40 minutes to Mesa and walk in the door complete with plenty of food and the sixth Combs member. It was Allen's job to have dinner ready but once in a while he keyed up the kids by bringing home the famous and local Pete's fish and chips for all to enjoy. The rarity of eating food beyond this kitchen was a luxury and for really special occasions Norma and Allen encouraged everyone to dress up for an outing to the favored Pepper Tree restaurant where the kids could have a big variety of scrumptious food to choose from. Finally, finances allowed family rewards. It sustained warm feelings of peace, wealth and tranquility.

"I'm sorry Norma, but we feel Larry shouldn't go home this weekend." She stepped inside his cottage and saw the scratch marks across her son's neck."

"What's going on?"

"Larry got in a fist fight with one of his roommates." The cottage mother explained.

"What?" She watched another young man walk around the corner from the hallway. He stood with a swelled eyebrow and forming bruises around the cheek. Both boys hung their heads in humiliation.

Norma walked over and lifted Larry's chin. "Larry, tell me what happened!" her command was strong and she needed immediate answers.

"Not my faut (fault), he stawded (started) it!"

The person in charge began to describe the events, though most of it didn't make sense. It sounded as if her son was the guilty one, but it was unclear what **really** took place.

"He steal my stuff, that's why! I don't like it!" Larry looked up into his mom's eyes as his lip began to quiver.

"He's had aggressive behavior all week and we notice it increases when he comes back from a home visit." The staff person stated.

"Why didn't anyone stop this? Who was supervising? Good grief! How did it get this bad, for crying out loud? Make sure these wounds are taken care of, for heaven's sake! This makes me very angry! Larry, I'm mad at you! Do you understand that?"

"Not my faut!" pleading his case again.

"Well, you can't go home with me!" she exclaimed. He immediately began to cry.

Norma glared at her child. She didn't know what to do next. Should he really be punished? Did these people know what was ACTUALLY going on? She just wasn't sure if she could trust their judgment. Discouragement and lack of professionalism about this place had been on her mind lately.

As she walked to her car without Larry she sniffled back the tears, questioning herself as to the decision in placing him here in the first place.

When she arrived home WITHOUT Larry, everyone was surprised. Spouting her aggravations to Allen, she hoped he would have some words of wisdom; but he offered, like so many other times, only a calm demeanor to assist in resolving her thoughts about their complicated child.

David looked at Larry's absence as a perfect opportunity to have the guys over to spend the night. The girls were sleeping at the Little's house and David would have free reign of the bedroom and backyard without Larry tagging along. Recently he had purchased the Beatles White album and some Mad magazines. It meant a party as well as using the sleeping bags in the latest groovy fort. He, again, planned on sneaking food out of the icebox to stock up inside his other house at the edge of the yard.

Ida and her husband moved out of their house and a new family moved in with a startling handsome son who was the same age as Carol. It was infatuation at first sight for the two and Norma was disturbed about the growing romance between them. They couldn't spend a moment apart. Carol received numerous gifts from her next-door-neighbor boyfriend; jewelry and stuffed animals showed his affections.

The silly behavior of the two caused the sibling's nausea, especially when they saw them kissing right behind the blossoming bougainvillea bush that stood between the houses. Little sister was now a pest to Carol when the lovebirds were together; but she was a buddy when it came to secrets.

"Come here, kid! " Carol pulled Debbie's arm inside the bedroom and shut the door. Making sure her voice was low and keeping eye contact with her little sister, she placed her hands on Debbie's shoulders. "Don't tell Mom and Dad, but Dick and I are going to get married."

"Are you kidding?" Debbie mucked.

"No, but you can't tell Mom. We are going to elope!"

"When?"

"I don't know but soon!"

"Mom is going to be soooo mad at you!" She wanted to bring her sister back to earth.

"I know, but she'll get over it when she realizes how much we love each other. We've been dating for two months now. Promise me you won't tell, kid, please."

"I won't." Her voice not so convincing! She was in wonderment over these two foolish people but it was just a matter of days when Carol tugged at her arm, again pulling her inside the bedroom.

"Now what?" Debbie said. She watched her sister gather all the presents she had received from her lover and placed them in her arms.

"Do me a favor and take all of these back to Dick. I'm breaking up with him."

"I don't want to do your dirty work!" she tilted her head.

"Please, kid, we are over and he knows it! I never want to see his face again! Barf!"

"Oh, good grief!" Debbie rolled her eyes and struggled out the door juggling what used to be items of endearment.

CHAPTER 32

REBELLION FORMING -1967/68

"Debbie! Linda, Annie and Rhonda are waiting at the door for you to play. Now go! It's a beautiful day and you need to get out of the house. Shape up!" Norma's youngest was still spending too much time inside her bedroom and letting fear run her life. " Stop your bellyaching"

Debbie unwillingly walked out the door and all four girls held hands and paced to the backyard. It was only a matter of minutes before Norma heard the familiar sounds of entertaining laughter again. She stopped at the window to peak at those tan, toothpick legs watching Debbie jump up to slap the tetherball. For the first time, these young girls looked like ladies. Where has the time gone? Her youngest would soon enter into her teens, right behind David. She always wanted the absolute best for all her children and yet she knew she hadn't always approached motherhood in the best way.

My mother spent lots of time in prayer over these kids and I have too, she spoke to God. Please God, continue to protect them and keep them from the evils of this world. Help me make good decisions as a parent. Finally seeing that Debbie was once again grinning, she was satisfied with the outcome of her demands.

"Mom, why do I have to be in choir at church? Debbie was mad. I hate it. In fact I hate church, period! I don't have friends there." Debbie bellowed as she slammed the car door.

Norma had just parked the car between the newly painted lines in the parking lot of the First Methodist church. "You may not like it now, but you'll be glad later," Norma responded as she opened the driver's door.

"David hardly goes to church and Dad doesn't either. Why do I have to be the one?" Debbie folded her arms across her chest while walking through the opened double doors.

Norma had already withheld her opinion of her daughter's short skirt, wild fish net nylons and straight stringy hair. Fashion was vital with her two girls but Norma detested the latest styles. At least the choir robe would cover her during the service, her eyes scanned up and down at her daughter. She reflected on her college years and the great Methodist choir she had the privilege to participate in. Those were some of my favorite times. I learned so much about the music world and how to read the notes. Debbie could and will do the same. It will be good for her. But the generational battles over clothing from both her and David were a sore spot and Norma had to choose one fight at a time. Allen stayed out of it. In her opinion, his silence sent a message of weakness.

But Norma figured if Debbie still attended church she'd let her wear her crazy outfits— as long as she maintained as least some modesty. It meant she had to swallow her pride and not worry about what other Methodist members may think of her.

David's interest in new fashion trends was the long hair. "No more hair cuts for me!" he quarreled. "And I like my jeans ragged. It looks cool!"

It was the complete opposite of how she was raised. Guys were to have short hair, nice pants and the shirt tucked-in with a belt. "My brothers would have never been caught dead going out in public looking like that!" she criticized.

David had been bringing home some strange looking characters to spend the night. With the slew of friends David had, no one could keep up. They too, had the "hippie" look.

"Lord, may this phase pass quickly." Norma whispered over and over. "I can hardly stand to even look at my children without opening my mouth about their appearance." She said under her breath as she watched them walk out the door.

Norma also had several deliberations with Allen as to his recent absences at First Methodist. "You used to teach the Sunday school classes there and now you barely go. What kind of message is that sending to your kids?" She questioned.

"I have to stay home with Larry," he said.

They didn't push the church thing on Larry anymore. It was different when the kids were younger. Norma always had her handy bag full of the quiet church-only toys to keep young hands busy, allowing the couple to concentrate on the words of the minister. Now that Larry was older, he had out-grown the toys and there wasn't anything that truly kept his attention for one full hour. He only picked up on small portions of the message, thus true boredom, restlessness and misbehaving manifested. It just wasn't worth the risk. Though Debbie and David understood bits and pieces of the sermon, they had no interest in it and simply couldn't relate; but Norma still couldn't get why Allen excused David to stay home with "the boys".

Carol had graduated from high school and was trying different jobs, as well as a typing class at the community college. She was ready to move out soon and hoped to room with friends. She needed her own space and wanted to make her own decisions without her mother "breathing down her neck." It was time to fly the coop. She and Norma had several heated discussions as to her goals in life, or lack of. Then there were the on-going car problems that caused frequent hassles and financial pressures.

If it wasn't Carol and Norma quarreling or Allen and Norma's disagreements about Larry, it was now David and Debbie questioning the rules and pushing for more independence. Tension was at an all time high.

The couple noticed repeated absences from the two youngest, especially when the heat got hotter between their mother and dad. Besides, they had places to go and people to see and weren't interested in those things that usually kept them home. Hopping on their bikes, they traveled to other houses, even other neighborhoods.

"I wanta go too!" Larry begged.

"Not this time! Besides you can't ride a bike," David and Debbie proclaimed as they let the door bang shut just inches from Larry's face. Standing at the screen, he watched them peddle away. It seemed he was staring at their backside more often and was depressed over his used-to-be playmates. Out of pity, Allen pulled Larry over to the dinning room table to play a game of cards.

"We should look for a large three-wheel bicycle for Larry to ride." Allen looked up at Norma walking through the living room. "I'll find one and will get a bike for myself. Then we can ride bikes together, Larry." He slapped his son's shoulder with the back of his hand and gave him the "OK sign" (a circle made with the index finger and thumb). Larry returned the whack and the OK gesture. He quickly picked up on the non-verbal humor and mimicked the same signal; his, however, was more embellished because he circled it around slightly with his squatty fingers, along with a goofy turned-down mouth and added the "uhhhhhh" grunt sound Allen had taught him. Allen was pleased with this comical boy of his, and jerked his head back with a belly laugh. "I get a kick out you, Wall-boy!" It was a new nickname that emerged from the still on-going Wallace and Ladmo show, for he was outgrowing the cute little Poody look.

For a boy who could rapidly put gray hairs on one's head, he had a contrasted way of keeping life simple. The two made up amusing and silly games together. It was obvious they enjoyed each other's company. Because of the different interests of the younger two and Carol seldom home, Allen and Larry found themselves together more and more. Everyone noticed a remarkable bond was forming. Despite the tension growing in this house, Norma knew Allen was trying hard to make sure Larry laughed in spite of the constrained family relationships.

It wasn't funny, however, the day they learned the Little family was really going to move from the 5th Avenue location. They now lived across town and attended different schools. Though the kids still spent the night at each other's house, it just wasn't the same. The planned picnics were fewer and farther between. Larry still spoke about Shari with a twinkle in his eye but didn't write, as many love notes.

"I still love her, anyway. She still,uhhh, my gilfiend." he told his dad. They thought about the patience Shari possessed over this "never give-up" infatuation of his. Larry's obsession over the opposite sex was a growing concern for his parents and an added new frustration for Larry. He wanted only non-handicapped girls and therefore the emotional feelings were never reciprocated . . . but Shari could fake it pretty well. She never held back the hugs he demanded and even added giggling to his silly sayings. She was sympathetic to his feelings. That's all he needed for now!

Washington public school had agreed to provide educational programs for Marc and give classroom space for the trainable children.[12]

Trainable was based on the IQ range and meant the child would NOT benefit from the educational system. Norma still believed Larry could learn to read if she could find someone who might have the knowledge and patience to teach him.

Some students stayed at the previous location; but the letter writing, discussions and repeated pot stirring from this core group towards the community was paying off. Norma knew if the squeaking endured long enough, things would happen in their favor and ultimately benefit the disabled.

Various terms of what to call her son's condition were continually in transition. Not only was Larry now considered in the "trainable range" but also Down syndrome was now the correct term, reminding all of Dr. John Langdon Down, the British doctor, who fully described it in 1866. It wasn't until 1959, however, that an extra chromosome was Identified as the cause. Dr. Jerome Lejeune, who was studying chromosomes (a specialty called cytogenetic), discovered it.[13]

It was established that the word Mongolism was an offensive term. In 1961,19 scientists suggested that "mongolism" had "misleading connotations" and had become "an embarrassing term".[14] Though one would still hear "retarded" used in a derogatory way, especially among young people, society was making progress in not only knowledge and acceptance, but also sensitivity to labels.

CHAPTER 33

LIFE'S BLOWS

The updates on Larry's behavior brought out the fighter in Norma. Valley of the Sun indicated often that he was lazy, worked very slow, touched others too much, was bossy and had babyish habits with frequent whining. The family had observed some of these inappropriate behaviors, but certainly not to this degree. She wondered if it was his way of saying "I want to go home". Was he feeling abandoned and rejected by his family? Surely by now, over a year of sleeping in a different bed at night, he would understand they weren't giving in. The good news was that his cottage parents could hang the going-home concept as a dangling carrot to reinforce good behavior. If he had a week of overall positive conduct, he could leave for the weekend; of course, it could also mean the opposite was certainly a possibility. Would Norma be okay with the strong chance of not being able to swing by on a Friday afternoon and pick him up for the abundantly loved 48 hours with friends, family gatherings, church and home-cooked meals? The big question was…will this work? Could and would he make the connections? Only time would tell.

During the seldom-quiet times she had to herself, the soul searching as to what she could do differently as a parent, erupted. He was a handful! But she wouldn't give up making sure people around him were doing the best for her son; her demands were going to be met, even if she had to write numerous letters! "By Golly!"

In contrast, Allen's sales were storming and he was winning prizes. The newsletters of the selling arena featured her husband's talents. The recognition for top sales in his district awarded the family a new car— Allen took the money instead! "Everything he touches turned to gold," the paper read. He won a trip and several small items. Maybe this was meant to be, for he certainly understood the art of selling, even though long hours and evenings were mandatory.

He finally is getting something out of it. Maybe, some day, I won't have to be the one who consistently provides the income. Maybe we will be able to get a better house in the near future. That would be so wonderful. She coveted in her heart the Little's new two-story home in an up-scale neighborhood.

As she pulled the pockets out of Allen's jacket for hanging, she noticed a folded piece of paper with the name of a local motel. Collapsing on her bed, all power left her body. The thought of infidelity inundated her mind. Was this woman back in the picture, again! Previous wounds were about to be laid open and bleed. She feebly picked up the phone and cautiously dialed the motel number. "Please, let my suspicions be wrong," she thought out loud. The question of Allen's presence at the motel was confirmed by a simple yes from the voice on the other end. Instantly hot tears burst from her eyes and she couldn't wait till he walked in the door for a colossal confrontation. Her emotions were uncontrollable. She wanted to slap him. Like always, he gave as little information as possible with very few words, never admitted to anything. Norma was older and wiser now and had to face the true fact that he could be lying. Her affections for the man she thought was her life-long partner, was dying a slow death. It was time to look reality straight into its ugly face.

In the meantime, she wanted desperately to talk to a friend, someone who would be willing to let her and the kids live with her. She had to get out of this marriage and now was the time to do it! Was she only dreaming? Should I call Nancy? She would understand! How can I possibly leave and go somewhere else? How can I arrange it all? I need to leave! I have to leave! How can I live this way the rest of my life? She shifted the culpability from the "crazy lady" to Allen. He is just as much to blame! He has too many secrets! He is just too quiet about things! What is he hiding? She could only imagine because he FORCED her to use her imagination!

They had four children, one whose many issues required attention from both parents. How could I do it by myself? She thought of the hours Allen spent with Larry; by now, Allen was considered Larry's best friend! For that matter, ALL the kids worshiped their father. They wouldn't understand. They would blame me. She also thought of the disappointments her mother would have, as well as her brothers and sister. I'm sure everyone has marital problems, but I bet not like this! It would be justified if I left!

When the dust settled, the only agreement between the two was counseling. But there was a new level of eeriness when Norma and Allen learned that this strange person sought information about them from extended family. The reality of a STALKER was an eye opener. They called the church and made an appointment for the next day. She had never seen Allen so disgraced. Maybe he truly comprehended the mess and potential devastation! It seemed he was finally waking up to the seriousness of it all. Because of this third party, Allen was on his way to ruining the great life he possessed (trials and all). Maybe he finally understood. How did the intertwining of complexity actually get Norma to feel sorry for her husband yet again?

"I recommend you get a restraining order in place. It will cost some money but its well worth it," the counselor told them.

Norma's thoughts were confirmed. Allen often told her she was an over-reactor but this time she was right. She was pleased with the wise words spoken in their session, but knew it was going to take lots of time and a miracle from God for healing. They agreed to attend church together even if it was only for Wednesday night bible study. It was certainly a start!

Broken Chains -1968/69

This underground friction was kept secret. The couple knew the children were clueless concerning the matter and they hoped it would remain so.

The house was quiet late Friday night. The parents being settled in bed stirred David and Larry to the kitchen. The family just got a new and much larger refrigerator, no longer an icebox. The two boys didn't see the innovation of it necessarily, but the massive size is what appealed to them. It meant more food!

When David rounded the corner from the dinning room, he fell on the floor laughing! "Larry! Debbie! Come here, you'll never believe it!"

Their jaws instantly released as they raced into the kitchen.

"Oh wow! She finally did it!" Debbie was astonished.

"Wha? Wha this all about?" Larry walked over and touched it.

Shining in the darkness was a gigantic silver chain and golden lock holding the long stream of links circling the fat, white box.

"Move over, Larry. I got to see this!" He walked up behind him and pushed him aside. "How many years has she threatened this?" David jiggled the lock and tried to pry open the door.

"She has really gone and done it this time!" Debbie shook her head.

"Wait. No. Look I can put my hand in." David had opened the door slightly, eager to see how much space existed.

"Yeah, but you can't get anything out, dang it" she responded.

"Oh yes I can." Now up for the challenge, David grunted as he reached inside and twisted his arm to pull out the bottle of catsup.

"Great! You get to eat catsup." Debbie laughed.

"Here, Larry, want some catsup?"

"Shooooot, no way!"

"No, really. Open your mouth; I'll squirt some in. You're hungry, aren't you?" David teased.

"No way!" Larry put both hands over his mouth and watched David inch the bottle back in the refrigerator while laughing.

"Well, we can still get the cereal" Debbie opened the cupboard door. "Just no milk . . .dang it."

She made a face, opened the box and put her hand down to pull out a Cheerio, then popped it in her mouth!" All three giggled with a screech forgetting about the sleeping parents.

"What's all that racket? You kids pipe down out there." a loud whisper came through the bedroom door.

"Yeah, Lar Piiipe down!" David poked Larry's chest and gave him a shhh signal.

Every night it became a new routine for Norma to "close" the kitchen making sure the chain and padlock were set before retiring for the night. David told all his friends of the pure gumption his mother had. It became a comedy act telling stories and imitating his mom's words using her overstated look. No wonder his circle of friends expanded each week. Not only was his wit contagious but he could also do the impersonations of several figures, famous or not, simply on command. It was instant amusement! Besides Barney Fife, Richachet Rabbit, Jimmy Stewart and Billy Graham simulations, copying his mother was among his best impersonations. Anyone who knew Norma instantly broke into laughter at David's great replication. Even Norma chuckled. David had a great way of getting his mom to lighten up. Everyone knew she needed it!

Carol had moved out. She had a decent job working at Motorola and Debbie finally got the new bedroom set she was promised, canopy bed and all. Spending more time in her own space, she was glad to get that Jim Morrison poster off the wall. The one Carol referred to so often as sexy.

David spent most of his time in the new fort in the backyard. It was nicked named by his friends as "Davo's Shack". This was no fort; it was a bonified building! The material was plywood and it stood 6 by 15 feet. It had a floor, high ceiling and a swinging door opening a few inches from the bushes. David slept in it several nights a week and Norma lost track as to how many kids came in and out. At least he was still at home, even if it was a few feet away.

Larry was requiring some of his own private time. He shut and locked his bedroom door and told everyone he was taking a nap. Was this really the case? Though his hormones were out of control, his behavior was under control, at least for now.

Norma's life was narrowing to simplicity: Carol was gone; Larry's visits averaged three weekends a month; and, Debbie and David's independence allowed her to focus her energies toward Marc, church and her social work. She and Allen still found time for square dancing and her true joy was organizing and arranging photographs into books.

But that peaceful routine didn't last long . . . "Lord, I just can't handle another cross to bear in my life, please!" she lamented as she hung up the phone after talking to the principal at Mesa Junior High. He told her that Debbie had been involved in a weekend drug party down the street from their house. The party was loud and the neighbors called the school first thing Monday morning to report the teenagers involved.

"Your daughter's name came up and we feel the parents should know," the principal reported.

"I can't believe my daughter would do such a thing! You don't know her! Besides what does it have to do with school, this supposedly happened on a weekend?" Norma retorted.

"Do you know where your daughter was on Saturday night?" he asked.

"Yes, she was spending the night at a friend's house. I called there myself and checked on her."

"Well, Mrs. Combs, I would look into this matter more if I were you. The neighbor said she suspected alcohol and drugs at this house and she came very close to calling the police. These are our students and we are concerned about them, even on weekends."

"Well, I appreciate that but I think you have the wrong person. I trust my daughter."

Norma slammed the phone down. "Ahhh!" she screamed.

"I know Debbie has new friends in this neighborhood and I don't know all of them, but don't you think she would make good choices?" she asked Allen.

"Yes. Let's just drop it. Don't be so strict on these kids. They're good kids." Allen's words were consoling.

Now worries over the children's choice of friends were unleashed. Really, the groups of relationships between the two youngest were one in the same. Norma felt she was looking at twins. She was glad they had always enjoyed each other's company; an advantage of having two so close in age, but what she feared was the way Debbie idolized David. If he made bad choices, Debbie would probably follow suit.

Larry also copied his brother. David's newest aspiration was to play the drums. If the family could put up with the designated times of pounding, they would purchase a set and place it in his bedroom, available for Larry as well. "Maybe it will keep David in the house more." they said. "And since Larry wanted to have his turn beating, maybe, just maybe it could be a good release of energy and even anger.

"Yeah, and you never know he might even spend less time watching TV, rocking on the couch and chewing on his finger." Allen agreed.

Norma was glad that finally someone was interested in learning music and she was willing to go as far as paying for lessons; hopefully, she could find that person who would have the patience to teach Larry with simplicity. If they made this big purchase, would they both be committed to practicing? Now, with this kind of loud instrument, Norma would have to talk to neighbors about the drum hammering and of course limit it to certain times to keep from making enemies on the street.

Larry at 2

Norma and Donny

Family of kids

Allen and Larry

Larry and Shari

Larry and David at the radio station

Larry and parents

Siblings

Debbie and Larry

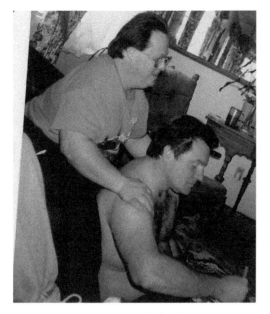

Larry giving Jeff a back rub

Funny face Larry and Debbie

Larry and Linda Carol

Larry and Russell

The two Davids

First Marc School building (Debbie, David and Larry are in this picture)

Norma and Larry at Debbie's wedding

Larry on his bike

Linda and Shari Little

Grandkids

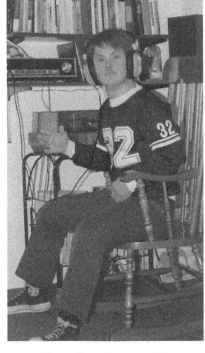

Larry listening to music

Norma and Debbie

Randy Gray giving Larry an award

Norma with her dad and siblings

Norma and Carol

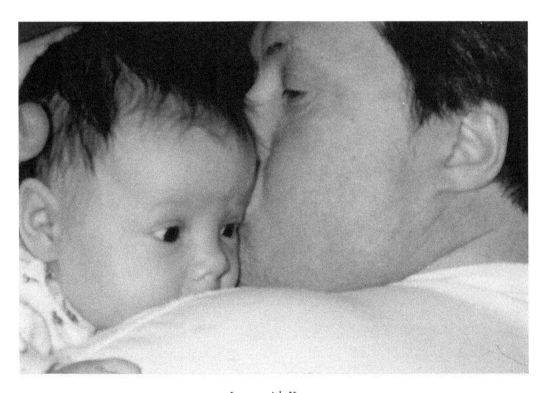

Larry with Kaysee

CHAPTER 35

LOSING OR GAINING CONTROL?

Norma reviewed the most recent report of Larry's accomplishments from the Valley of the Sun school. His IQ was 52. He could read at a pre-first level, knew the alphabet, could add combinations of 6. In the vocational area, he folded clothes, made his bed and cleaned the bathroom. His social skills were still an issue: he took things that didn't belong to him and then lied about it. His newest trick was faking of seizures. School staff responded exactly as he wanted… with immediate action and then sympathy. Finally, they caught on to his new attention-seeking behavior and by the time he had pulled this stunt for the third time, realized they had all been fooled. He could turn it on or off in a snap. Funny how quickly he could fall to the floor when doing a hated task, then close his eyes, lie down and jerk his body.

"Of course he's trying to get out of his work; he has to make five beds in the morning." Norma defended her son. "Who wouldn't? He may have an IQ of 52 but he's no dummy!" She always had some kind of rebuttal in his defense; but no matter what, the closing remarks from both parties and always written on paper were: NEEDS CLOSE SUPERVISION!

Norma was wondering the same about her other children. She had received another call saying Debbie and her friends were caught stealing at the new Tri-city Mall. When Norma drove downtown to get her daughter at the police station her cheeks were stained with tears thinking about the sweet little girl she used to have. Debbie hated to see her mother cry and expressed her remorse.

David had a rebellion all his own. He was more blatant with his ideas of freedom around the house and certainly didn't want his mother telling him what to do. Rules were not for him he expressed to his parents.

"I feel like I'm losing control! What am I going to do? I deal with this kind of stuff at work and now my own children?" She sought the face of God and her prayers were on the rise.

When she thought things couldn't get any worse, Mr. Cain came over to the house. He was a junior high math teacher whose son was a good friend to David and he made it known that he was furious about the structure in their back yard.

"You need a building permit for that thing! You better find out what's going on back there. I suspect some hanky-panky, drugs and alcohol!" The man's fists rested on his hips. The worst of it all was that his son and David were gone!

"What do you mean? Our sons ran away?"

"I mean, they are gone! Do you know where your son is?" Mr. Cain's voice got louder.

"At a friend's house." She replied.

"How long has he been there?'

"I don't know. A while, I guess."

"Exactly, he was at our house and my daughter told me our two boys were planning on running away together."

The adults conceded to calling the police. And, as predicted, David didn't return home that night.

"Do you have any idea where he might be?" Norma and Allen asked Debbie.

"Probably at some friend's house but who knows which one, he has so many."

David's magnetic charm drew others to him. Norma and Allen were proud of this quality in their son but apparently he was attracting the wrong kind of people. It was time to find out who they were. She began making phone calls. No one slept that night. They wanted to hear from somebody... anything. Instead of going to work, they spent the day driving the streets. The sun set and still no David.

"Fourteen years old and he thinks he's twenty." Norma bellowed.

"You are too strict on him!" Allen argued.

"No, you are not strict enough!" she yelled. "He runs the show. He thinks he's an adult." The quarrelling wouldn't stop and Debbie plugged her ears. She never heard such friction between them.

The next morning required yet another Circle K trip. Debbie walked behind the oleanders and onto the dirt field. The tumbleweeds were extra thick that morning because of the wind the night before and as she paced towards the convenience store she screamed! Instantly in front of her, a head popped out of the thicket. David laughed and stood to pull his ragged sleeping bag off the stickers.

"Man Davvvid! You scared the hell out of me!" she slapped her chest. "What are doing? Did you sleep here all night?"

"Yeah."

"Mom and dad have been looking all over town and you were just right here?"

"I've been everywhere, parties mostly. I was going to sleep in my shack but someone locked it."

"Yeah, mom did. And, mom and dad have been fighting and arguing a lot cause of you. You need to go home."

"Well mom needs to chill out and get real!" David was mad. " Crap, I'll go home when I'm good and ready. And when I do, mom better not bug me with all her stupid rules!"

"Are you stoned?" Debbie's eyebrows turned in.

"No, not now, but went to such a cool party last night by the river!"

With a half smile she shook her head and begged him to go home and to do it now!

There was a new covenant made that day when David finally opened up the kitchen door—-making himself visible. After much debate, a declaration had been established between Norma and Allen. Allen would be in total charge of David and he would have to answer to his dad. Debbie would be under Norma's direction and as long as she left her son alone, focused on Debbie, and allowed Allen to handle one rebellious child, she would handle the other. They felt like this might work. Allen was rarely adamant about anything, but today he took charge and Norma was in agreement. That's just how it had to be!

CHAPTER 36

DIVISION/WHOSE KIDS ARE THESE?

David and his dad pulled the nails from the walls of the legendary Davo's shack. Under inspection, the police officer said it had to come down. The backfire, however, was that David spent more time elsewhere. He ignored his curfews for the most part and Norma's constant prayer was that he stayed out of trouble, wherever he was. Debbie was close behind, but at least she asked to spend the night at her friends and Norma knew where she was even though her choice of friends was not what Norma had hoped for.

Their parents were desperate in finding balance. Allen sought to crackdown in the mild manner way he knew how and with an opposite approach Norma tried to let up on her rigorous rules. The distress of seeing two self-indulged teenagers was like watching someone else's kids. Norma thoughts carried her back to those little bodies sitting in the carport playing jacks and marbles. They had been lovable, carefree, and best of all, had occupied their unique brother for hours. She had been so proud at the time. Now they didn't have the sensitivity, nor did they respond to Larry the way they used to. They hardly brought friends home when he was in the house and Norma and Allen knew it wasn't coincidental. They realized that David and Debbie were embarrassed of their brother more than ever. He just wasn't cool! Norma and Allen sensed that their kids were worried their friends might make fun of Larry; something that wasn't a strong concern before.

At least David and Larry still sang Beatle songs together and took turns playing drums. Though David was up on every new group that came along —Santana, Jimmy Hendrix, Cream and the Doors—no one topped the Liverpool gods. Music sure wasn't what it used to be when Norma was growing up and she was worried about the new influences her children were continually exposed to.

Debbie was still going through the motions of church but Norma suspected she was ditching her Sunday school class. The three males were totally un-churched and they liked it that way! She found consolation in that Allen still read his Bible and connected with the Methodist clique from time to time. Carol was struggling to get along with her new female roommates and Norma was desperate in finding answers.

"We need to get away," she proclaimed to Allen.

"How about we go to California and visit Lee and Laura this Christmas? They have invited us and all my relatives are going to be there."

"Nope, staying right here!" Allen commanded. "Besides who would watch the dogs and cat?"

"Fiddlesticks! That's just an excuse!" She knew he wouldn't admit to his fear of travel, especially flying. Her eyes were opened to this when he refused to get on a plane to attend his own mother's funeral. In fact, Allen had many phobias that he wouldn't admit to and all the nagging on her part only produced more stubbornness on his.

He once again faced friction with humor. "The best way to travel is to go to the public library and read about it. It saves money and you can go anywhere in the world. Just find the right book uuuhhhh" he cracked a smile at her. She rolled her eyes, turned her back and walked away.

Except for his job and the Odd Fellows and Toastmasters groups, Norma thought he could easily become a recluse, keeping his nose in books and shutting out reality. But either way, SHE was going on this fun adventure and taking whoever wanted to tag along.

"I can be just as stubborn as you," she affirmed.

Only four of the six Combs' members flew to Salt Lake and hooked up with Uncle Don for the rest of the trip. Carol, Larry and Debbie were having a great time finally getting to know those relatives they knew only from looking at pictures. It was Christmas morning when it hit those in Arizona **and** in California that this family was divided in more ways than one. The happiest day of the year and they weren't even together. Unwrapping a few gifts certainly didn't fill the void. Things were on the brink and all family members powerfully sensed it. Norma wanted to make the right choice in bringing her family together but often her obstinacy clouded her conscious. She knew her strong-will got in the way. Sometimes being the fighter that she was became her downfall. She once again asked God for guidance and humbled herself for some much needed self-examination.

"I need you to be her friend, Debbie." Norma spoke to her daughter a few days after returning home. "Her name is Karen." It was a good Methodist couple that had just taken in a foster child.

"She will be lonely and away from her family. You two are the same age and she'll need new friends."

"Oh, Mom, I don't want to!" Debbie's face grimaced.

"Just meet her and help her at school. It would really be a blessing!"

Karen came over for a visit and, yes, they related right away. She had some quirks about her, however. "When she takes off her shoes she has tattoos all over her feet." Debbie told her mother. "She is embarrassed and always covers them with band aids. She says her mom put them there when she was a baby. I've never seen anything like it. I would be ashamed too!"

This girl was very different from anyone they knew, she lacked extreme confidence and was always fearfully looking over her shoulder as if someone was about to grab her.

Debbie did feel sorry for her and Norma was disappointed in her daughter when she heard the two had ditched school together.

"I thought you would be a good influence for Karen. That's what she needs!"

"Mom, she hates school and it seems she is always hiding from someone. It's really weird. When she asked if I would go with her after lunch, I said okay but once we got to this house, I felt uncomfortable and wanted to leave right away. I'll never do that again!"

"What was at the house?"

"An older man and a very young girl, I thought at first it was a dad and daughter but then it just didn't look right."

Norma was scared and asked for more information from the church couple as to Karen's past.

"It doesn't matter now; she ran away and went back to her mother." they said.

Norma decided to forget about it but more information surfaced in the coming weeks. She certainly wasn't going to tell Debbie of the knowledge she now knew about Karen. This young 14-year-old girl was steeped into child prostitution. It was her way of life as well as her mother's. Norma had petitioned her daughter into something way beyond her own comprehension and into darkness she hoped Debbie would never understand. Remembering Debbie's explanation of this house, she had a sick feeling it was a pimp's residence. "Boy, did I jump into that one way too fast." she told herself and spent several nights tossing and turning; thinking of what could have happened because of her bad judgment and thanking God for His ultimate protection…yet again!

CHAPTER 37

PARADIGM SHIFT-1970

"Man, this wedding is boring!" Debbie said to David. They were sitting in a corner and away from others in the church fellowship hall for the reception. Debbie's "I'm- better-than-anyone-here" mindset was not communal by the stranger sitting next to her. David had recently revealed humility towards his parents and acting unlike himself.

Debbie questioned his bizarre actions, "What's gotten into you, anyway?"

He was about to tell her but first pulled a small booklet out of his pocket. "Have you heard of the four-spiritual laws?"

"No and don't think I want to." she said.

"Let me just tell you something very important, Debbie." he said.

She rolled her eyes and patted her cheeks holding heavy make-up as if to say, "Let's get this over with."

Norma glared across the room at her defiant children and wondered what they were up to. She noticed Debbie's slight attention, as David was deep in thought. He was turning pages of a booklet while conversing with his sister and the wrinkled lines near his eyebrows told her that he was serious about the topic.

"Man is sinful, I'm talking about everyone! There is a great chasm between human beings and God . . . because of sin! Do you understand that?"

"I guess. What else is new and what's that got to do with me?" she replied.

"This is why God sent His son to bridge the gap. Jesus took upon himself our sins, everyone's sins . . . past, present and future. He died for you and me. There's hope, Debbie. There's hope for our lives. It says in the Bible "I am the way, the truth and the LIFE." I'll tell you what's gotten into me—it's Jesus! He is changing my life and He can do the same for you. We need change, Debbie. All you have to do is pray and ask Him to come into your heart. Are you willing to do that?'

"Not now" she said sharply and stood to refill her punch cup.

David had recently stopped all communication with most of his friends. No one could figure out this new behavior. He began a journey of weekend activities and attended a weekly Bible study at a different church. His new friends were odd. Some came over to the house to pray for Larry's healing. Larry wasn't sure of the happenings around him when they laid their hands on his head and prayed out loud, even spoke in a different language. Initially, Larry had an uncomfortable look, but stood still and closed his eyes. Upon completion, he relaxed and hugged each individual.

Debbie didn't like that she had to answer to the constant questions at parties. "Where is your brother? Why isn't he here? Is he a Jesus freak now?" they hounded her.

"Yeah, but he'll get over it. Give him some time." She tried to appease them and just wanted the bugging to stop. He was severing this style they had going together and Debbie was bitter!

Norma couldn't sleep at night when the recent upheaval of Carol moving across the United States was proclaimed. She had met a guy and they were on their way to Chicago. This was embarrassing and Norma certainly wasn't going to tell friends that her oldest was living with a boyfriend! It is unheard of and extremely sinful!

How much deeper can this hole get? she thought. I feel like my life is nothing but a war. Every relationship is strained . . . Allen, Larry, David, Debbie, and now Carol is gone. She reflected on the beauty her daughter possessed. It was her mother's dark eyes, her dad's rounded nose, light brown hair and a tiny body that made up an attractive young lady. I hope and prayed that she isn't being taken advantage of by the wolves out there—such a big bad world and Chicago of all places!

Now . . .

Norma was shocked over the obvious transformation evolving inside David's soul. Was it authentic? Everyone had the same question as they watched, waited and analyzed his every move.

"Debbie, really, just go to this Bible study with me." Norma heard her son beg his sister for the third time.

"No thanks!" she said. But she noticed Debbie was softening with each plea.

David had spent several evenings talking with his mother. It was when he asked her forgiveness that she truly listened.

"Mom, will you forgive me for all the wrong I have done and hurt I've caused you?"

Mom, you need to become a Christian." David stared into her eyes.

She laughed, "David, I am a Christian. I've been one all my life. Where have you been?"

"I'm not talking about religion, Mom, I'm talking about having a relationship with Jesus. You have been religious all your life. There's a difference."

Norma couldn't believe how bold yet immature he was as to spiritual matters. Again, just a punk who thinks he knows it all! She said to herself.

His audacious words were making everyone feel uncomfortable but watching his actions was truly convincing. The verification of a genuine concern for all the family members was a complete 1-80 turn from just weeks before.

He was NOT letting up and Debbie, now weary of the pressure, finally went to this infamous Bible study hoping to get him off her back.

Upon walking into the house later that evening, Debbie couldn't stop talking about how "cool" it was. "It's in a large room, called the fireside room, and was behind the pastor's house (Strigas family). You sit on the floor and you can be barefoot. Lots of people have long hair and they are really, really nice. It's **not** like church, you sing these really great songs, but not out of a hymnal, people have guitars and it's different and so much better! I think I like it!"

Every time David opened his mouth to anyone, even strangers, he spoke about the importance of having a relationship with Jesus. He was on fire! He listened to his parents without attitude and followed any parental direction. What a shock!

"Boy, this is a far cry from the day he held his fist to my face and said I'll fight you, B!" Norma told Allen. "I was really scared that day and suspected he was on drugs."

CHAPTER 38

WHERE DID I GO WRONG?

David and Allen had several father/son discussions about the Bible. Though David wanted to pray with his parents, praying out loud was foreign and felt awkward. Everyone was trying, but this new person in their home was on fast forward and pushy. Still cautious about this drastic change, either way it was positive, no one could dispute that a revival was rumbling within these house walls.

Though Larry was trying to fit inside the change, Norma was unsure if he was experiencing more separation. It seemed the more he tried to change, the harder it was. When his extreme behaviors showed up frequently, it was just speculation as to why. Should he spend more time with people like him or mainstream into the real world? Both produced repeated defeated attitudes not only for Larry but others around him.

Comfort, whether large or small, came through discussions with other parents, whose handicap child had their own acting out procedure. In Norma eye's, Larry's was the worst. His body was growing in both directions. He was strong and healthy. Upon a sudden shift of anger over something insignificant, he was uncontrollable. He would run outside as fast as his short legs would carry him, banging the front door behind him with full force and usually ending up by a busy street, his face red with fury and fatigue. If someone chased him, he enjoyed the game. If he was caught, it became a wrestling match. Often a known neighbor would come along and assist in bringing him home. It would take hours to calm him and his demands for attention wore everyone down. Trying to discuss his feelings meant a merry-go-round conversation. The more discussion, the more misunderstanding and basically getting no-where!

Valley of the Sun provided counseling for parents and Norma and Allen agreed to join. Now getting some relief, summer camps specifically for the mentally handicapped were offered and Larry was going whether he wanted to or not. The parents just had to have the break! Everyone, for that matter, needed the break!

But the real excitement came over the news of another camp, directed by Coach Carl Heath. This exceptional individual attended the Methodist church. He spent his time around the young people at church but was also a basketball coach and teacher at the local High School. During the summer months he conducted weeklong camps in the mountains and his love for others and for God made him standout among the Methodist group. Debbie and David took notice of him, even months before. He was different! He told everyone he met that Jesus loved them and that he also loved them. It was out of the ordinary and even somewhat strange, yet very genuine. Norma came home bubbling over! Now there was a possibility of her two youngest attending this youth getaway.

"I've heard about this camp at Mingus Mountain and would love to go." David said, agreeing with his mother. "Yeah, I heard it's really out-of-sight."

Though her kids were now attending another church, Norma was still pushing for hers. The weekly fireside Bible study group, however, represented various churches and some often referred to Coach Heath's fabulous camp. The news was that it was highly spiritual and life changing.

The inspirational week went by too quickly. It was not only nice to be with other young people, but not having parents around brought an independence Debbie and David longed for. They didn't want to come down the mountain and away from the familiar surroundings of their childhood days. The popular "Toothacher hall" and the hikes up to the lookout point, viewing God's creation at it's best; this time seeing it through a keen consciousness of the Almighty! Just walking around the grounds gave the two continual flashbacks to those early Methodist family camps. Like then, this camp also included young people from other Methodist churches around the Phoenix area and so new friendships were surfacing.

Coach taught how to have quiet times with God, read His word and tell others about Jesus dying on the cross; but most of all, just love people the way Jesus did. The hilarious skits that took place in the dining hall after dinner showed this group that it is fun to be a Christian and goofiness was welcomed. Friendships and connections were indescribable. They had never met such a Godly man as Coach. He embodied Christ-likeness in ways they hadn't seen but now desired.

"Mom, Coach wants us to give our testimony at church for the Sunday night youth." her children told her when exiting the camp car and still walking on air.

"What do you mean?"

"Well, you stand up and talk about how your life was before Christ and then how He has changed it. Hopefully, others will want the same."

"Oh, okay!" Norma was not quite sure how this would look or sound. Will they say embarrassing things? How much information will they give? She nervously sat at the edge of the pew with a group of 50 or more individuals scattered throughout the large room. Her body was tense as she listened to what her son had to say.

"Well, I got involved with drugs. It started when I was in 7th grade and smoked marijuana with friends," David began.

Norma gulped and held tight to the armrest.

"I really hung around with the wrong kind of people. I not only gave into peer pressure but what my parents really didn't know was that I was one of the leaders. I gave the peer pressure! I could talk others into trying the stuff. Marijuana led to stronger drugs. Both my sister and I started dropping acid just for fun!" Norma's head hung, she closed her eyes while listening to this horrifying account and swallowed hard.

"My rebellion was making life very miserable for my parents and I even ran away for a few days. The worse of it was that I not only took drugs but dealt them . . . right outside our backyard. I became a drug dealer! I had friends that bought off of me right from my backyard fort. Some of my older buddies would drive on a dirt road behind the oleanders, to get it. It was the first drug drive-through." Everyone laughed. "I'm not bragging. I'm ashamed of what I did. I never got caught but came pretty close until Jesus got a hold of my life. It was when I went to a Campus Crusade meeting with my good friend, David Little, that I heard about Jesus and how he could change my life. So I invited him into my heart. When I prayed the sinner's prayer I suddenly had no desire to take drugs and especially didn't want anything to do with my hippy friends unless it was talking to them about Christ. Some of them were open to it but some didn't want anything to do with it.

That's sad for them but maybe they will come around later. Coach talked about planting seeds and how we don't really know how much we are affecting someone's life. If we just do our part by telling them about Jesus the rest is up to God. I've talked to lots of people, including my family, about this change and I'm now going to a Bible study and church, something I've never had a desire to do before. Coach helped me see how I need to grow in God, read the Bible everyday, pray and love others. He also talked about asking forgiveness of people we've offended and I hope my parents will forgive me!"

Norma wiped under her eyes. She was crying from delight mixed with a massive dose of grief and embarrassment. She had to gulp down these feelings of failure as a parent and hope that her friends wouldn't talk behind her back. She knew other families in this church who had problems with their teenagers as well; perhaps this would become prevention for them. The overpowering feeling of David's true repentance was real!

Debbie spoke of similar accounts. She often stayed out most of the night with girlfriends and walked from one drug party to another. "I now know God was working in me, when all my druggy friends were asleep in the early morning and I was still awake from the acid. There were some times when I thought I was going to overdose. That's when I reflected on my life and thought about how much I was hurting God and my parents. But my heart was still hard. When David talked to me about asking God to take over my life, I thought he was out of his mind! I didn't pray right then but I noticed a big change in his life. I soon realized that I needed the same! So I prayed at camp and asked Jesus to be in control. When I closed my eyes to go to sleep on my bunk that night, I saw all kinds of demons in my head and couldn't sleep. It scared me and I just started praying like crazy! I know Satan was mad. The reality of darkness from drugs and all that goes with it showed me that I was doing exactly what the devil wanted and I never realized it until Coach talked to us. When I gave my life to Christ, there was a battle in me and I could feel it."

As young people mingled afterwards, Norma exited the sanctuary with her head down and promptly walked to her car. How could my own children do this to me? She sniffled and snapped open her purse, graveling around for a tissue. The reflection on the last few years and her failure as a parent caused a churning in her stomach. She felt ill and weak. How could I have let things get so out of control? Allen certainly didn't help me and he didn't back me up when we needed to set boundaries!

She thought back to the night Debbie came home with a cut above her eyebrow and needed stitches. Allen helped her clean the blood, put a bandage on it and told her to go to bed. Though Debbie said she fell while running, Norma suspected something beyond that simple story and wanted to check into it more. Allen poopooed it! I don't even want to know what really happened. She must have lied about everything and David a drug dealer in our own backyard! How? Were we

SO blind and foolish? She began to cry and reflected on their family home movies, the silly behavior of darling and blameless children. Their Sunday drives to Sky Harbor and Falcon Field airports were Allen's idea for a great adventure. Those free excursions to watch the planes take off and land brought the family such pleasure. The innocence! I wish I had those years back.

We did so many wonderful things with our children when they were little, all caught on our 8-millimeter. We've laughed so much in those days. How could they have turned on us? And, WHY didn't we see it coming?

Ugly words from a doctor, long ago, came to mind, "A Monolgoid child will take attention from the other children in the family." Is this the case for our family? Who is to blame? Had we spent too much time with Larry? Other thoughts circled her brain: My job was so demanding, too; I should have been checking on their friends. What about our neighborhood? And, Do we have too many bad influences even around our own home? Lord, I'm tired! Please help me!

Days passed and Norma and Allen had much to think about; but it was the day that Norma and Debbie were shocked to see a photograph of her daughter's good friend on TV and the announcement that she had been murdered—all due to drugs. This tragedy was a rude awakening and dread penetrated Norma's soul. "I'd rather suffer a little awkwardness from these testimonies than have my son or daughter's body lay in a casket like her friend," she said to Allen. "Our kids have changed and that's all that matters now."

They both conceded to support this unusual but better quality path the two youngest were now setting before them. The change was authentic!

CHAPTER 39

EYE-OPENERS AND CONFESSIONS-1971

Summer was ending and their baby was ready to enter high school. The last sibling would be attending the same school as her brother once again, this time with a new fervor of life.

"Since your school doesn't start for another few weeks, how about you come with me to work and file papers? It would be such a great help. I have so much to do to get ready for the year." Norma faced her daughter.

"That's an idea. I guess I can do that."

Norma's chest expanded with pride as she took her daughter around the school and introduced her to co-workers. Working so far away, her Phoenix friends knew about her family only from verbal stories and numerous photos. When they buckled down, Debbie hid herself in her mother's office and filed away. She took her daughter to lunch upon completion, at a nice Phoenix restaurant, and inquired about going on a home visit after eating. Those two words, "home visit", were very familiar to the family for they frequently heard them come from Norma's mouth when she arrived home each day. By now they all understood that it was a big chunk of their mom's job description as social worker, but no one really comprehended the details.

"You want to go?" she asked her daughter and hoped for a yes reply.

"I guess." It was obvious Debbie was edgy about it.

While driving back to Mesa, her daughter was silent. They had previously entered a near cardboard structure without any kind of doors or floor. Debbie had watched her mother's enduring motions and job skills play out towards this large family living in a hut-type dwelling. Her daughter's expression was solemn. Norma figured she was still in shock over the fact that there were people in the world who were really that destitute.

"Mom, when we came home that day our house never looked so large and felt so warm!" Debbie finally said a few days later. Her eyes were opened to the grit of her mother's work, giving her a new appreciation of the strength and stamina she possessed. It was mainly the picture of the barefoot, dusty children walking around wearing very little clothing and clutching a piece of bread, that was embedded in Debbie's thoughts. Norma knew it when she heard her daughter describe it to friends. "I never thought a family could really live that way or **had** to live that way! I felt so sorry for them. Some of the children were actually naked!"

"David, what are you doing? Mom and Dad are sleeping. It's late!" Debbie interrupted her brother tapping the parent's closed bedroom door.

"I know, but Coach told us we need to tell our parents we love um, remember?" (It was the challenge this respected man often gave to young people- to use those three words-I love you; which seemed foreign to Debbie and David, especially since they were not little anymore. They hadn't said or heard those words for quite some time).

"Now? While they are sleeping?" Debbie asked.

"Yeah, that's the best time." He laughed and slightly tapped the door again,

"Mom? Dad?" He whispered. He paused and heard nothing. David slowly stepped away from the door thinking they were in deep sleep.

"Whaaat?" Finally, they heard a barely audible murmur on the other side. David swung back, held his head to the wood and took a deep breath to let it out.

He buckled, couldn't do it. "Never mind!" he said.

Debbie threw herself across the bed laughing! Tears streamed down her face from pure exuberance of this great entertaining scene. "Oh David, you are something else! You crack me up!"

David watched his sister and laughed himself realizing that it was pretty funny, alright. "Oh, I'll tell them later." he chuckled then flopped on his bed and turned off the light.

"Debbie," he whispered across the hallway, not ready for sleep.

"What?" she replied, still laughing and wiping her eyes.

He waited a few seconds for her to stop. "You know what I did today?"

"No, what?"

"Walked over to circle K and told the owner I used to steal from them and to please forgive me."

"Are you kidding?" Surprised at his pure bravery or possible stupidity. "What did they say?"

"He thought it took a lot of guts and thanked me. I think it really affected him. I shared Jesus with him."

"Wow, way cool! What did he say?"

"He listened and was open to it."

"I actually talked to Mr. Reed, my favorite teacher at Lowell (elementary school) about Christ. I rode my bike to the school yesterday." Debbie said.

"Yeah, what happened?"

"He got tears in his eyes. He told me he was having a lot of problems with his son. I told him I would pray for him and his son."

"Wow! Man! I did so many bad things before I'm not sure how to make it all right." David was deep in thought.

"Sounds like you are doing the right thing but what about that big orchard fire you started a few years ago?"

"Yeah, thought of that too but have no idea who owns the land. Hey, I wouldn't talk! You got kicked out of Tri-city Mall, of all places, for stealing."

"I didn't steal! Roberta did and I happened to be with her."

"Yeah . . . right!" David turned his body over while letting out a big yawn. "Too much to think about right now! I just have to keep praying and asking for God's help. Night."

"Mom, how about you and Dad come with us to Church of the Redeemer?" David said the next day. "It's just down there, close to the Little's new house." He pointed out the window to the north.

"Sure, we can do that!" they responded. They already knew a sprinkle of young people who attended there, the same frequent dinner guest their third born brought home every week.

"What exactly is the denomination again?" Allen inquired.

"It's not! It's what you call non-denominational. They just teach strictly from the Bible." David replied. "Just go and you will find out. I know you will like it."

"Do you think Larry could go?" Norma asked.

"Yeah, why not?" David answered with excitement.

It was a done deal! The entire family would attend together —well, nearly, so Norma adamantly prayed for her oldest to come home. She talked to her son about her concerns and he affirmed his prayers for her as well.

"I'll tell Jamie to pray her home too." David's relationship with this young enthusiastic Bible scholar, the one leading the remarkable fireside Bible study, was taking shape. Jamie's charisma was also infectious. His deep knowledge of the Bible opened the eyes for many young people.

By now Norma and Allen were expanding their circle of church friends to include another church. They decided it was okay to attend two churches. Redeemer had a different feel and the best part was the "killer" youth group that included Larry in everything!

Norma and Allen were never so excited over full acceptance! This young crowd not only had fabulous leaders, but the continual slew of activities gave Larry a "typical" countenance. There was the prom-type dance, eating out, hayrides, costume parties, games and swimming. He was included in all of it and treated like the rest. "Hey Larry, you want to come? You want to join us? I'm coming to your house and I'll see you there. Love ya Larry. Give me a hug Larry," were the words she heard over and over from this incredibly spirit-filled gathering of young people. He smiled, he laughed, he joked and he dressed his best. He even shaved, slapped on a generous amount of cologne and was continually aware of his open mouth forcing him to intentionally press his lips together. With the idea of watching surfers on TV (one of his favorite pass-times), he unbuttoned the top button of his shirt in order to show all two-chest hairs.

This young man never looked so good! But the self-consciousness of his chunky body was on the rise; he told everyone that once he lost weight he would be tall and he truly believed it! Although this thought was a funny one, everyone indulged Larry by saying he looked great. The awareness of his short stature bothered him to the point that he obsessed about it, especially because now he had to look upwards for eye contact with his new friends. They were much taller and height was something he aspired to attain. Norma tried to get those around him to change the subject when he brought it up, but often they milked it by letting him talk, saying the same things over and over.

"Someday, I be tall like you."

"Yes Larry . . . someday."

Though his newfound arena of inclusive friendships had wonderful motives, Norma knew there would have to be some educating of the do's and don'ts in relating to a mentally challenged individual, specifically a Down syndrome teenager who had a strong consciousness of his differences.

The Jesus movement exploded everywhere, not just in this household but all over the nation. That's why the buzz of a Christian Woodstock-type gathering taking place in Texas was called Explo 72. The youth group planned on traveling in a bus and taking as many as they could. David and Debbie desired to be sitting on that bus with their friends but they had to resort to spelling when Larry was around. This was one activity he couldn't be a part of.

They were going to be gone for one entire week and "what Larry didn't know, wouldn't hurt him." His self-esteem would certainly be injured if he did have knowledge of it. Larry wanted to be included in everything. He was Mr. Outgoing and thrived off the energy of others. Secrets had to be said and done behind his back or the tantrums could be in full force.

The motivational speakers and musicians heard on this trip brought the kids home inspired again. They had more bonding friendships to add to their list but one was very special. David now had a girlfriend, a **Christian** girlfriend! He had experienced numerous female friends in his "old" life, but this dark haired, full of life, young and assertive girl was like no other.

NEW DIRECTIONS-1971/72

Carol walked in the door with boxes and a wounded spirit. She was moving back home for now and didn't speak much about the last year. It was obvious, though, life's blows were pushing her to maturity and she was ready for change. That's why David wasted no time talking to her about the family's new found life; she was ripe and ready.

Thank you, God! You not only answered our prayer about our daughter coming home, but she is changing like the rest of us, Norma smiled.

"Everyone, this is Teona Bailey." David announced. When in her presence he had a glimmer in his eye. It was a clue to everyone that this relationship was special.

The still familiar face hanging around, and one that was always welcomed, was David Little. Some members of the Little family were also attending Redeemer and now a new bond connected the Combs and Littles together again. Bill and Nancy had divorced, however, and both had remarried. Bill and Beverly attended the church with their children. Bill taught bible classes: sharing his knowledge and wisdom to many.

David Combs' influences wouldn't stop either. The magnitude of his turned-around life affected numerous people and the domino reaction kept going. Every person he encountered heard about Jesus whether they wanted to or not. He had a boldness that stood head and shoulders above his Christian friends and that's why he was elected president of the high school club called C.Y.A. Christian Youth of America. Debbie was proud of her brother and was once more willing to endure the title of 'David Combs' little sister." Twenty or more club members met once a week before school to pray for guidance and the lost.

"Why can't I drive?" Larry brought up the subject for the tenth time this week. "I can do it you know, I not batarded!"

"Well, Larry, umm, yeah, Larry, ummm, yeah, you are." David and Debbie spent hours trying to reason with their exasperating brother. He watched his younger siblings drive a car and constantly questioned when it was his turn. It just wasn't logical to his simple mind.

"Why, why not? I can do it. I oder than you!" He just wouldn't stop."

"Larry, you have to be able to read in order to take the drivers test. You take a test to drive."

"I wead, really, I can do it. You won't let me, that's all."

It was this strange belief that it was his family who were keeping him from getting his license and keeping him from reading. So many conversations with Larry were like hitting your head against a wall trying to produce better results. Everyone tried various ways to battle it: ignoring, reasoning, changing the topic, and even just a pure reality check. Nothing worked. He wasn't satisfied. Larry's heightened jealousy caused an extreme self-pity and he talked about it to anyone who would listen—and even to those who didn't want to listen. Now that the friendships included so many young people trying to exemplify their lives as Christ, they gave way to Larry's whining. They thought sympathy and patience were the correct reactions; it was a learning process for all, even for Larry! Though he didn't realize it, he was finding out what behaviors got the best results.

The Combs family had a new problem on their hands. How were they going to tell these pure-of-heart friends that they were not only letting Larry wallow in the mud, but were jumping in with him? Debbie and David were puzzled. Was it better to include him in our lives or did it make matters worse? This ignited a different dialog between Norma and Allen, one about professional counseling services, this time for Larry. Maybe if he had one set of ears, allowing the circular discussions to linger, he'd speak his peace and then hopefully drop the subject to the public. It was another "Lets try it and see."

"Mom, we're going to Jeff and Luanne's to swim, and we're taking Larry!" the door closed. David Little had introduced the four Combs' kids to another family—the Draytons! They had their own swimming pool. Pool volleyball in their backyard was not only good exercise, but also provided association with another set of Christian teen-agers. The young men had the strength required to wear Larry out in the water with plenty of wrestling. He came home content with the generous compliments about his volleyball game and was ready for rest.

"They say to cut my hair. They're driving me insane. I grew it out long to make room for my brain. But sometimes people just don't understand. What's a good boy doing in a rock and roll band? I know what's right. I don't confuse it; all I'm really trying to say is why should the devil have all the good music? Cause Jesus is a rock and he rolled my blues away."[15]

David sang the words to a new song and sound. Contemporary Christian music was beginning to trickle into the Christian bookstores and radio. Finally, the Beatles were taking a back seat and a different resounding tune came forth.

"I love wok and woll!" Larry said as he hit the drums and jerked his head, swinging the long blond bangs to one side. He knew every word from this new up and coming singer, Larry Norman.

"He has the same name like me." Larry boasted.

"Yep, he does!" they answered.

"And he cool like me."

"Yep, Larry. Whatever you say."

If the family could endure the ear penetrating sound of drums banging, it was a good release for Larry's exuberance, pounding with forcefulness. No one really understood Larry's frustrations. Leaving his true family and entering the world of the mentally disabled at Valley of the Sun week in and week out was rough. Though he laughed, joked and giggled with friends, he endured long periods of sadness, separation and loneliness.

"Larry, how about we go on a bike ride?" Allen had put training wheels on a bike for his son and now the two could ride the streets of the neighborhood.

"Sounds good . . . auchabottom!" he answered.

"What?" Allen's light blond eyebrows turned down with confusion. "Off your bottom?"

"No, I mean, I mean, um, ummm aucha, auchabottom!"

"Off your bottom?" His tan face tilted. "Hoooowws that? I don't get it"

"You will someday!" he looked up at his dad, smacked Allen's chest and turned down the corners of his mouth. He jerked the okay sign around and grunted. "Uhhhhh!"

Allen laughed and called his daughter from the other room. "Debbie, come help. What is he saying?"

"Say it again, Larry," Debbie listened.

"I say, I say, umm, I say auchabottom. You know auchabottom!"

"Oh! He's saying up and at 'em; copying mom when she says 'Let's go! Up and at 'em!'"

"Yeah, that's what I mean…auchabottom."

The two watched their dad give his famous kick-the-head-back gut laugh; he caught his breath and through the lingering chuckles said "Okay Wallboy. Auchabottom!"

In 1972, Marc voted to change its name to Marc School for the Handicapped in order to include children with physically handicaps. [16]

CHAPTER 41

ANYTHING FOR ATTENTION.

"Larry, who was that girl you had your arm around during church?" David asked.

"Umm, I can't member her name. Uhh, I can't think it out."

"Larry, you can't just put your arm around any girl you want, especially during church! You don't even know her. You just can't do that." Debbie, David and Norma were lecturing for the sake of this uncomfortable young lady and once again trying to reason with Larry concerning appropriate social behavior.

"Why not?" he tilted his head.

"Well, because you don't know her, Larry, and she doesn't know you. It makes her feel uncomfortable."

"Well, I not want to do that! " he responded. "Uhh, I know her. I do. She, umm, she my gilfrind."

The three looked at each other and shook their heads. Again! No Comprehenda!

"Larry, I want you to sit with us during church!" Norma demanded. Besides, the church elders told me you took money out of the offering plate when it passed by.

"Uhh, oh no, I did not!"

"Larry, you stole money. That's stealing! Offering is for putting money IN, not OUT! Now give me that money! " Norma held out her hand. "Where is it?" she said firmly.

"I don know!" his voice got louder!

Crimany Larry! What's gotten into that head of yours?" By now they had him cornered in Lloyd Hall, the room next to the church sanctuary.

"I, I umm a Chistian now. I no do that!" He turned his hands out and stressed the words.

"Well, you have to sit with us from now on! Do you hear me?" Norma boomed.

"I no want to!" Larry got louder. He was just getting used to his independence, sitting wherever he wanted in church and definitely desired to continue.

"Yeah, Larry, you sit with me, David or mom from now on." Debbie tried her best to convince him. He usually listened to his siblings better than his mom but apparently not this time. He walked away swinging his head back while shaking his bootie and turning to give a dirty look to his family. Secretly the three weren't sure if they could pull this off; making him sit in a specific spot each week, next to the family, would be difficult.

"He may make a scene." Norma said while watching his pounding steps. "We can talk to him till the cows come home, but it probably won't do any good."

"Maybe we shouldn't push him coming to church so much." Debbie said. Like always they needed to know, dependent on Larry's moods, what would work.

Whoever this girl was, she had a gorgeous face; Larry's taste in women was excellent which made matters worse! It certainly didn't help when he watched his brother and his new girlfriend holding hands. Sensitive to this, David tried spending more time at the Bailey's house, so as not to flaunt his affections for Teona, in front of his envious brother. Debbie and Carol were spending more time around the opposite sex as well, dating was becoming the thing to do and Larry noticed every detail.

"Why wouldn't he have such strong feelings himself? He'll be in his twenties soon and he's a guy with hormones like any other guy. It's all around him!" Allen reputed, almost excusing his son's deeds.

"Well, should I not let him come home from Valley of the Sun as often?" Norma wanted answers.

"Not sure. Don't know. Maybe." Allen said. "The problem is he still doesn't like living there."

"Yeah, but I think he can tolerate it," she said. Numerous future conversations under this topic brought out all options . . . still no solid answers.

"I take care a myself!" Larry said trying to get everyone out the door. Allen was going to First Methodist that morning, Norma and David to Redeemer. The girls had other commitments. Larry wanted to be alone. Everyone was weary of the battles so they decided to actually let him try it. If he found some good shows on TV, it would keep him occupied for a few hours. It just might work.

"Let him watch his favorite show, *Emergency*. I'll hurry home from my church and it will only be a little over an hour," Allen persuaded the others. Though it would be a short period for Larry to be alone, still it was longer than anything they had tried in the past.

"Let's keep our fingers crossed." Norma glared at the shifty look on Larry's face, hoping he didn't have anything up his sleeve.

Allen pulled out of the driveway in his green Datsun pickup truck that was used for hauling vacuum cleaners and parts. Norma and David were driving away as well. With the little Down syndrome expression, he peered out the window with the drape behind his head. A half "I got my way" grin and his fat fingers moving back and forth right next to the darling look, made it difficult not to smile back.

Norma and Allen had figured out the back and forth of two churches. Allen was back to teaching the adult Methodist Sunday School class and Norma was leaning towards attending Church of the Redeemer more than ever. She and David greeted old and new friends and settled into the blue-cushioned church pew. Closing the hymnal after the last song, "The old rugged cross," she looked up to see a church usher motioning to her.

"You have a phone call," he said. "You can take it in the foyer."

"Oh, No! What now?" she whispered to David and rolled her eyes. Slipping out through the side door, her thoughts got the best of her. Is someone hurt? Is Larry okay? What did he do? This better be important enough to get me out of the church service.

"Hello, this is Norma." she said.

"Norma Combs, this is the Mesa Lutheran Hospital calling." She listened to the authoritative voice, held her breath and looked around for a chair. "We have your son, Larry, here at the hospital and it appears he had a grand mall seizure at your home. He called an ambulance and he is now resting here at the hospital. We think he is okay Nor…." Before the caller could finish speaking, she slammed the phone down, swung her purse around her shoulder and marched to the exit doors, slapping them open. Seeing her face beating red, one of the church elders briskly followed her and yelled across the lawn—inquiring if everything was okay.

"Please ask David to get a ride home. I have to go. And, yes everything is okay!" She turned back around and directed her swift steps towards the car; squealing tires broadcasted her quick departure.

"I knew it! I knew it! We shouldn't have left Larry home alone. A seizure! Yeah right! Boy, howdy, he fooled them. This beats all!" She planned to give those people a piece of her mind. "He actually took a real ambulance ride to the hospital? How could they fall for such nonsense, Good Heavens!" She griped out loud to herself.

She knew Larry had no history of seizures but he DID have a history of scamming them. Now she knew what Valley of the Sun had endured and hated the fact that Larry had become such a good actor. After all, he lived with people who truly had real grand, mall seizures and by watching how it worked, could mimic it well. Norma couldn't wait to get to that hospital bed and pull her son out! She quickly found a parking spot and stomped into the emergency room, not caring who was watching.

"Larry get out of that bed! We are going home now!"

"Wait a minute, Mrs. Combs, he has not been discharged!"

"Boy, have you people just had the wool pulled over your eyes. Larry DID NOT HAVE A SEIZURE! He completely fooled you all! Larry get out of that bed now and let's go home!" She shook her finger near his face. Turning back around to those who were now watching this entertaining show she bellowed, "Why didn't you people call me from my house? I could have told you then that it was all an act."

With confused and puzzled looks, the medical people were stunned, shocked and speechless.

Jerking the bed covers off Larry's supposedly weak body, she lifted the plastic bag holding his belongings from the floor and slammed it on the foot of the bed. Larry was now realizing that the much-loved basking and relishing of the overabundance of attention, was coming to an abrupt end. The young pretty nurses would no longer be giving him popsicles or drinks at his every whim. "You all have been suckered by pure manipulation." she was proud to announce and hoped to shed some light on their stupidity.

A doctor stood behind the machines and spouted off Larry's vitals in order to justify their actions. Norma completely ignored his remarks and insisted on his discharge papers! Realizing that this lady was not giving in, they rushed around to meet her demands.

Norma's thoughts were racing; the sooner I get out of here, the less embarrassment I'll have to endure since I've already had my fair share for the week! She picked up the receiver to the hospital phone as Larry reluctantly put on his shoes. The big bang *Emergency* show Larry had independently written, produced and starred in was over … and he knew it. She took a deep breath to think clearly for a moment and dialed the church number. It was now necessary to communicate this surreal story to her other son and again, could care less who was listening. They could stare at me all they want to. Maybe they will realize how gullible they 've been over this whole senseless performance! She was satisfied, however, that her very commanding presence was causing a fair amount of hustling and she became hard-pressed toward her goal … to quickly get the heck out of there and take her bratty and conniving son with her. The stewing and fury kept tears from coming and if she buckled now it would only ruin what she had going.

Larry lay in the back seat of the car, still pretending to be frail. Norma was too mad to talk and he sensed that "big trouble" threat she often told him about. Usually Larry didn't think much about future consequences, he was incapable of that, but today his silence conveyed some consciousness of something bigger.

Allen's truck was in the driveway. He walked out the front door as soon as he saw her vehicle, opened the back car door, pulled his son up, pushed on his back and directed him toward the house. David had already called and explained the event of the day to his dad.

"When I came home from church, the rocking chair was turned upside down." Allen said.

"Yeah, he was lying under it when the paramedics came. Can you believe it?" she scowled at Larry standing close to his body and pointing. "You go to your room young man. Now!"

Allen guided him there. The house had a smell of emergency crews and equipment from just hours before, reminding both of them of this unrealistic and thought to be fiction story. The confirmation of having all those strangers in their house – unnecessarily – angered both of them even more.

"Sometimes I could ring that boy's neck!" she spoke out loud while walking to the bedroom. "You can answer the door." Norma turned to Allen. They both knew it was the neighbors inquiring of Larry's ordeal. "I'm going to lie down." She ran her hand against her brow. The need to hide herself in the bedroom, calm her nerves and pretend this day was over was essential to preserve any sanity she had left.

Allen gave the least amount of information to curious but sincere neighbors. The Combs family had endured a lot of embarrassing "Larry" moments, but this one would certainly go down in the Combs history books. This one would definitely take the cake!

Allen closed the door, made dinner and cleaned up the kitchen. No one could talk for several hours. Even Larry kept quiet. Pure silence!

CHAPTER 42

MOVING ON-1973/74

Jeff Drayton and David Little often brought their guitars to the house. They had numerous songs and tunes to practice in front of the Comb's members before playing at the popular venues called Christian coffee houses; an exciting hang-out for young people but without the alcohol and yet, still, good music. They asked Bob Schlesinger to sing harmony and join in playing his guitar. The three modeled their sound after the latest Crosby, Steels, Nash and Young (mostly Young) style and Jeff's creative song writing produced words the forming fan club quickly learned. "Jeeesus, I'm not worrrrithy, to untie the straps of your saaandles."

The Maranatha house was in Tempe, a city only 25 minutes away. Word traveled that this great place for Christians on a Friday night provided prayer groups, singing, food and fellowship. When David, Debbie and Carol took Larry to listen to the trio, a group of "prayer warrior" friends circled around their special brother asking for any kind of healing. Often the prayers were extended into the night.

Norma took Larry's money he earned from the Valley of the Sun and made him pay for the notorious ambulance ride. She wasn't sure this would work because of his limited understanding of money, but if he counted out sixty dollars, one dollar at a time, perhaps the magnitude of this deception would sink in. He now had no money for any future indulgences and everyone hoped he would make the connection.

The new agony, though, was an expanding battle concerning finances at his residence. It pushed her to keep better records than ever before. She had suspicions that Valley of the Sun personnel weren't giving her honest answers concerning Larry's monthly Social Security Income (SSI) checks and that's when she sought out an attorney. It was now necessary to demand extra copies of records. This was taking way too much of her time but she realized she had no choice. It just had to be done.

She wrote, "I'm enclosing a three page report which I prepared for Mr. Legg, my attorney, regarding our problems with the Valley of the Sun school and our son's social security checks." (Now trying to hunt down two missing checks produced massive headaches!). "This is a case of fraud! Allen and I should be the payees of Larry's money, not someone else." Her written statements were essential to recover missing funds through the court system."

The venting towards her husband was on the upswing. "When it comes to Larry's finances, we always need to be on the lookout. I'm going to fight them tooth and nail if I have to. After all, the continual change in staff seems to mean the right hand doesn't know what the left hand is doing. You've seen the big notebook I have of all the letters and correspondence over these last 7 years, well we have to constantly stay on our toes! The administration is sloppy in my opinion and now these so-called 'lost' checks are just the handwriting on the wall. This whole thing stinks to high heaven."

Allen thought she might be blowing things out of portion again, but since she was so stressed, he gave in and decided to help her look into the matter more.

Now a new conversation brewed between the two —bringing Larry home for good!

They decided Larry could work at the new Marc sheltered workshop and it was promised a group-home would open in the very near future. Larry's name was on top of the list for Marc's first residential program. The workshop would be an 8:00 to 3:00 job. Contracting with various companies for sorting, assembling and packaging of items was how the mentally and physically disabled adult could contribute to society and still earn their own money; most people would be bored with such tasks, but could possibly be a challenge for Larry. The clients would have their own workstations and payment would be according to the production.[17]

"The incentive to work fast in order to earn more money would be good for him," the family agreed.

Once Larry was out of their home and in his own place with co-workers, managers and other trained employees, a van would provide transportation and staff would make sure Larry packed a healthy lunch the night before. In addition, major reorganization was happening at the Marc meetings, including electing a new board of directors, rewriting the constitution and bylaws; and forming committees.[18] Marc was much more than just a school facility. The need for various services was a demand: one that a very large city couldn't ignore.

Debbie had graduated from high school and she and David attended the community college together. They were once again enjoying each other's company driving back and forth to their various classes in one car. David continued to keep both of his sisters in stitches from his creative and new comedy routines.

"You should go on the radio, David, really! I bet lots of people would listen to you."

Debbie said through the lingering giggles.

Carol was working full time and now able to pay rent on her own place. Larry would soon be working all day and he would have plenty to do between Special Olympics, church, youth-group volleyball and picnics.

Since Jeff Drayton was spending so much time at the house, he helped taxi Larry around town. Norma wasn't sure whom Jeff hung around the most . . . Larry, David, Debbie or even Carol. For now, he seemed to be an overall family friend and was generously available, not only to assist but to also just hang out and willing to provide last minute transportation when needed.

"He sure is good to him, don't you think?" Norma said to Debbie.

"Yeah, he is! He's patient, yet he keeps Larry under control."

"How refreshing!" Norma responded.

"He play, uhh, he play uunor with us." Larry said.

"Yeah, he sure likes playing Uno with you and your dad, huh Larry? Norma repeated his words. He even understands your humor, Larry! And, that's hard to do." She whispered.

"Wha you say?" Larry turned toward her.

"Never mind Wall-boy."

"Don't call me that, I no like that! I not, um, wall-boy!"

"Hows that? I'll call you Larrywyemiss? How do you like those apples?" Allen laughed

Larry looked at his dad, "shoooooot, no way!" he smiled and gave his funny look.

David and Teona had broken off their relationship a few times but were now back together and talking of marriage.

"Oh, David, you are too young and you need to finish college." Norma hoped he was kidding like usual.

"I'm serious, mom," he said.

She never knew how to interpret his comments, especially when he was able to easily trick her. One day he called imitating a segment from a recently purchased comedy album.

"Norma? Norma Combs, do you have a son? A son named David? David Combs?

"Yes!'

"Norma, we have your son down here at the police station."

"What?"

Now changing his voice back to normal. "Just kidding, Mom. It's me!"

"Oh, David, don't scare me like that!"

He delighted in playing jokes on his mother and her perfect reactions, and laughter from others, encouraged him to do more. Like his dad, humor demonstrated love.

But the true fluttering in Norma's heart was for her other son the day she and Allen walked into Larry's cottage, cleared his closet and drawers, packed the boxes full of his belongings and said . . . "Come on Larry. You're going home and not coming back!"

"Oh, boy! Bout time!" he grinned and squeezed his mom and dad.

CHAPTER 43

HANDLING DILEMA-1974/76

David and Teona set their wedding date. Debbie finally saw the light and was now seriously dating Jeff. Sensitive toward Larry's feelings of separation, the two often took him along. Carol was attending a different church and visits with family were less frequent.

"I wan a gilfirend! Umm, you not the only one! I have feelings too!" Larry said to his siblings as if it was a new concept. David and Debbie were trying to reason with Larry on a Sunday night after church. The friends were all going out for ice cream at the famous Farrell's Ice Cream Parlor. Larry had just stormed the church doors, when he saw Shari talking to another guy. Usually they could ignore these jealous fits but tonight, because their parents were out for the evening, they were in total charge of him and couldn't just drop him off at home. Often in situations like this they weren't sure what to do next. If Larry went along with the group in a foul mood he was capable of putting on a show and was usually impossible to work with. If they took him home it meant they gave up their social outings with their friends. No one had the nerve to leave him home alone, even for 30 minutes. The younger two wanted to help support their mom and dad but often it meant sacrificing their own desires. The kids knew that their parents needed social and emotional release times just as much as anyone, especially since they were frequently invited to parties with the Methodist couples.

"You not the only one, I have feelings too!" Norma made a Larry face and gave a sarcastic laugh as she talked with her kids.

"Good one, mom." (Norma's humor came forth in rarity so the kids had to encourage it).

Though some in the Redeemer youth crowd could assist with Larry, when it came down to the nitty-gritty, many didn't understand, thinking the only solution was to sweet-talk him which was just another way of giving into his childish tantrums. Once more, the inconsistencies and total frustrations gave Larry mixed signals. But his persistent whining of needing a girlfriend combined with a bad attitude was usually aimed at his family.

"Larry, you sound like a broken record," was often his family's response, which was actually code for "We had heard enough!" Now that he was home from Valley of the Sun, he had reminders everywhere he looked. It was a world of couples in his mind and so the broken record played over and over.

Larry's special job at the wedding was to take the gifts and stand at the book-signing podium.

Everyone was in suspense, hoping Larry would remain calm and demonstrate happiness for his brother and new sister-in-law.

"I gong, um I gong to be a, uhh, bother-n-law," he declared with a smile.

"Yes, Larry, Now get ready. We have to go soon." Norma bent with anxiety.

"Help him get ready!" she demanded of Allen. She was worried about the task David gave his brother for the celebration. He had to greet people walking through the door. Norma worried about his ongoing bad breath and teeth issues. Lots of money, in years past, had been poured over dental work for this young man, and she feared much more would be in the future.

"Make sure Larry shaves, brushes his teeth really well, and uses mouthwash!" she nagged at her husband.

"Here Larry, eat an onion. It will help your breath!" Allen laughed and put the onion back on the kitchen counter.

"Oh suuuure." Larry reciprocated his dad's humor and gave the notorious Allen-Larry "uhhh" signal! Shuh-lup, (shut-up) he laughed.

The more Norma stressed, the more Allen played. He had to overcompensate for his wife's angst. But, this day his son cleaned up nicely in a tuxedo and blue ruffled shirt and remained decently social (and very handsome), especially after all the previous lectures from his mom.

In 1974, Larry re-entered the Marc program. Three days a week Larry participated in an adult workshop. At least his time would be occupied a few days each week and they hoped down the road that it would turn into a full workweek, which would mean less idle time for Larry to conjure up mischievous things to do.

In 1975, another landmark accomplishment occurred: the federal Education for All Handicapped Children Act, later known as the Individuals with Disabilities Education Act (IDEA). The law was passed to meet four huge goals:

1. To ensure that special education services are available to children who need them.
2. To guarantee that decisions about services to disabled students are fair and
3. appropriate.
4. To establish specific management and auditing requirements for special education.
5. To provide federal funds to help the states educate disabled students. (https://en.wikipedia.org/wiki/Education_for_All_Handicapped_Children_Act)

The law was intended to make sure all children with disabilities obtained a free and appropriate education. An Individualized Education Program (IEP) document was implemented to provide special education services.[18][19]

Then, in 1976, the first Marc group home finally opened and Larry's childhood friend, Russell, was his roommate.[20] Randy and Kathy Gray were the first resident managers. Reflecting on the Marc timeline, Norma was proud of the accomplishments: Mamie Eisenhower's visit in the 60's; the infant and preschool programs; the summer, day care and training programs; habilitation; attendant care; respite services; a vocational program; and, now the first group home. The Marc school's new title turned to MARC Center for the Developmentally Disabled.[21]

Norma thought back to all the letters she and many other parents had written to the public schools in previous years. Oh, how they wanted public education for their own children! Yes, it was now a few years too late for her son, but she was grateful for the future of others. She appreciated the direction this great nation was taking towards children all around the country who were disabled. "Bout time" she had to imitate her son again.

It took several months, even after Larry came home, before Norma and Allen were reimbursed the social security check deposited without their permission or Larry's signature. Norma published a letter to the Arizona Republic in order to make others aware of the goings-on at this school. They had even involved Senator John Rhodes office.

"What a fiasco! They sure sent me on a wild goose chase! It's too bad things had to end this way." she said to Allen. "He did have a few good cottage houseparents' especially at the beginning. I thought there were some years out of the seven that he was well taken care of. He learned how to write his name in cursive, tell time to the half hour and recognize some safety signs."

No matter, it was behind them now and Norma hoped Larry would be satisfied working at the Marc workshop and happy with his independent apartment living. The rental of a triplex was the organization's first group home endeavor. Larry would live with three other men next door to his resident managers a separate, but connected apartment, was home to four women. The family thought this new living arrangement demonstrated that Larry was all grown-up—well maybe!

"I want to, ummm, take evybody out to eat. I got, I got my paycheck. David, my sisser-in-law-Teloynya, Carol, Jeff, Debbie, evey body." Larry announced on a Friday.

"How much did you get paid, Larry?" his mother questioned.

"I not sure. Umm, Six dollars. Somethun like that." he responded.

Norma had tried to teach Larry how to count money on numerous occasions. It was also an annual objective in his schooling. He just couldn't fathom that six dollars wouldn't pay the bill for that many people. She and Allen decided instead of squelching the excitement of this little boy in a big body, they would secretly pay the tab and make it look like Larry had foot the bill. Everyone met at Allen's favorite place, the Royal Fork.

"I like going there cause it makes me feel young." Allen laughed and combed back his straight hair.

Snowbird was now the term heard throughout this expanding city of fifty thousand. It was becoming a winter haven for retired people, certain restaurants attracted the silver-haired population, and enhancing Allen's young look but still sun bleached light-brown hair.

"Thank you, Larry. Yeah, thanks Larry." Everyone took turns hugging him after dinner, while they winked at each other behind his back.

"I wok hard, umm, at the workshop, that's why."

"We know, Larry, and we appreciate it!"

"Well, I, ummm wok hard, you know! I try my best I can."

"Yep. Thanks!"

Norma's excellent money management skills afforded a savings for Larry. Often she picked him up on a Saturday afternoon, brought him home and allowed him to mow the lawn. He loved it! His face lifted when she handed him a five-dollar bill. She told the other kids later that it came out of his own savings account.

"So Mom, in other words you pay Larry for mowing your lawn with HIS money?" they laughed.

"Not in **other** words", Allen said. "Those **are** the words!" He grunted, "Uuuhh."

"You better believe it!" Norma responded.

"Remember . . . what he don't know, won't hurt him." Norma made the "okay" sign this time and tried desperately to emulate her amusing husband. "Uhhh!" she said. Everyone laughed but she suspected it was more **at** her than **with** her.

CHAPTER 44

MEETINGS, MEETINGS AND MORE MEETINGS-1976

Larry moved in his semi-independent apartment and now only one child was left at home. Soon Debbie would be flying the coop. She and Jeff were engaged. Marrying off a daughter was a much different story. Norma was troubled over the lack of finances to help this couple and the fact that Jeff worked two jobs to earn wedding money—-made her feel guilty. Having one entire year to plan at least afforded time for bargain hunting.

Debbie and Jeff often supported Norma and Allen by attending one of many Individual Support Planned Program (ISPP) meetings. These Marc meetings were required every six months on behalf of their son/brother and now soon-to-be brother in law. It could take hours as each person around the table shared past goals met and future goals for Larry to accomplish in that particular setting. His workshop supervisor reported that Larry worked hard, but not fast and that it was his constant flirting with staff members that was an ongoing problem and just had to be addressed.

Relief was in sight when Larry met Susan. She was a tall smiling girl and was very high functioning. She was the one! Finally, Larry was facing reality only as he knew it. He initiated his focus toward Marc activities as opposed to church events. Now he was spending less time talking with other girls, knowing "Susan not like it."

"I just think they are feeding a flame already in progress!" Norma couldn't wait to call Mabel after walking into the triplex living room. She had seen Playboy magazines on the coffee table and was infuriated!

"I'm going to call Randy and give him a piece of my mind!"

Mabel agreed and said she'd do the same.

"These adult men have rights, Norma, and they are allowed to look at anything they want. Why should they be denied these pleasures? They also have desires," Randy responded.

"Well, I think these types of pictures will only enhance those desires and cause more frustrations" was Norma's immediate come back. "There are parents who don't want those types of magazines available for their sons. What about our rights? What about my son's right NOT to have those magazines around?"

155

She and Mabel kept pressing for complete removal but the compromise was to make sure the "dirty" magazines stayed in another room and away from tempting their boys.

An additional meeting was called but this one was concerning Larry starting a small fire in the backyard of his apartment.

"Who was supposed to be watching him? Where was the supervision? Yes, Larry was in the wrong but where was the group home manager. Larry has too much idle time! This could have been very dangerous; he could have burned the place down! We're talking safety here." Norma refuted!

Larry had lived there six months and already had way too many close calls. This latest fire episode, however, would become the deciding factor for removal.

"Maybe he just has too much freedom. He can't handle it! It gives him time to think these things up." Norma said.

The next group home was promised to open soon. This one would be set up differently. All clients would live under one roof with 24-hour supervision. Larry could share a room with one other person and be strictly monitored. His name was once again put on a list of clients for the closely supervised home. Unfortunately, he would have to move home again until the new place was ready.

Jeff gave Larry the job of ushering for the second wedding. Another great surprise that he kept his cool throughout the ceremony. Arm in arm he walked the young girls to their seats; making sure to keep his lips closed and shoulders back. His slight smile revealed he was full of glee and enchantment but had to keep it under control for this job was serious.

The family made sure to pat him on the back and tell him how proud they were. One more wedding to go! Carol had met Rollie at her church and the two were spending lots of time together.

Larry still had Allen's undivided attention at the Fifth Avenue home. Since Allen could pick his own work hours, he chose to be home when his son was not at the workshop. If the two weren't playing board games or riding bikes, Larry, Allen and Jeff hopped in the car and drove to the local theater: a newly discovered pastime. Larry was becoming a movie-fanatic just as long as they were G or PG rated: his two favorite influences in life. . . romance and comedy. While watching the silver screen, he ate popcorn, drank his diet soda (so he could "get skinny then tall."), smiled a lot and laughed along side his movie buddies.

"I like momantic" (romantic) he looked at his mom.

"I know Lar- you like it when they kiss." She made a silly face towards him.

"You bettcha! That's why, umm I like momantic."

Allen continued his gifted way of redirecting Larry's attention down other avenues, which gave only temporary relief but at least it was some kind of momentary escape from his sometimes-painful reality. Norma was grateful but was now bothered by the already sporadic Marc meeting attendance by her husband.

"Why don't you want to come to Larry's meetings anymore? He's your son too and we should be there together."

"Just don't want to," he said.

She asked the question, but deep down inside already knew the answer. He was embarrassed by her brash remarks and bold comments in front on all those people. She made sure her voice was heard even if it hurt the feelings of others. Her husband told her that she needed to calm down. In her judgment, however, HE didn't speak up enough which forced her to do all the talking.

"Well I'll get Debbie to go to the next meeting with me. She doesn't mind going and she says she learns a lot." Norma quickly responded.

"Go for it!" Allen was irritated!

It wasn't that long ago when she brought a full paper bag to a meeting and pulled out Larry's "nasty shoes and ragged clothes" to make her point of Larry's inappropriate dress to church functions.

"This is what he wore to church because NO ONE paid attention to his appearance at the triplex."

Staff knew this woman was not going to back down especially since she often popped into his apartment unannounced to check on her son (really, to check on many things). Seeing the condition of the place gave her more reason to complain for lack of cleanliness

"That bathroom is filthy! You need to be teaching these boys how to clean and use disinfectant-talk about gross!"

Each meeting required certain people to be in attendance. Norma made sure Larry's caseworker from the Division of Developmental of Disabilities was notified way ahead of the date. The caseworker's job was to advocate for the rights of the family throughout the designated time. His/her presence was crucial! Continual change of Marc Staff meant no one was sure how many new faces would be in attendance; thus, the exasperations of repeating previous topics (very wearing on the family). Larry could contribute at anytime. He was allowed to express his thoughts, desires and concerns. It was his RIGHT, of course!

The space between Norma and Allen's differences would widen with each encounter they had about their son. There were now just too many to count. The feeling that Larry was stuck in his teens even though he was in his twenties was on everyone's mind and seemed to be one of the few things the couple could agree upon. He often acted like that sneaky 14-year-old who only said he was sorry only if he got caught.

CHAPTER 45

ROLLERCOASTER 1977 TO1979

Larry and Susan's relationship was cut short!

"She can't go, um, she can't go on a date. Her mom don't let her date. I don't like that." he said. Larry was now back, playing the field. Though his siblings were no longer involved with the youth or college groups, Larry still attended whatever activities he could, scouting out the ladies.

The second move took place. Norma liked the new format of this group home but now worried about its location. It was right down the street from Church of the Redeemer. Since Larry was a "wanderer," would he take off to the church at all hours of the evening and weekends? Some church activities were not for him but he was not aware of such a concept. If there were people and food, he not only wanted to be there, but also figured he could.

"You'll really need to watch him! I don't want him walking down the street at eight o'clock at night and enter any ole activity, an elder's meeting or something like that!" Norma affirmed at the next meeting. The good aspect, though, was the walking back and forth to church, attending the allowed events. It would provide much needed exercise. Larry's continual weight problem concerned the family and they were now insisting on physical activity beyond the once-a-week Special Olympics training.

"His weight is getting up to over 200 pounds and that's uncalled for! He's too short to carry that much weight."

Since this group home setup was different, his supervisor was pushing for more alone time on Larry's behalf. "Three hours of alone time? Are you crazy? Larry couldn't handle that! What are you thinking?"

The group home supervisors would need to taxi other clients here and there and if Larry couldn't stay at the house by himself, he would have to tag along. Repeatedly, Larry became obstinate to the plans. It took too much time to convince him to get into the vehicle and because of his complete stubbornness; the others would be late to their destination. It was just easier not to fight that battle and let him stay home by himself.

The topic of alone time became an on-going dilemma and heated discussion at the Larry-focused gatherings.

The latest family announcement was that Teona was pregnant. A new passion came over Larry. He added new words to his vocabulary of communication.

"I gunna be a, a, a uncle!" he told everyone, "he gunna be, umm, my, a my, a my nep, nephew!"

Uncle Larry. It had a certain ring to it and he liked saying it repeatedly. How would he react to a baby? Especially one he was related to. Everyone was curious. Larry did have such a gentle way when holding a kitten or puppy and somehow understood about fragile beings.

Carol and Rollie also announced their engagement and for the third time their brother would take part in a wedding ceremony. Carol was going to borrow Debbie's wedding dress, change the look with a large sun hat and alter the size 5 waist to a 3. They, too, were looking for ways to cut financial corners.

Norma still had a talent for planning short trips and picnics. She had such a unique way of bringing people together and made sure her children's other families were invited: the Baileys, Draytons and now the Pomeroys. It was remarkable that she had time for social gatherings and some how could squeeze it into her busy weekends.

Her expertise as social worker was at an all time high. Growing callused to the harsh parts, she knew how to do her job and do it well! Adding to her involvement at Marc, she continued to help with decisions and to keep communication open with those in the public eye, all while the keeping copies of every documentation, newspaper article, photograph and letter. Amongst all of this, she fit in some therapeutic hours organizing her own family photo albums and, as if she had the time, recently volunteered to archive the Redeemer church functions as well.

She and Allen would be grandparents for the first time and the two set out to find a new and improved camera for all the pictures they would be taking. Both were anxious to tell their own fathers the news that they were to be great-grandfathers and hoped that someday the men would visit.

Once Larry settled into the second group home working out the related kinks brought on more stress. The biggest issue was finding good resident managers! The couple they interviewed and hired seemed competent at the time but Norma later noticed they needed anger management classes, especially the husband.

"Where do they find these people, anyway?" she told Allen. "This guy shouldn't be working with the mentally disabled! He lacks patience, to say the least, especially with Larry. I think he targets him." It was time for the Community Living committee, of which Norma was a member, to revise the clearly written criteria for hiring. It was also necessary to add to the next agenda the need for more training, especially for life skills instructors who usually, on a daily basis, enter the group homes.

Norma wondered if there was ever going to be a time when she would be able to relax in this life. She was always on guard and ready to fight for her child—much like a mother lion does for her cub. She thought that some days she would burst because of nervous anxiety and Allen was too comfortable in her shadow.

"Someone's got to do it cause you certainly won't" She and Allen were once again in conflict. Allen figured the best thing to do was just walk away from her argumentative spirit and not give her the satisfaction of refuting; just letting her bicker with herself since he believed she enjoyed a good fight way too much!

Though she had become a spokeswoman for other parents and knew of their appreciation, she reflected on the times Allen told her that she too often looked at the glass as half empty. In his opinion,

Marc people tried to help Larry and did focus on some of his positive behaviors, but no one doubted that he had ongoing difficulties causing total frustration for all involved. Some problems surfaced more than others and at different times. It was a rollercoaster with lots of twist and turns. He could actually move along nicely for a few days, than was caught stealing a co-worker's lunch, or taking money out of employers' belongings. He was devious all right! It made others feel he couldn't be trusted even if he was on an uphill swing of proper acting. The only thing consistent was his inconsistency. Grounding him from events was usually the only consequence that spoke to him . . . at least for a short time. This proved tricky, though. The state rules in running group homes tied the hands of resident managers trying to carry out consequences.

"These people have rights! They have rights! That's all I ever hear and now Larry's saying it too!" Norma said. She had just had one of those round-and-round conversations with him on the phone.

"Larry, you can't just take other people's belongings whenever you feel like it. That's stealing! Do you understand that?"

"Oh, sure I do! I, umm, don't steal!"

"You already did, Larry! You stole from Ron at work."

"Yeah, riiiiigt! ."

"Well, you are grounded! I'm not going to pick you up to go see Debbie and Jeff. You just stay home and think about what you did."

"I think aright. I, um I have rights, you know."

"I mean it, Larry! It's not funny! **I** have the right to ground you, mister!"

"Well, I have rights too, you know. Umm, you, you not the only one. Besides, I see um, I see Debbie tomorrow!"

She was now a supervisor at the workshop. Larry was seeing her more and more during the week. She and Jeff were also helping out at the triplex as relief managers on weekends. His younger sister's interest towards the handicap population inspired her to take special education classes at Arizona State University.

"Well, you won't be able to go on the church picnic coming up either! You need to learn."

"You learn!" Larry sassed and hung up the phone.

Gabriel Ryan was born and Larry's quiet hands held his new nephew. Norma's camera flashed over and over and the photographs would be shown to anyone who paid attention. She often tucked pictures into her purse to pass around at church. Larry liked carrying a few pictures in his back pocket too. Those at church indulged Larry by complimented his handsome look. "I um,I un uncle." Larry remained proud and now his sister, Debbie, was pregnant.

"I gunna be un uncle two time." He held up two fingers with a smile. "I wan to get married. I need a gilfriend." The broken record started again. "I need a college gil, and she, well she, umm,she drives and she, she tall!"

"You want a college girlfriend that drives and is tall," was how people responded, along with a laugh.

"Put in your order, Walboy. I mean Larrywyemis!"

Since Susan no longer existed in his mind, he paid attention to Michelle at the Marc functions.

She didn't drive, but was another high functioning girl and, best of all, was very tall. Yes, Larry once more found romance and Michelle returned the love.

"Miiiiichelle, my Bell!!" The words to the well-known Beatle song were perfect. "I love you, I love you, I loooove you!" Shaking his head this way and that, straining his voice, he knew each word and sang it from the heart. It provided joy to those watching.

Working with his new girlfriend at the workshop created an added concern to the list for monitoring. The two walked around the back of the building and often were found "smooching" during lunch breaks. Just visualizing this created giggles from the family—Michelle was tall and slender and Larry was the opposite so he probably had to stand on his toes to just barely reach her lips.

"Please, keep a close eye on these two." Norma begged once again.

"It doesn't matter now, Michelle is getting a job at the Pizza Hut and will no longer be at the workshop," the supervisor said.

A new component to the Marc program opened which allowed some clients jobs in the community. Now providing a job coach and the chance to intermingle in the real world, doing remedial tasks at a restaurant or grocery store; it was another great push towards inclusion and full mainstreaming, benefiting everyone. [22]

"I want to get a diffent job." Larry said.

"You have a job!" his family responded in another stab at realism.

"No, you no understand. I mean, um I mean, a real job, uh like my gilfriend, Michelle. She wok at Pizza Hut. I wanta work, umm, I wanta work there." Larry complained.

"I, um I um going to talk to my boss Randy Gray (now CEO of Marc) cuz I known him a long time and he, um, he yistens to me."

Though Larry and Russell spent way too much time "bugging" Randy about what could be viewed as insignificant matters, Norma was impressed with the enormous amount of patience Randy possessed, always allowing these two men to vent. Some Marc supervisors told her that no matter what grievances Larry and Russell had, they wouldn't talk to anyone but the big man himself. They always chose to go straight to the top- Randy Gray's office.

He's been the constant one in their life, Norma thought. Or maybe they just feel entitled. But no matter how busy Randy was that day, he took time to be a listening ear for these two young men. Norma was grateful.

Having a community job was not a reality for Larry, for now anyway, but what was reality was Norma's generous action of taking her son and new girlfriend out on dates. She often talked to Michelle's mother on the phone about her going to dinner with the family and even got as daring as dropping the two off at a movie afterwards; but, only after lecturing Larry about appropriate touching in public. She realized the talking-to did absolutely no good the day Larry and Michelle were kicked out of the theatre for unsuitable behavior and asked not to return. "Oh, Goooood Niiiight!" Norma yelled.

He moved back to the triplex. The Stapley house was not working for the needs of her son, but this time the triplex was restructured and would be closely monitored. Once again, Norma hoped for these assurances to **really** come to pass.

When Allen was out, and Norma had time alone, the house was quiet. It was then that she heard the laughter in the walls: the laughter of her small children; their arguments and intense conversations about Larry; the slamming doors; the music and pounding drums; and, silly games with giggles of tiny voices. She cried, she laughed and she searched within. Purpose! God has a purpose . . . remembering the pastor's words!

She spoke out loud to her Lord. "I have a purpose. I know but sometimes I doubt. Sometimes I wonder if Allen and I are going to make this marriage work. You gave me a heavy burden, Lord." She opened her Bible to Proverbs 3:5, "Trust in the Lord with all your heart and lean not on your own understanding. In all your ways acknowledge Him, and he will direct your path." Memorizing these two sentences, she said them under her breath when life gave her too much weight. They were repeated over and over.

CHAPTER 46

REVERSE PSYCHOLOGY

Norma had mixed feelings. She struggled to find balance in her decision-making. "Should I rescue my son or let him learn from his mistakes? If, that's even possible." That's why she listened carefully at the next meeting about Larry's desire to smoke.

"I can't believe I said okay," she told a friend on the phone, "but it sounded convincing, you know that reverse psychology bit."

"If he wants to smoke, then let him. He'll soon lose interest, especially since he enjoys the game of sneaking behind backs," was the advice given at the latest meeting.

But she put her foot down when it came to the bars. Larry had walked down the street to a nearby bar and drank alcohol while smoking his cigarette. Again, the question was asked: "Who's supposed to be watching him? Why didn't you notice Larry's absence in the first place?" She had accidentally found out that it was one of the managers who took the clients to this setting a few weekends prior.

"Of course he would walk away from the triplex and go the local bar! Lo and Behold, you guys put the idea into his head! What a shenanigan!"

Exasperated, she wrote another clear and strongly worded letter; demanding that Larry not go to any bars, have access to dirty magazines or attend "R" rated movies. Her angry words penetrated the paper: "They hire any Joe blow off the street, pay him a few cents and Larry can manipulate whatever naïve house manager happens to be working that day. Staff doesn't know what's going on! What a joke! I even saw one of your female employees dressed like a chorus girl! Her rear end hanging out of her shorts! What kind of example is that?"

"Chorus girl! Mom, really? That's such an old term!" Debbie said.

"I don't care! They need to change their ways or I'm going to give them a piece of my mind!"

"Sounds like you already did."

"Well, I'm going to rattle more cages then. If they think I'm going to back down, they have another thing coming! Ahhh!"

Larry's Social Security money, after paying for his board and care, paid for the usual clothing needs. Because of his distorted feet, he had to have particular costly custom made shoes. Extra money was also needed for frequent dental visits and then there were the on-going eyeglasses saga. (Since his first pair back in 1965, Larry often lost or broke them.) Once more, Marc employees didn't pay enough attention in Norma's opinion. When going shopping with a staff member, Larry had whims like a small child and "needed" whatever he saw in the store. Too often a new inexperienced person would feel sorry for him and allow him to purchase his wants.

She added to the letter: "He doesn't have the money for anyone to give in to his desires that often come when shopping at K-Mart and I refuse to keep paying for those purchases! I will decide what he needs! I give Marc center a certain amount of spending money for Larry and now I want a complete breakdown as to where that money is going or I will have a breakdown myself! I've been burned before, and it's not going to happen again. Larry gets a new feather in his cap about something he thinks he needs, almost on a daily basis" The words were yet again, unyielding: "Church events often call for money and yet you drop him and Russell off without food to contribute to a potluck or money for a certain event. Because I'm at the gathering myself, I usually end up paying their part which I shouldn't have to do. This is when you **need** to provide the funds!! Things have got to change! You're teaching them to be freeloaders!"

"I bet they just cringe when you walk in the room." Allen said with annoyance.

"Big deal!" she pushed her lips together making a "puffing" sound and gave a flippant swat with her hand.

CHAPTER 47

WHAT A LIFE!

Debbie, David Little and Patty (a mutual friend) started a Redeemer special education Sunday school class. They were given a specific room in the building and now Larry not only could learn about Jesus through a simplistic curriculum but was also encouraged to invite anyone from the triplex. Initially, a few came and over time the group began to grow.

It didn't make Larry happy, though; in his mind, it was another reminder of separation from the people he preferred.

Handling one or two mentally disabled persons from the church population was manageable but the time had come to embrace several. It wasn't going to be easy. Each individual was unlike the next and most with little social etiquette in place. Many attended the main church service afterwards. They seemed to enjoy the larger group events but had a hard time sitting long periods in the service: especially, because they couldn't quite comprehend the words spoken by the pastor. They squirmed while rudely staring at those sitting around them and some even scratching private body parts in plain sight; all while the churchgoers were listening to a message about God's forgiveness. Everyone had something to learn. The group home young people needed to focus on proper manners while out in public and the church members had to be tolerant of the challenged individuals. Those who were used to a predictable controlled environment were forced to accept humiliation and give up some comfort for these new attendees.

Unlike Sunday mornings, Sunday nights were much more relaxed. After spending the afternoon with family, many members came back for the evening service. Jeans and casual attire were accepted. Once another sermon was given by the pastor, a church elder would then stand holding a microphone in preparation to hand to anyone in the audience of 300 or more. This was a time of sharing, prayer requests, talk about God's blessings, or just anything that was on one's own heart. Sunday after Sunday, it became a comical routine when Russell immediately raised his hand then stood and talked into the mic asking prayer for Larry. On several occasions, just hours before the service, the roommates had gotten into an argument and in Russell's opinion Larry was the one who needed prayer! Then, Larry raised his hand when Russell was finished and when given the microphone he returned the favor. This casual church service was becoming a way for both these Down syndrome young men to vent their resentments to a larger group. It was a droll act! Because Debbie was teaching the Sunday school class, the pastor asked her to talk to the two about their problems.

"Try and reason with them as to when and what to share with the group at church. " he said. "Help them understand what's appropriate and what's not."

It was the next Sunday night when again Russell's hand went up immediately.

"What is he going to say?" Jeff elbowed his wife as the two sunk into the pew, holding their breath and crossing their fingers for no more indignity. Debbie glanced at her good friend, Maryann, and watched her snicker. She had the same thought. A few rows behind, David, Teona and Norma shot each other a glance. They, too, looked down at the floor and hoped for some kind of decent communication to come from their good ole pal, Russell.

"Uh, Hi. Uh I want, I want, to ask, to ask prayer. I gong, gong to have an op, op operation on my, my down belows." He finally got it out after several seconds of stuttering. Most people hung their heads from pure awkwardness, not sure if they had heard him correctly. What exactly was Russell was trying to convey? He was asking prayer for himself this time. It was an upcoming vasectomy that he was concerned and very serious about. The family had their hands over their faces and was now practically sliding under their seats. This was to become another one of those "grueling at the time, but funny later" memories.

"At least it wasn't Larry making the request." the family stated after church that evening, still rolling their eyes and not yet ready to see the humor.

Larry was also scheduled to have a vasectomy. He just didn't exactly understand the concept like his buddy did! Norma and Mabel had recently decided this had to be done and scheduled the procedures for their sons.

"Yeah, and at least Russell didn't say, well you know, say ummm. You know the P word!" Now, **that** comment brought laughter.

What a life-that Larry and Russell! Oh, what a life!

CHAPTER 48

BIRTH AND DEATH -1980 TO 84

Everyone was relieved to know Larry would not be able to father a child. The only babies he could claim as family were his two nephews. Kelsey Justin was born to Debbie and Jeff. This family of three lived across town. The exercise routine of Allen's became peddling miles on his bike to see his new grandson and then picking up fruits and vegetables at the farmers market on the way home. Once again, Norma observed Allen's love for small children, this time the second generation. Though Allen was getting Larry to ride his new three-wheeler further away from their neighborhood, his sister's house was yet too far.

Watching their children start their own families was a reminder of letting go. The empty nest season of life happened for all their friends but the difference was that the Combs parents would never be letting go of one in particular. Though Larry's future of living in a separate dwelling provided some relief, he would not ever be on his own . . . not in the same way as the other children.

People didn't understand a new reality for the Combs couple, only those in the same situation, but a few Redeemer people approached Norma about allowing Larry be a part of the upcoming college and career trip to California . . . without her. Wow! Talk about really letting go! Could she do it? It definitely was something she would need to think long and hard about but it would surely make Larry happy. Would he behave himself? Who would help him with his hygiene? Who would make sure he didn't get lost or wander from the group? Someone would need to make sure he went to bed when he was suppose to and get up on time, take a shower, even dress appropriately, take care of his belongings and follow directions from his peers- but really his authority. It's not like people can always be his friend. Someone has to take on the parent role. What if he gets angry over something and storms off? How would they handle it? Who would monitor his eating and make sure he doesn't constantly eat sweets and junk food? He is pretty much addicted to diet soda now and gulps down a can in four swigs, only to grab another. Someone would have to be close by to say "No more soda Larry!" What if he tries to steal something? It's not like I could just run over and get him, if there was a problem. It would be an eight-hour drive and I'm not even sure if Allen would go with me. The inner questions started up again. She wanted him to have his independence but contemplating such a decision was bringing on a vast amount of fretfulness. Yet, the fact that they approached her with this question: Larry joining them on a several-day trip so far away? Wow! It showed how caring –and somewhat daring- this group was. These were the same people who had known Larry for a while now and most were aware of his ups and downs . . . even had witnessed his tantrums and anger outburst. What a demonstration of their true character. Whatever she and Allen decided, she would be grateful for their willingness.

David was changing jobs frequently and Norma saw a pattern that she hoped wouldn't reveal itself like Allen. It was restlessness. She wanted her son to find his niche and stick with it.

Beckie Lynn and Rebecca Jean were both born in 1980. Norma and Allen now had a total of four grandchildren. Beckie was David's second and Rebecca was Carol's first. Rollie's job was in construction work and they too, had a house in Mesa. God had blessed Norma and Allen repeatedly with healthy and attractive grandchildren. Allen spent lots of time holding and playing with his kids. He wore the grandfather attire well and without wrinkles. They called him "Tombez", a name Gabe started in his early speech and so it stuck. The two continually thanked God for all the bestowed blessings. Now, Allen split his time between his needy son and the grandkids. Larry didn't seem to mind as long as his dad still had time for a round of Uno. If the other families were at the house, they too joined the game. In Larry's mind, the more people around the table the better. Large groups meant more jokes . . . and more jokes meant more laughter.

Despite the joyfulness, the Combs members ached for the Bailey Family. David's father-in-law had been in and out of the hospital. Doctors couldn't figure out the reason for his high fevers. Teona was beside herself but no one was prepared for what was about to happen to this exceptional family.

Norma walked inside the house to see Allen hang his head and slowly put down the receiver. She had just come back from visiting her friend Ouida, Teona's mother, in the waiting room at the hospital. She had gotten the latest thoughts from the doctors as to her husband's condition and more testing was to be done. It didn't look good.

"What's wrong?" Norma asked Allen and thinking it was about Teona's father, Bailey, as they called him.

"That was David. Bill (Teona's brother-in-law and a highway patrol officer) was driving and pulled over to help a fellow officer dealing with an accident along the side of the highway. Another car came over the hill, a drunk driver lost control of the car crushing Bill between two vehicles."

Allen looked up into Norma's eyes, "They air-vacced him in a helicopter."

Norma grabbed the car keys and the two rushed out the door. They returned to the hospital where Norma had just been, but now to comfort Ouida over her son-in-law. The next crucial hours were spent in prayer by anyone who knew this family. Bill died the next day and, yes, Bailey died shortly after. Teona's dad and brother-in-law died within the same 24 hours, at different locations. The shock was unbearable!

It hurt to see this wonderful family endure such intense pain. Gwenn, Bill's wife, was a few months into her second pregnancy. The twin girls were only three years old and now had lost their daddy. What a horrendous tragedy!

Though Norma had a way of reaching out to all three in-law families, her and Ouida had a special chemistry. Oh, how she longed to take this unbearable pain from her friend, her daughter-in-law and especially her son, who himself was trying to provide comfort and support to his wife and in-laws. People walked around at both funerals asking the same questions: Why? Why? Why would God allow this? No one had answers; they just shook their heads in wonderment.

Unable to nurse baby Beckie due to stress, a nursing mom and friend of Teona's took on the task and fed her newborn in the adjacent room during Bailey's funeral. Upon completion of one ceremony, another was to be organized and attended. It was when Gwenn lifted her arms up to the heavens as she sat in the front row and heard the honoring words about her husband, which caused uncontrollable tears to echo throughout the large room. In spite of the sheer darkness in her life, she was exalting God . . . A bold testimony to the rows and rows of men in uniform. They had come from all over the state to show respect for a fallen warrior and fellow officer.

The church wanted to extend their love to these two widows in the months following, especially after hearing news of Gwenn's miscarriage within days of the incident. No one knew what to do or say. Norma frequently dropped in on Ouida hoping to lift her spirits with a book, a written poem, or a message on tape. Observing the loneliness of her friend, it caused a new freshness towards her own life and she began to gratefully thank God for her husband, despite their many, almost daily, disagreements.

Debbie and Jeff moved to Sunshine Acres children's home. They were eager to do missionary work and took the house-parent job. It meant they were in charge of taking care of 10 teenaged boys. Debbie was pregnant with her second child and Amber Renee was born just days after moving to this "miracle in the desert."

"Amber is going to grow-up thinking she has eleven brothers." Allen laughed.

They all lived in a large dorm together as a family. Several other dorms housing children of various ages were positioned throughout the 130 acres of desert land. The founder, Vera Dingman, was among the godliest women they had ever encountered and faith was what kept this home for distraught children in place. Serving on the Sunshine Acres board was the famous Coach Heath and the well-known Dr. Kerr (Dr. Kerr also served on the Marc board). The Kerr's offered their mountain get-away home to all house parents during their scheduled days off. It was welcomed for the highly needed R and R. The Drayton and Combs families took advantage of the nice offer.

Amy Joy was born to David and Teona; and they too, for the second time, moved to the Acres to parent the little boys' dorm and then later, the girls' dorm. Now most of the cousins were together daily! Norma, Allen and Larry spent many weekends playing with five out of their seven grandchildren in one location. Carol had given birth to a baby boy, Michael Aaron. Norma and Larry were more than happy to paint the nursery in preparation. The two realized that they were a good team in helping others- especially if Larry was in one of his good moods.

Norma decided to make herself available to assist with the Acres kids. Since David and Teona managed the girls, she could act as one of the relief house parents providing time off for the couple. She spent quality time with these girls and began to establish solid relationships. It was a world of children everywhere in a camp-type setting; riding bikes, swimming, a 4-H club, eating at the dining hall, building forts, sports activities, summer programs and lots of wilderness space. The grandchildren were having a ball but Norma could see her own children wearing down. These needy boys and girls that they were in charge of had extreme dysfunctional backgrounds and were not easy to wrangle. Debbie wasn't getting much sleep, Teona gave of herself to these females who needed lots of positive attention and David and Jeff had to consistently carryout consequences. Most of the Acres rebellious children were not used to rules and continually tested the limits.

"I don't know how you put up with us when we were like this." David told his mother.

Norma grinned and uncommonly kept her thoughts to herself.

CHAPTER 49

UPS AND DOWNS

Larry hopped on his three-wheeler and rode to Pizza hut. "Michelle is going to get fired, if you do that again, Larry! Is that what you want? Do you want her to get fired?" Norma spoke on the phone, scolding her son for the third time this week!

"Oh I don't want that." He replied.

"Don't do that again! Her boss said you two were behind the building making-out. . . kissing!"

"I know."

"That's not appropriate Larry, do you understand that?"

"Wull, corse I do, I know all,umm, all bout, bout propriate!"

"I'm going to bring your bike home and lock it up if you do that again!" She reputed.

"Well, umm I want a job." He argued.

"You have a job, Larry."

"Ya but…"

"Ya but nothing."

"No, no, I mean… not that kind job, I mean, I mean, um a job at Pizza Hut, like,um my gilfriend."

"Just be happy with what you got. If you don't listen to staff, you won't have any job. Just cool it!"

"Shooot" was often the reply when Larry didn't know what else to say and had been caught red handed.

She wanted Larry to have a community job just as much as **he** did. When walking through the workshop, she viewed lower functioning disabled adults working along side her son. It sort-of magnified Larry's disability and she knew he sensed it as well. Watching, she wondered if he could carry on any kind of decent conversation with his co-workers. The topic at recent meetings was that Larry had no desire to talk with those around him, unless it was to tell them what to do. He himself wanted to be a supervisor and was determined to take on that role.

At least upon arriving at his apartment, he conversed with Russell in a somewhat regular manner. They were on the same level in several ways but she was noticing more and more fights between the two. From one day to the next, one didn't know if they were friend or foe. After an argument and then residing to friendship again, they were in cahoots, planning something together. It became a sort of sick scheming in a competitive way- like brothers… very competitive brothers!

While at church the two asked for rides home after the service. Seems they could find and prey upon the ones who felt sorry for them. They both had the intelligence to use their disability to their advantage. Russell even asked the church secretary to advertise it in the Sunday bulletin: the two would need a ride home every weekend.

"We don't mind, really, Norma." She had marched into the church office and told them the boys were conniving again.

"They have a ride; the van from their group home picks up all the clients! That is their job. There's no reason Larry and Russell can't ride the van home. That's just nonsense now take it out of the bulletin!" Norma had to endure the dirty looks even from Church members. Her reputation was always wavering with those who truly didn't understand.

As long as the sun was up, Allen canvassed. The large retirement communities were endowed with opportunities for selling door-to-door and so Allen, again, on a winning streak. Finances were cushioned, at least for now.

The evening phone calls were usually a customer but tonight Norma suspected someone else. She followed Allen to the bedroom. He stood still and didn't speak for a long time. Norma knew by the look on his face it was HER!

"I don't want the money," Allen said.

Norma's forehead wrinkled, sustaining a baffled look aimed at her husband.

Allen hung up the phone. "She died and left me some money." He turned to his wife.

It was just recently **that** woman had sent a letter in the mail explaining her poor health and with the letter, a picture of Allen's alleged granddaughter.

"You call them back right now. I want the money!"

"What!" His eyebrows lifted.

"I mean it! With all the hell that woman put us through! I want the money! I've always wanted a backyard-covered porch. We could use the money for that."

Allen gazed into her eyes realizing she was serious and like a whipped dog, dialed the number.

Norma spent the next few days inquiring to others about a contractor for the soon-to-be and newly laid covered back porch.

Within a few weeks it was completed. The kids and grandkids came over for more backyard fun, slip and slid, eating around the picnic table, this time under shade and of course not knowing where the money came from for such a luxury. Debbie made the comment of why we didn't have something like this when we lived at home?

"Yeah, you guys think you're cool now that you don't have kids at home and have lots more money-huh?" David joked. Allen laughed as he pulled his white handkerchief out of his pocket to wipe his pretend tears through the chuckles. It was his way of making fun of the pity and an " I don't feel sorry for you." gesture. (Plus it was a good cover-up for the real thing). Such a familiar sight!

If the grandkids weren't laughing with Tombez, they were riding bikes along side him. It seems he always had the time to take a trip to the Reed Park recently built only blocks from the neighborhood. Peddling together on beautiful sunny days, they took breadcrumbs to feed the numerous hungry and annoying ducks. He showed them how skip rocks across the pond and acted as if he had not a care in the world and nothing but time on his hands.

Norma's favorite times with the grandkids were the quiet moments of reading together. She found good deals on used books and kept a small children's library at the 5th Avenue home, always ready to introduce another intriguing story.

Life had so many warm fuzzies; it lessened the day-to-day drama of the Larry planet. Though they couldn't escape it completely, the second generation softened the blows. The two lost themselves in the pleasures of grandparenting, anticipating each day to see and talk to these seven cutie pies, each with distinctive and fun personalities.

"Sometimes I wonder if it's worth Larry having a girlfriend." Norma questioned.

The newest and latest was the physical fighting. Larry's jealousy was at its peak when he viewed another guy talking to his girlfriend. It sent his fist flush into the eye of his co-worker. Larry's new response when confronted about it was…

"No… you know me…I'm a, I'm a lovr, not a fighter." (Something he got from a movie). Yet Tony had a black eye as proof that Larry was a fighter, not a lover.

Norma had had it! "I'm going to the beauty shop to get my hair dyed, so many of these gray hairs have Larry's name on them, anyway!" She looked at her husband.

When she walked in the door a few hours later, she was beautified!

Allen joked in front of the young ones. "Was the beauty shop closed?" He grinned at his wife.

The same state of affairs was playing out for the next generation: Allen joked, Norma rolled her eyes and the kids laughed.

All the kids looked at their grandpa and showed the Tombez sign, turned it around and adding the Uncle Lar face. Uhhhh!

Oh, how he taught these little ones, well!!

"Phooey" Norma's hand flipped.

NOW WHAT?

The next Marc board meeting was focused on much needed financial assistance for the group homes and Norma agreed to type up another letter this time to state representatives asking for additional funds. The legislature has chosen not to increase taxes; therefore, the response she received mentioned a slight cut in support for most programs. State representatives specified that they were under the impression parents contributed their own private resources, along with the resident's monthly social security income, to help run the group homes. The letter also indicated there were no monies in the state budget in the current year, or the next year, to increase any agency funding.

Despite this, Norma was bold enough to ask the Marc organization to set up an account to compensate for lost or stolen items in the group home. She listed all the things she had bought for Larry in the way of clothes and items that were now missing. Though Larry could have misplaced them himself, her suspicion was they were stolen. She knew he wasn't the only one with sticky fingers in that apartment and respect for property was a needed lesson to be taught for **all** the residents. She even had uncertainties toward the ins and outs of employees.

A desire to get her son out of the ongoing group home chronicles, prompted her to pull him out for vacations with the family, weekends at home, and helping around the house. He had so many life skills in place and loved to load the dishwasher, fold laundry and, of course, mow the lawn. When special projects were called for, like painting, Larry couldn't wait to put on the grubby clothes and mouth mask; then, with brush in hand, paint away under the supervision of someone hired from church, someone who knew Larry and certainly didn't mind his "help." For the most part, he did a good job but was so meticulous that he didn't get much accomplished, painting the same area over and over. One of the few consistent values in Larry's life was his hard work ethic, only when motivated that is. It gave him satisfaction when he was paid for a job well done and, more importantly, received words of encouragement from friends and family.

"I, um, I hep paint!" he told visitors who came over and as a result got yet many more pats on the back. Every time Larry heard, "That's good, you did a great job!" a huge smile showing his jagged teeth, verifying his delight. He lived for those tight squeezes (of course favored any pretty female doing the squeezing). It was too bad he didn't have the desire to work that hard during the weekdays at the Marc workshops. He didn't want to be called "a client" and certainly didn't see himself as one of "them." At the latest review meeting his supervisors vented their frustrations and for the ump-teenth time, expressed that they couldn't get him to stay seated at his station, focus on his **own** piece-work and mind his own business! And. . . for the ump-teenth time, the discussions went round and round as to what to do.

Allen's honey-do list included, but not limited to, taking Larrywymiss for haircuts, dental check-ups and glasses repair. For the most part, Allen didn't mind as long the list wasn't exhaustive and he didn't have to face the Marc crew . . . that was Norma's job. Often her list was on going, however, and sometimes impossible to complete. "I'll get to it! I'll get to it!" he told her. Yes, even Allen's patience could be stretched thin and if anyone knew how to do it, it was his demanding wife. There was always something more that she wanted! "Never enough!" he told her.

"Yeah, she a um, she, um a slave diver (driver)!" Larry repeated a term he often heard from family members.

"Mom, I've got to talk to you about something important!" Debbie called.

"Yesterday, when you brought Larry and Michelle out to the Acres, Jeff noticed the ring on Michelle's finger looked just like my wedding ring!"

"What are you trying to say, Debbie?" Norma was now disturbed.

"I'm saying I'm pretty sure Michelle is wearing MY wedding ring!" Debbie replied.

"Aren't you wearing your own ring?"

"No, I take if off every time we have karate class, put it in my jewelry box and now it's not there."

"Oh dear! What a sneaky brat! I'll go over and find out what's going on!" She hung up the phone and immediately hurried to the car.

Larry, of course, tried to deny the allegations initially, but when he saw his mom steaming, he gave in, admitting to taking the sparkling diamond.

"I soooooorry," he confessed and once again thinking those two words would smooth things over.

Norma called Michelle's mother and told her what happened.

"We're coming over right now to get the ring."

"You are not going to talk to her or kiss her or anything, Lar, just get the ring and get back in the car. Do you hear me? Lickety split!"

"I know, you tod me!"

Michelle walked out the door and apologized.

"I didn't know, Norma, really."

"I know, Michelle, it's not your fault," she said.

Michelle handed Larry the ring while he looked up at her. "I love you anyway my honey," he said. She smiled and blew him a kiss. Larry handed his mother the piece of jewelry.

"You drive me beserk!" Norma said under her breath.

But hearing her, he said the words again. "I soooooorry. He turned his palms up. Um, um I not know!"

"Michele has a jewelry fetish and even though Larry tries hard to please, he should have never stolen his own sister's wedding ring. That kid is so mischievous!!"

Allen listened to another emotional tirade from his wife. "How did he get it?" he asked.

"Went into her room and took it out of her jewelry box. I tell you, I can't take him anywhere without having to watch him like a hawk! Ahhh!"

Now Larry was indefinitely grounded from seeing Michelle. Norma had control over this consequence, since most of the visits were through family outings. Except for the occasional Marc dances, talking on the phone was all the love birds could commit to. Larry made kissing noises into the receiver of the phone showing off his affections. His parents snickered in the other room while overhearing these amusing conversations.

"Well, I love you anyway. You know, um you know that, don't you?" And following a pause replied, "Well corse I do!" he kissed the receiver again.

"What a goofy couple, those two! They are something else!" Norma looked at her husband, giggled and shook her head.

Marc center now opened their twelfth group home.[19] Norma offered up the challenge of having too many; there was still so much to be accomplished in running the homes already in place. She was pushing for quality not quantity. Yet she understood there was a real need in this highly populated city.

"Now, Norma, you know that each group home goes through a site-review process to keep us accountable. In fact, our latest one from DDD at your son's group home was very positive and stated that we have many good quality services in place. We are following protocol for each group home and if we are called out on a certain recommendation from any of the agencies, we are swift to take care of it."[23]

Norma undoubtedly didn't see it that way. When Marc hired a promising supervisor for Larry's group home, she listed on paper many of the things that needed repairs and/or cleaned up around his apartment and handed it to the newbie; hoping that maybe this fresh and energetic employee would respond appropriately.

Lately, Larry was experiencing cold symptoms or fighting diarrhea on a regular basis. Norma felt the cleanliness, or lack there of, around the place certainly didn't help; especially, noting that other group home clients were in the same situation. This would be another reason to drive over, pick Larry up and take him home so she could nurse him back to health. Larry had no idea what medicines to take and often the relief staff was clueless. Again, she felt, the home had revolving door of personnel coming and going, little communication, lack of knowledge and just plain laziness on their part!

The most recent financial crunch for Larry was his phone. Complaint letters were getting easier to write and each one bolder than the previous. Lately many of them were under the topic of budgets-specifically Larry's phone bill. The split of phone and cable fees was too much! Funds were pulled from one account to go to another; Larry was paying his fair share and more. Some residents were making long distant calls and people were confused as to who needed to pay what. It beat all, however, when there was a porn number which showed up on the statement and no one in the group home would fess up.

"I thought this place was going to be better supervised?' she said. "I have to make up the costly difference too many times."

"Broken promises, always broken promises! Things like . . . If you pay for Larry to go to International Fitness, we will make sure we take him three times a week." Their good intentions were short lived.

She again was wasting her money on the lack of integrity. "What is the exercise program at the triplex, anyway? Is it TV, going to the movies and eating out? No wonder they, the clients, have rolls of fat and pot bellies!"

It appeared the more aggravated she was, the less she held back. She wasn't known for any kind of constructive criticism and hadn't been for a long time. Everyone knew that by now! It was after this meeting and seeing the looks on the faces that Debbie scolded her mom.

"Mom, if you complain about every piddling thing," using her mom's words, "then no one will believe you when you have a really valid compliant. Like the boy who cried wolf; you need to choose your battles."

In her opinion there were too many battles. She had no idea which ones to pick, if she was going to take that advice at all. The frustrations were mounting weekly. She was growing weary of educating "the new person" knowing it would only be a few more weeks before starting over. "Sometimes I feel I'm entering the cuckoo's nest when I go over to that group home . . . and I'm not necessarily talking just about the clients," she had to laugh. "Some of these hired people are just plain nutty! Yet, every so often a high-quality employee comes along; neither one sticks around, however"

Russell loved to tell Norma all the things Larry was doing wrong as soon as she stepped into the apartment. Larry enjoyed tattling on Russell as well. These two were driving her to the crazy house! They were like a couple of grumpy old men. She even suspected Russell listened in on her and Larry's phone conversations using the kitchen phone. He was such a meddler and it was putting a strain on the close relationship she had with his mother, Mabel.

Their most recent fourth roommate had just moved in. He had anger issues. Larry called his mom the day this new roomy put his fist through a window and there was blood everywhere. She swiftly drove over the moment she heard her son crying on the phone. It was a scary sight all right and that's why she stuck around to make breakfast for the guys while the manager rode in the ambulance to the hospital.

Norma thought if she could just get away from it all she might get a better perspective. But, how would that ever happen? Even while on vacations and away from Mesa she stewed over the problems. The best release was for her to verbalize to others.

David had listening ears, but often didn't know how to give advice for such unique situations. He comforted her by praying with her over the phone. Carol was preoccupied with the stress of raising her own children and Norma was careful not to add to it by bothering her with Larry issues. Debbie's area of expertise was in special education and often the two conversed for long periods of time even if the end results led to no solid solutions. When she talked with a few other Marc parents who had the same concerns, it gave her comfort knowing she really wasn't going mad. And then of course she always had her daily release of journaling. She wrote it all down: the conversations, encounters, reactions and daily routines. It seemed to put things back in perspective before realizing that maybe things weren't as bad as they seemed.

When she contemplated past accomplishments, she continually told herself that if she hadn't made others aware of needed improvements and hadn't become the squeaky wheel, along with other parents, services wouldn't have progressed the way they had. Secretly, however, she contemplated the way in which she approached others and knew Allen might be right. Maybe I could be the one causing some of the staff turnover?

Larry's Marc file was becoming thicker and thicker with documentations, letters, forms and correspondence. Her conversations about her son, and other "trainable" adults like him, were mounting. She was introduced to more and more pertinent individuals and was trying to keep it all-straight. It was becoming a second full-time job and her difficulty in sleeping was again routine.

The Xerox copy machine at the nearby grocery store was now her buddy, especially since her memory wasn't what it used to be. She made copies of everything. Friends and family scoffed when she got out the tape recorder and even recorded personal and professional conversations, labeled the cassette tapes and then filed them away in her home filing cabinets. Allen thought it was silly when she recorded her grandkids conversations; her explanation was how much they would get a kick out of it later. Reminding Allen of the paper in her possession, it listed twenty facts for parents and stating her rights as a parent when attending the ISPP meetings.

"Here, right here, number nine: 'Bring paper and take notes or bring someone to take notes for you. Remember, you can tape record the meeting if you want to.' Ha! See I have rights too!" She proclaimed.

Despite all the protesting, she had to admit that from time to time Marc was starting to find some decent, well-educated, somewhat professional-type people. She was sad when they actually found competent managers for the group home and then they left for higher ground. The job was just experience on their resumes: a stepping-stone for the next part of their career and rightfully so. Though she and Randy Gray had numerous debates over Marc subject matter, she was thankful he stuck around too and endured the trials. She knew he truly cared about all the clients and had their best interest at heart. There were a handful of personnel who didn't jump ship and for that she was grateful.

"It does say something for their character," she declared.

CHAPTER 51

BEND IN THE ROAD

Financial cuts were also imminent in the Wilson school district. The social worker position would be dissolved, forcing early retirement for Norma. Once she got over the anger, the thought of having less pressure in her life was appealing. It had been eighteen years and she had put in her time. Besides, she was getting weary of all the Arizona State University classes she had to take in order to keep her certificate current.

"Redeemer school is always looking for substitute teachers. I could do that!" She told a friend on the phone, "Eighteen years and never in an accident driving all that way, back and forth on the freeways. The Lord has been good to me!"

The wear and tear was not only on the vehicle but her body was feeling it as well. Phoenix was growing by leaps and bounds and now there was so much more traffic to fight each day compared to the early days. The route was becoming intimidating and the freeways more complicated with so many entrances and exits. That alone, was unnecessary stress she could definitely live without.

If she worked out her budget to the penny, retirement would prove itself doable, that is, if Allen kept working. Selling always had dry spells and getting used to the inconsistencies was never easy. But now she had other ideas for directing her time and energy and she began reflecting on an Old Testament story: "You meant it for evil, but God meant it for good." It was one of her favorite lines from Joseph towards his brothers. Many of her co-workers thought she had been done wrong by the district and they were willing to speak on her behalf. She walked into her office and saw a note lying on her desk from a close co-worker.

"Norma, our district has made some foolish mistakes in the past, but to RIF (reduction in force) you takes grand prize. I'll be at the board meeting tonight . . . all for you!"

The only good result after the frenzied discussions was that she would get full retirement benefits. She could live with that! Now realizing the freedom for doing more of God's work, she knew it was meant to be. And so a new journey and direction took a turn. Teaching a class to young mothers about child rearing, attending CBT (Christian Biblical Training through Redeemer Church), and occasional substitute teaching at the Christian school. Her newest adventure was the nanny position with the Morrison families. Both of these two wealthy and kindhearted couples were generous. They made her feel important with extra bonus money and lots of verbal praise. It was revitalizing to spend hours in a huge well-kept house and with children who had manners and were courteous, so unlike many of the children she dealt with at her Phoenix job.

Now that she was her own boss, she heightened her journal entries and when skimming the pages, was so proud of what she could accomplish in just a 24-hour period. As far as Marc, the current situation allowed her to take on new assignments: namely, Parent Group coordinator. On more than one occasion she shared, "Are you aware of the many benefits of respite care? I remember the days when it was very difficult to find a babysitter and often siblings or other family members were the only ones available. Now respite workers have been trained to care for your child when you and your family deserve a much needed break."

In addition, she was pleased with parent attendance and certainly welcomed input from others to share ideas, concerns and issues, while problem solving together. Norma's desire was to make sure parents were informed of all the benefits they were entitled to and that's why she collaborated with others to make it a point to schedule speakers from the state department.

Her nearly new garage-sale typewriter was used for necessary correspondence. She typed letters to continue advocating for her son and encouraged other parents to do the same.

To all Marc Staff:

At each annual staff meeting which is held for Larry, there seems to be a "big push" to increase the time that he can be left alone at the group home. In a discussion at Larry's staff meeting on January 24th, I reluctantly agreed to a maximum time of 4 hours even though our daughter and I both stated that neither of us would leave Larry alone for that length of time. Since we have Larry home almost every weekend, we are able to observe his behavior and we do not see that it has improved as to his dependability and trustworthiness. If Larry is bored or restless, he will think up weird and unpredictable things to do. Therefore, we do not agree with the staff's decision to permit Larry to stay alone for four hours. Two hours would be the maximum amount of time to which we would approve.

Signed by Norma Combs, Allen Combs and Jeff Drayton and Debbie Drayton.
(Norma later told Debbie- "Why do I have to confront this topic over and over)

Norma's new schedule also gave her more time for second-hand store shopping; allowing her to put together care packages for her grandchildren. Her favorite place was Gracie's Cottage in Tempe. It branched off of the huge church called Grace Community. Debbie, Carol and Norma had already learned of opportunities for women at this beautifully decorated church building by attending the daylong annual retreats. They benefited from the spiritual giants in the Christian world of public speakers: Joni Ericson-Tadda, Corrie ten Boom and Joyce Landorf provided an inspirational message that would live on in the hearts of the many females who were present. This particular church could afford to bring in speakers from other parts of the country and the vast sanctuary held over a thousand women each year. Large churches (or mega churches as they called them) were beginning to pop up in the densely populated regions of the Valley.

A week at Redeemer's Prescott Pines family camp was also vital. Norma took the kids by alternating summers between the boy and girls. These growing and long-legged grandkids could hardly wait their turn and were grateful to their Nena.

The Draytons had moved to the mountains of Flagstaff, only a two-hour drive, and the second Combs family (along with one particular girl from Sunshine Acres who would now live with the Combs family) would soon be doing the same. The Schlesinger family would follow months later. Bob, Kathy and the three boys were like family. The memories they shared dated back to the Redeemer youth group days.

Now Norma, Allen and Larry were excited to spend numerous opportunities away from the unbearably hot summer months in their growing town made of concrete. Soaking in the cool breeze of the Ponderosa forest was refreshing before returning to the heat again. Now that Norma didn't have the stress of an 8:00 to 5:00 career she pulled Larry from his environment more frequently, giving increased time for travel and eating out.

"I love um, I love to be with. I love my famly." He smiled at his mom.

Allen's hours of work were his own choosing and his free time was spent on reading. He was gone much of the day, part of it hanging out at the public library. He brought home different books, although quite often he chose history books to expand his knowledge. The heavy books he walked in the door holding were finished within a week and quickly replaced with another.

Was his reading becoming an escape mechanism? Norma wondered. Some of the books looked strange and she feared they promoted far-out thinking; however, her own reading was also taking on a different form. She picked up books by Christian women authors who weren't as well known. It forced a different kind of conviction, one that was beginning to gnaw away at her heart.

She wrote in her journal a question she hadn't thought of before: "Am I robbing Allen of his leadership in our marriage? I think God is showing me a more realistic picture of myself in this relationship. He seems to be opening my eyes."

Allen's lack of interest in church was on the rise again and she knew he had some bitterness about relationships that had gone sour among other Christians. Redeemer had endured several changes, including pastor turn-over. Some had fallen into enticing sin and Allen used an age-old excuse, "Too many hypocrites in the church."

The phone rang and Norma heard her daughter's unstable voice. Norma was glad Allen was not home at the time because the two seemed to have a long conversation ahead. Debbie relayed to her mother an article in a newsletter they had received in the mail that afternoon, The Free Thinkers publication had been addressed specifically to Jeff and featured a small write-up by a Mr. Allen Combs. As Debbie read the words out loud over the phone, Norma was silent.

Quoting Ingersoll (a prominent atheist) volumes and relating Christians to the movie The Music Man, she read her dad's explanation of how the people in the movie visualized a real band only because they wanted it to be true. It was a dream and not real. Debbie paused making a comment of the numerous times they had watched this movie as a family and knew it was her dad's favorite. Was he now using it as an example of the fantasy world that Christians live in? Debbie continued reading more quotes from atheistic thinkers and finished with her dad's ending: denouncing his belief in God and Jesus. Norma paused a while. Finally, she spoke expressing her concern and then added the statement that she knew nothing about this. "He has been reading a lot of junk lately and you know what they say . . . 'garbage in, garbage out.'

The publication was going to change everything, though. Their relationship was already hanging by a thread and now they wouldn't even connect in spiritual matters? How could this be? How would it affect the entire family? Prayers around the table and just general circles of praying out loud had become a common occurrence with all three families. Larry even contributed his simple, repeated and earnest prayers.

"Well, this is a lot to swallow! I suspected something, but never imagined it like this!" she replied.

She knew the children and grandchildren would be grieving over his spiritual faithlessness. It was just the other day when little Beckie asked why Tombez didn't go to church anymore; another one of those few times in which Norma was speechless. Though they loved their grandpa, understanding him was going to be tough. Sending this article to Jeff was making a statement they knew he wouldn't do verbally or face to face. So much of his life was secretive anyway and he hated confrontation or debate.

As Norma shared the information with friends, some had already received the publication in **their** mailboxes and were sorrowful. Many tried to talk to him one on one, others wrote letters in response to the article, but no one could get through to his way of thinking. Norma's intuitions were coming true about this, sometimes, distant man she had married. She hurt for the lost spiritual being within him. Will I see him in heaven when we die? Will he get over this? Will this pass? She had been forced to spend more time reading her Bible and writing down applicable verses.

"Think of all that God has blessed us with and how we have had so many miracles in our life, our children, and our grandchildren. You have spent hours studying and teaching from scripture, you're willing to throw all that away?" she boldly proclaimed and tried for eye contact.

"How can a loving God send people to hell?" he asked.

"He loves us enough to give us free will." she reacted.

"You have been brainwashed! We've all been brainwashed!" He walked out of the room.

Norma wondered if the inner struggle of his sister's death contributed to this darkness. Though he wouldn't admit it, word from family members said she overdosed on prescription medicine: in stronger words, committed suicide. The stronger words weren't use, however, because no one knew if it was intentional or not.

The Odd Fellows received Allen's resignation letter. He had dedicated so much of his life to them and Norma lay in bed at night thinking of all the organized commitments he gave in years past. She remembered him heading up the Salvation Army bell ringers each Christmas and pictured him standing in front of a store ringing away. With camera ready she clicked it while watching the grandkids giggle at his long green and white silly Santa hat.

He visited the sick only to report back to the Odd Fellows group of the patients' health progress. Rewriting the bylaws was also a major contribution by this man who never bragged about his own accomplishments. She thought of the top honors he got for his outstanding and faithful service, surely he still had a heart for the sick and the poor. This was who he was, Christian or not.

THE BODY-1987 TO 1989

Larry's on-going health issues kept Norma and Allen busy with doctor and dental appointments. By now they were familiar with many medical offices around town. A sleep study was scheduled. Larry was to be observed throughout the night. If necessary, he would need a C-PAP machine to help with breathing. The lack of clear nasal passages and a wide tongue (or maybe small mouth), kept him from a good night's sleep and it was time to do something about it. The couple hoped this might solve some grouchiness during the day and possibly alleviate continual mood swings. They thought it was quite interesting that the conversation with the doctors at this great Phoenix hospital revealed the frequency of sleep apnea among people with Down syndrome.

"People think they are lazy in general, but really it is probably due to low energy because of a lack of a good night's sleep night after night."

Larry had a new evening ritual. There were several steps to getting the machine ready before bed. Norma was proud and even a little surprised by how "pesonsible" he could be when he really put his mind to it.

Grandson, Gabe, broke another bone, this time playing basketball. He was often on Norma's concerned list, between the frequent broken bones, surgery and headaches. David's family increased Norma's prayer time: her son and daughter in-law's financial difficulties and the strain of marriage problems, kept her talking to David and to God on a regular basis.

Because of the breast cancer history with her mother, Norma's frequent check-ups and self-exams for her own body were vital. That's why she made a doctor appointment the next day after finding a lump. It hadn't been that long since she had the popular mammogram the medical world claimed essential, and therefore, was not too concerned about it. Her disciplined life was evident in other routines like exercise, proper eating and control over food portions. She ordered vitamins every month and read the latest information concerning diseases. People complimented her slim, beautiful legs, which she always took pride in and believed she had inherited from her mother.

Allen was troubled when the doctor wanted to see both of them at a follow-up appointment. He didn't like to be inside a doctor's office and avoided it whenever possible. Norma thought back to the disagreements they had when the children were small and came down with a flu or cold virus.

"Just let them sleep it off," he told her. "Stay away from medications and allow it to run its course. A fever is the body's way of fighting the toxins. We don't need a doctor!"

It was a perspective that came from his previous Chiropractic training in the holistic and natural approach.

After the breast biopsy, the recommendation of a mastectomy of her left breast gave no other options. The cancer was in the very early stages and Norma strongly stated that she did not want to pursue radiation therapy afterwards. Allen agreed. The operation was set for July 3rd and now came the task of telling the children and grandchildren.

"Nana just has a sick boob," she told little Amy hoping she wouldn't pass that information to too many people in her tiny, adoring voice. "Dear God, I need to be there when my grandkids graduate from high school, marry and have their own children. Please grant me long life."

All family members were at the hospital. Surgery went well and the doctor stated that he had penetrated the cancerous area. Allen did his part taking care of his wife once they were home. Any other concerns were put on hold for now. This crisis was bringing the two together in powerful ways.

Norma often reflected on her own forcefulness and questioned her possible dogmatic contributions to her husband's spiritual rebellion. Perhaps she was too legalistic. She had always seen the world as black and white with no gray areas of conviction. She spoke them out loud whether people wanted to hear or not. After all, it was just a few days ago that she had to call Carol and ask her forgiveness for the rude things she said the day her daughter had stopped in to visit.

"Lord, help me with my mouth." she wrote, "I need to think before I speak. It's an ongoing problem I have." Turning to the book of James she read: "If anyone considers himself religious and yet does not keep a tight rein on his tongue, he deceives himself and his religion is worthless." Trying to control such a small body part, she now had to contend with an actual piece of her body missing. It felt strange and she was willing to seek assistance through group therapy. It wasn't going to be easy getting use to prosthesis, but there was no time for self-pity and she forced herself to remain optimistic. She thought of her friends who had also endured an illness of some sort and possessed a kind of "learned helplessness." She wasn't willing to succumb to that! Her own mother was strong through this same affliction. Previous friends in Kansas often stated that she possessed the same grit that her mother had. She was proud of that!

CHAPTER 53

NO! PLEASE GOD! 1990

Since David and Debbie had moved to Flagstaff the holidays were engineered through a different kind of memory builder. The Draytons, Combs, Schlesingers and sometimes Pomeroys were graciously invited to the Schlesinger dwelling. Kathy's hostess talents and large "great" room provided a place for everyone to sit during a fabulous dinner. Games, laughter and delicious food brought the families together. The cousins, especially, contributed off-the-cuff jokes. This Christmas was no different. Norma had healed on schedule from her surgery and the three were ready to head north on Interstate 17 for the holidays. Nonetheless, fretting over something kept her from packing. Allen couldn't kick flu-like symptoms and Norma began to think his projectile vomiting was perhaps food poisoning. She made an appointment with the doctor but after a quick look, they sent him home. . . said he'll be fine.

"I'm going to take him to the doctor, again." she told David. "He has continual hiccups now. It is very weird. This time we're going to ER."

She called the kids back several hours later and gave the latest, "The doctors have checked him: same thing, told us he will be okay." Their plans were now on track. Yet, still, she called back a third time, this time from the hospital.

"Your dad is very sick. I think you better come down here." From the sound of her voice, they concluded something was terribly wrong! "I had to call an ambulance to the house", she continued, "Your dad fell unconscious."

The weather report of a massive snowstorm in Flagstaff forced slow traffic. The roads were packed with ice. They would have to take their time, although they had no time to waste. Kathy offered to drive Debbie and David and the rest of the family would come later. Throwing their duffle bags into the back of the vehicle, they kept quiet riding downhill until coming to warmer weather. Kathy's skills in driving a school bus everyday gave them confidence of arriving safely despite periods of whiteout conditions.

The two finally pushed open the hospital doors and profusely thanked their driver for her selflessness! Carol showed them to their daddy's room in the intensive care unit and now the children were fighting the heartache and emotional pain of seeing their usual funny and laughing dad in pain. A tube down his throat and nose and machines all around his skinny, naked white body, only slightly covered. No one could speak. The sight was grim. Their mother's face was extremely serious, the corners of her mouth turned down more than ever and her forehead was creased with tension.

Allen was pale, his eyes were sunken into the sockets and his legs were restless. There was a male nurse sitting by his bed with a notebook and pen in his hand, watching the monitor carefully and precisely writing down notes. The puckered brows of faces standing around his bed were what Allen could see for he was fully alert now and his restless body made it obvious he was extremely uncomfortable. The kids stood at his side rubbing his arms and looked into his desperate eyes.

David spoke. "Dad, we are concerned about your soul!" Allen rolled his eyes up.

Norma walked out of the room. They followed and she informed her children of her weariness. They motioned for her to go home and get some rest. The day's events were pulling their mother into a dream world and everything seemed surreal. She couldn't even remember what day or time it was.

"He seems to be stable right now and we can call right away if anything changes." they told her.

"If I could just get a few hours of shut-eye, I think it would help."

The family talked with friends who had come to the hospital upon hearing the news. Many wanted to go to the hospital chapel and pray. Somber faces and bowed heads were everywhere as people tried to be a comfort to the family without breaking down themselves. Members of the Little family had arrived. On their knees begging God not to take their friend/father was the picture in the quiet and serene chapel that cold December afternoon. Returning to their father and seeing that his condition hadn't gotten better, but still not worse, gave them hope of some kind of miracle. Yet, lingering thoughts of losing their amazing dad and friend who contributed so much to their lives was unbearable to think about. Norma was back after a while and lots of people were still standing around asking questions with pure puzzlement. She had rested only as best she could and was ready to face this nightmare with the little bit of courage she could gather.

"How did this happen?"

"Did you notice anything a few days ago?"

"It's all so sudden."

"I just saw him last Thursday and he was fine."

As the sun set, friends hugged over and over. Phone calls and return visits were promised for the next day. Throughout the night Debbie, David and Norma kept checking on his condition but most of the night was spent lying on the uncomfortable chairs in the small waiting room down the hall. Only short visits were allowed in the ICU unit.

When the doctor conversed with the three of them, he stated the same comment: "No changes." He also remarked of how baffled he was that Allen was even conscious. "With this kind of condition, most people would be in a comma. He is fully awake and seems to know what's going on."

Norma's thoughts to the previous doctor's visit replayed in her mind. The outrage welled inside her from the poor advice she received. "Sending him home and he was gravely ill with poison in his blood!" What a hideous mistake!" Everyone thought the same.

Christmas music played softly in the long hospital hallways. The family decided this to be the worse holiday ever, no matter the outcome.

Norma once again drove home to rest. Debbie and David returned to their father's bedside and he began mouthing a word they couldn't understand. "What? You want something? "He tried again, pressing his lips together around the tube and mouthing the word "mom."

David understood and said, "We sent her home to get some rest" Allen acted as if he didn't like that answer but everything at this point was pure speculation. He tried to communicate with his eyes and barely with his body. A doctor came in and motioned for Debbie and David to follow. Leading them into a lit room with x-ray pictures illuminated on the wall, he showed the double pneumonia and offered another tactic. It would require taking the tube out for a few seconds. The kids thought this may be the answer to their prayers and it just may work. They hadn't slept all night, though, and making rational decisions seemed to be out of the question at this point. Nodding their heads for approval they exited the room and found a phone to call their mother. Just as they placed the receiver on the hook, they heard a code blue over the hospital intercom. It wasn't uncommon in a building this large but the running was nearby. The two slipped out into the hallway and watched medical staff running towards their dad's room. The doors swung wide open and they could see the commotion of the nurses and doctors surrounding the bed. Their dad's jerking body moved up and down from the slamming of the paddles on his chest.

David and Debbie doubled over with grinding faces! They wanted to scream! Time stopped! The doors closed and a doctor stood in the hall. He looked up at the two and gave another motion, this time to a private room. Shutting the door to the outside world, the doctor gave a regretful stare.

"We tried to save him. I'm sorry."

The two cried out "No, God. No!" Just then, Norma slowly opened the door. David stood to hug his mom.

"Mom, he's gone!"

"WHAT?" her limp body fell into the chair.

CHAPTER 54

SHOCK!

Bill and Bev Little stood outside the door. They always had a way of making themselves available at just the right time. Desperately needing a rock-type temperament to offer emotional stability to this now fragile family was extremely welcomed and exactly what was required.

"Come in here and let's pray." Bill motioned to the four kids and Norma.

Allen's cold body, nearly covered with a white sheet, lay on the gurney. The nurse and doctors agreed to step aside and allow the family a few minutes with their dad, husband and friend. Larry wasn't grasping the magnitude of what had just happened. He walked into the room, set his eyes on his daddy, stared for a moment and cocked his head to focus. Soon the tears began to stream down his red cheeks. He shook his head back and forth while lifting his fingers to his face, squeezing water from his eyes. Bill and Beverly held hands and motioned for everyone to do the same. With heads hung low, Bill graciously begged God for His Holy Spirit to comfort each family member's broken heart and wounded spirit. His words were rich and penetrating.

The Fifth Avenue house became inundated with people coming and going. Disbelief and utter shock was the common reaction. "He was so healthy just days ago. What happened? How could this happen? We don't understand! Didn't he ride his bike something like six miles everyday? He was in such good shape."

Coach Heath came by and circled everyone around. With eyes closed, he petitioned His Lord with pleas of comfort. This spirit-filled man had a connection to God everyone longed for. It brought a peaceful relaxation to weary souls. Coach then shared a story of how Allen knocked on his door at 2:00 in the morning a few weeks prior . . . just wanting to talk. "He told me that he had been driving around all night thinking and questioning life. We prayed together and spent a long time talking. He had so many questions," Coach revealed.

In the days that followed, no one felt like opening Christmas gifts but did as if they were robots going through the motions. For now, they temporarily brushed aside the emotions. It was necessary for they had a large gathering to organize, phone calls to make and meetings to attend. It seemed feelings were completely nonexistent as their bodies and minds were in distress mode but the physical pain felt in the chest was real; they understood the reality of true heartache.

Norma, David, Carol and Debbie met at the Mortuary. Larry wanted to tag along. The person assigned to the family for business, showed the items listed on the package deal and led the children into a small showroom of caskets. No one paid attention to Larry walking away from the group until they heard a jingling noise. All watched Larry walk from one casket to another scoping out the marble handgrips and then pulling up slightly on each one.

"Larry, Larry, what are you doing? Don't touch. Those are really expensive." His siblings were tense.

"I know," he paused. "But I need to be, um, I need to lift it, um my dad. How am I,um I gunna do that?" He turned to his brother and gave a solemn look. They all knew, immediately, what he meant. He was worried about the weight of the casket and would he be able to carry it. He was thinking ahead this time and taking very seriously, yet obviously nervous, of his future role at the funeral.

The siblings looked at each other and let out a quiet and controlled laugh. It was too weird to giggle in this setting . . .almost sacrilegious. Even the mortician seemed to get a kick out of Larry's unusual request but the smiles immediately straightened once they saw that their brother was not joining in.

Just one more day and the funeral were to take place at Church of the Redeemer. Plans for the event had been finalized with the church staff and the children had just a few more hours to refine the short eulogies they would give.

That evening Debbie was fumbling around in one of the spare bedrooms at her parent's home: now an office. She opened the file cabinet drawers and found a few folded handwritten letters. As she unwrapped them, a picture of a young girl fell to the floor. She bent down and gazed at the child. With confusion she began reading the heartfelt words and was perplexed as to who the author might be. That person stated strong frustration of Allen not being involved with his granddaughter. Debbie read the letter through and then again. She strolled into the living room seeking her mother and hoped for a perfectly good explanation.

"Mom, what's this?" She held the paper and pushed the small photograph towards her.

Norma looked up, pressed her lips together and paused. "Debbie sit down, I have something to tell you!"

While staring into her mother's eyes, Debbie slowly bent her knees and slid into the chair.

"This letter is from a person that has chased us down our entire married life. She claimed she was carrying your dad's baby before we even got married. Your dad swore up and down the boy wasn't his, but she just wouldn't give up!"

Debbie looked down at the picture and silently inspected the photograph again. "And, this is supposedly the granddaughter?" she finally responded.

"Yes"

While looking for Allen-like features, Debbie replied in a whispered voice "She does kind of look like us."

"Really! I don't see it at all." Norma grabbed it from her hand and calculated it again.

"Remember the story I've told you over the years about the black eye I had on my wedding day? " she questioned and slowly handed the picture back to Debbie.

"Yes, you went to the post office and someone opened the door and it hit you in the face?"

"Yeah, I was coming out of the post office because I was so upset at this emergency letter I received.

I was in shock after reading how I shouldn't marry your dad because she was pregnant with his baby. And, can you imagine, this was just days before the wedding? I put up with so much over the years," her voice strong and confirming.

Debbie again reasoned to herself as she kept her head down and continued to study the photograph.

Norma looked at her daughter's hurtful expression and was reminded of how much of her own dad's personality she possessed.

"You don't remember me crying all the way to Mingus Mountain one summer in those early years?"

"No, Mom, I don't," still mulling over the biting information just handed her. The wonderful father who made few mistakes; Debbie wasn't sure whom to feel more sorry for: Allen, Norma, or the kids.

"We should have had ongoing marriage counseling. I regret that we didn't!" Norma said. Then she proceeded to tell the story of how she got the money to pay for the backyard patio.

"Well. . . I guess he was human, just like the rest of us!" Her daughter couldn't take on another punishing thought.

Norma felt better about her daughter's response and now that it was out in the open the two talked about when a good time to tell the others might be.

"Should we wait until after the funeral or tonight when everyone comes over?" Norma questioned.

"I say tonight. We will have to send the grandkids outside."

"Good idea."

The plan was carried out even with Larry sitting with the family. Of course, the words were carefully chosen and questions were asked in such a way that Larry couldn't follow the conversation. Because the family had practiced this so often in years past, they were experts at keeping him from unneeded information. When Larry walked out the door, the picture was passed around. They discussed the possibility of trying to find this so-called half-brother if in fact he was but the consensus was to leave it alone, at least for now.

Larry soon walked in the front door with the newspaper in his hand. "I got, ummm I got this for you." He handed the newspaper, which he just picked up from the driveway, to his brother. David opened it wide and turned the pages to the obituaries. There it was! The family viewed a picture of their handsome and striking father and underneath, a paragraph of information. Cutting through the protective shock, now this horrible nightmare lay opened on the very table Allen had played games, ate his silly bowl of cereal with chopped nuts and milk, conversed with his children through groaning jokes and laughter; but most of all, this was the table at which Allen spent copious hours playing cards with his very special son. The family stared at each other and a feeling of eeriness silenced all in the room.

CHAPTER 55

THE FUNERAL

People gathered in the blue highlighted sanctuary: the irony, a place Allen had become scarce to the last few years. Norma's renowned photo albums were placed on oblong tables in Lloyd Hall and showed the sequence of a life consisting of humor, humility and honor.

Family sat in the first two rows with the Littles and Schlesingers' close behind. The scene in the church was somber; friends and family hugged and tears flowed freely. Jeff and Teona sang a duet; David Little a solo and Bill shared the wise words he was known for. The sentiments pierced listeners' hearts and some were now reaching for tissues. But it was when Larry stood and walked to the microphone that the sniffling echoed throughout the A-frame structure.

"Umm, my dad, I known him a long time. Umm, I use to, umm, ride my bike everyday to my dad. And, umm, my dad, umm, he was so good to me! I went to a movie. I went to a movie to my dad and I, um, I just I love him real bad. We played Unor. I want to say, umm, well, ummm, I miss him real bad, Uhhh, I love him real bad! I went to my bike to my dad, to love him so I went whatsyoucallit, but I love him anyway, I really do. I love him!"

Debbie, Carol and David also walked to the front and spoke of the great attributes of their father. "I never felt I was in the way, he took time for us and we knew we were loved, not by the words he spoke necessarily, but by his actions. We were important to him and he made it known." Debbie revealed.

David's funny stories were desperately needed by now. The kind he always delivered with wit and a calming voice. The confirmation that Allen's humor passed to the next generation was obvious, but most already knew the comedy torch had been handed from father to son.

"Anything new and creative that he could do with his hands, " David's memories came effortlessly. "When we were young, we had an electric go cart that he made out of a vacuum cleaner motor. It had an extension cord on it and we could run it around the carport. He used a sewing machine pedal to act as an actual accelerator. He told me one day 'if you keep it floored around that curb, I'll give you a dime.' I thought to myself, 'I'll fall over, I'll get hurt.' My dad looked at me as if to say 'whatever.' Well . . . I did and . . . I did . . . but it was very fun anyway! He was such a kid at heart himself and enjoyed homemade things. No need to spend money. He loved fatherhood . . . that was what he left for me."

Carol graciously thanked friends for coming and announced how much she loved her father!

The sanctuary held old friends from the early days, neighbors, Methodist buddies, coworkers, customers, and even recent acquaintances. Annie (that freckle-faced girl who lived across the street and frequently knocked on the door at dinner time) approached David at the gravesite telling him how she could actually see and touch that go-cart when he talked about it. Danny, another long ago neighbor, handed Norma a letter written from his heart; it was a beautiful account in enduring words of how, as a child, he had idolized Allen and wished he was **his** dad.

The outpouring of love flowed in abundance. Many, however, were also concerned about Larry. Norma knew that just as soon as Larry became aware of no more bike rides, movies or long hours of games, he would need professional help for his depression. Although she would do her best to keep his time occupied, this enormous loss would leave a large emotional hole, one that would nearly be impossible to fill.

CHAPTER 56

ALONE-1991

The days unfolded slowly and painfully. Norma didn't want to be alone. She heard every crack and tiny sound in and out of the house; the pipes, the traffic, the heater, birds chirping, and children playing. These walls, the same structure that held six people not long ago, kept them warm and comfortable, now offered nothing but isolation. Conversations of life, the discussions of major and exhausting decisions, laughing, games, teasing, washrag throwing, sassy voices and attitudes, Beatle songs, drum pounding, Debbie cart wheeling through the living room, fierce knocking on the bathroom door, even thinking of the toilet as the same one her children were potty trained on made their way through every fleeting thought.

When walking out of the bedroom and into the living room, she saw Allen sitting in his chair, reading while holding his magnify glass; it still lay on the end table, exactly where he positioned it. She opened the closet doors in the bedroom and could smell his cologne. Several bolo ties hung on the hook revealing the many clothing ensembles; some matched and some didn't. His wrap-around sunglasses lay on the dresser, ready for grabbing. The toothbrush, shaving cream, razor and washcloth had been used just days prior. It felt too odd to move them.

Nights were the toughest and she wasn't beyond taking pills to assist sleeping. Otherwise the reality of her arm laying across his side of the bed and feeling nothing, hearing nothing, snoring or breathing . . . stung! She whimpered throughout the night and screamed out for God's help. Experiencing loneliness at its deepest, darkest level, she saw no end in sight.

Bringing Larry home more often, provided some comfort for the both of them. They needed each other! Sitting by herself at the dining room table, eating and looking across the way at no one was another reminder of the piercing silence. Larry came over to share her meals. She wanted him to spend the night. Having another person in the house, especially during darkness, gave a bit of relief from these foreign emotions. Larry cried when he walked into the house and didn't see his dad. Norma hugged him repeatedly.

She replayed the events of the last few weeks in her mind over and over again. Piled on top of the mountains of seclusion was an overpowering guilt, the why's, what ifs and how comes? Why wasn't I there when he died? He was asking for me, I should of never left his side. Why didn't I listen more? Why didn't I listen to what he was saying and pay attention to what he didn't say? Why didn't I learn to relax? He tried to teach me to be calm, not get so worked up over things.

Why didn't I think more clearly? Why didn't I insist the doctors' check him over better and more thoroughly? If they had drawn blood at that first doctor visit, they would have known how truly sick he was.

She made phone calls to friends offering to meet for lunch. Not sure how well she would handle widowhood, calling her daughter-in-law's mother, Ouida, more frequently somehow helped. Her friend knew of these exact emotions. Norma reconnected with long time Methodist friends and spent hours talking about Allen to others. In her times with God, she opened her Bible to read His words and hid them in her heart. The Lord is close to the broken hearted and saves those who are crushed in spirit." Psalm 34:8.

The family went out of their way to come over, realizing their mom's loneliness would be unbearable. Even their usually sturdy mother could buckle and their hearts throbbed for her. They stayed with her while she boxed up Christmas decorations and took down the tree. This holiday would never be the same. Oh, if only she could turn back time.

When the grandkids called, it helped change her thinking to something more pleasant. She was desperate to occupy her thoughts elsewhere but at the same time, desired to comfort them, choosing the right words. Reminded of Kelsey's continual crying at the viewing, it hit her of the profound sadness from the two oldest. Gabe and Kels had gone on several bike outings with their Tomez and because of being first-borns, had spent the most time with their grandpa. Everyone, though, had his or her own unique connections.

She decided it was time to pick up around the house. Lifting the bed skirt for vacuuming, she spotted the Christmas paper around a box. While pulling it towards her she read the words, "To Norma with love." Wiping the instant tears now flowing she slowly tugged on the paper. The blood seemed to leave her arms and she could hardly break the tape. Her hands shook. She never thought she would be opening her Christmas gift from her husband in an unspoken and emotionally cold house. Remembering the discussion a few weeks back about Christmas presents, she expressed the desire of having a juicer for healthy shakes throughout the day in order to keep her energy up. This package proved that he was listening. The wetness under her eyes and runny nose forced her to stand using the bed mattress to brace her weakened legs. She then pulled a few tissues from the box next to her bed and quickly plopped down on the mattress to wipe her face. Now trying to gain control of her breathing, she sat in the stillness.

The phone ring broke the moment and she considered not answering it. With a soft hello, she was glad to hear her daughter's voice, "What's wrong Mom?"

"I just found your dad's Christmas gift to me. I sensed him standing here watching me open it."

"Oh, Mom. I'm so sorry!" she heard Debbie's voice crack.

CHAPTER 57

THIS TOO, SHALL PASS.

It didn't matter what **she** bought for Allen for his Christmas present, he ultimately returned it: a running family joke. "Don't bother buying dad a gift, he'll just take it back," One of those many quirky behaviors with no explanation, other than . . . "Don't need it!"

Norma had been on the phone to her Kansas family. She looked forward to seeing her little brother, for Don and Marilyn were now on their way. Oh, how she longed to wrap her arms around this couple. They, too, would be hurting deeply, but not necessarily over Allen, they recently lost their young daughter to cancer. Norma and her sibling were in a whirlwind of emotions at different locations of the United States and at the same time. The loss of a child! She couldn't even imagine their pain: so much more in comparison to hers. Her thoughts raced back to that horrible day she received a phone call from a relative stating that Nadine (her sister's daughter) had taken her own life. She spent many hours in prayer over this solemn situation and was now feeling ashamed of her own grieving. Her siblings had experienced stinging heartache at the most horrific level. She knew their lives would never be the same and yet they were reaching out to her this day. Lee promised of coming to Arizona at some point as well. He would help her with organizing required financial papers and she was eager to get the sound advice her brother frequently gave.

David told her that he had set up a meeting with the head person of the intensive care unit. After the autopsy there was still confusion of what Allen actually died of, why he died in the first place and how it came about. This was not acceptable and they needed some answers! Thankful for David taking charge, she just didn't have it in her this time. Arrangements were made and Norma asked a friend who was a nurse to join them as a medical supporter, one who would know the right questions to ask.

But walking away from the meeting that day, she and the children weren't satisfied at the "it was a judgment call, and we didn't make the right call," answer. Most of the blame was put on the insurance companies.

"They want us to do as little as possible deeming unnecessary things like blood work. In hindsight, we now realize we should have run more tests, but at that time didn't consider it crucial. Now we know that he aspirated/breathed stomach content into his lungs, which then spread to other organs.

"So as a result it took a human life: husband, dad and friend. What a terrible and needless loss!" Norma said her peace (piece) before exiting the conference room.

"You don't need to do anything else," she told her son. A short discussion arose of possibly taking it a step further, court perhaps. "You've done enough, besides I feel bad that you already missed out on your NAU graduation."

"It's okay; I'll just walk with Debbie in May. We can have a double party and everyone can come for both. I just wish Dad could be there!" David's degree was in radio broadcasting and now he was looking into work around the Phoenix area.

"Oh, I would love it if you lived close by again." Norma divulged.

So grateful to God for having a non-disabled son, now that she had wills on her mind, she would make sure that he would be her power of attorney. The insight as to the importance of keeping matters in place upon her own death was a devoted promise. Her lonely days were now, not only occupied with thoughts from the past, but also about the future. She knew that it was the time to actually put together a folder of Larry's life history and to make sure each sibling had a copy; something she had thought about often and in previous years. It would be a condensed version of Larry's past and would serve as an easily accessed documentation for those future review meetings that the children would someday attend without her. (The idea of Larry outliving her was now a very real possibility) She thought about how much time and work it would take, but she just had to get started—the sooner the better. She jotted down in her journal all the items she would include: his early training and developmental years, vision and health check-ups, personality profiles, activities and special events, psychological evaluations, employment and, of course, all the past financial and funding records. Just the thought of all that toiling made her tired.

A few days later Norma took the grandgirls shopping at the mall. Upon arriving home, the girls followed behind their grandmother walking into the living room. Norma noticed the blinking red light on her new answering machine. Pushing the button, they all listened intently.

"Hi, Mom. I just want, I just wan to say, I miss him, I miss him real bad. I love, umm. I love my dad and to love, I miss him so bad! I just wanna tell you, ummm, I miss him, real, ummm, so bad. My, umm, Allen Combs."

There was a long pause before the girls responded.

"Ohhhh, poor Uncle Lar."

"That's so sad."

"Poor guy! He hurts so much."

Gazing at these princess ladies, Norma knew they were moved with sensitivity towards their uncle's pure and sincere communication style.

It was times like this that he demonstrated true normalcy, and his venting was actually a good thing.

Other phone calls came, even months later. Dreamland Villa retirement community customers inquired about vacuum cleaner check-ups and was shocked to find out of Allen's passing. Norma had to tell the story over and over, even to friends who had been gone for the holidays and just now learning the horrible news. Each time it was as though she was re-living Allen's death: a drain to her already, weary spirit. Along with the calls were the mounting sympathy cards, many with comforting Bible verses. The words were like ointment to her wounds and she was consoled by the outpouring of love from numerous and caring people.

After several mornings of meditating, she sat under the back porch, straining to hear the birds between the horns and motors of intersection traffic. She looked around at her covered porch, reflecting on that initial letter, the phone calls, counseling and the rough interactions concerning the very reason for this structure. "Wow, she spoke out, over 40 years of someone hounding us, nearly breaking us, and I got a covered porch out of the deal. HoopDeeDoo . . . she swung her finger around and laughed! What a sense of humor you have, God!" As soon as she said the words she realized something profound. She was beginning to reflect on memories with a half inclined smile and even slight laughter. Though she and Allen had some doozy arguments, she was finding herself reflecting fondly on the humorous happenings. At last, replaying the fun times . . . enjoyable trips to Grand Junction, Colorado (where her cousin, Donna lived), visits with extended family, the square dancing, going out to eat, attending parties with friends, and cherished memories of raising those goofy kids . . . all the laughing and more laughing. She thought about how well she and Allen worked around the house and made lots of improvements. The lawn never looked so good.

And then there was the frequent "sentence finishing." Her long pauses during a conversation pushed Allen to finish the sentences for her. They laughed together over their oneness of mind. Being married so long definitely had its benefits. Sometimes it was just a look or gesture and they knew the thoughts of the other. When Norma was looking for something around the house Allen could find it for her. Oh . . . and his special way of loading the dishwasher. She was more than happy to let him do it **his** way. She cleaned and mopped the kitchen floor, only in her certain manner, yet vacuuming was his job and, of course, they were privileged to have the latest cleaner models.

A picture of heaven entered her mind and she struggled to view it. All those years of studying God's word but only two years of questioning the validity, Surely God has mercy on my husband. She thought back to the story Coach told her. He had driven most of the night and ended up at Coach's house with questions just days before his death. Did he truly make his peace with God? The recent arguments seemed now so trivial! They were meaningless in the whole scheme of things but there was no going back. Complete reliance on God was all she could do.

A good friend at church spoke to her in private. "Norma, you have new things to look forward to, stop looking back." It felt like cool water to dry cracked lips and a very thirsty soul. She knew it was time to heed this great counsel.

Other friends had more comforting words. "It's never too late for new beginnings in your life. Allen didn't like to travel, well now is your time to travel. Allen didn't want to move to a new location, now is your time to relocate and even downsize. You always wanted a nicer, more reliable vehicle; we can help you find one. Allen didn't want to be involved in church; you have a family here and can spend as much time as you want with your Christian family."

Yes, it's high time to start cleaning out his backyard shed, she told herself; the one he, the junk collector, kept under lock and key. She knew some of the vacuum cleaner parts wouldn't be of much value so it was time to start pitching. Tackling such a task, though, meant pacing herself by doing a little each day. What a nice surprise of finding envelopes with cash: thirty dollars, fifty dollars and even one hundred dollars at the bottom of some seldom touched boxes. She figured he didn't even remember having that money or did he? She decided to use the extra cash for more house improvements and so a new list was formed. Rollie showed up several days at the house, using his expertise for a few of the repairs. Tech savvy Michael set up her new VCR and other items she had recently purchased. Pushing the right buttons was foreign to Norma and she not only needed repeated instructions but also requested a good amount of patience when demonstrating the latest technology.

When at the NAU graduation ceremony, Debbie looked out at the audience and for a split second thought she saw her dad sitting there. Norma watched her wipe her quiet tears.

Despite, the double graduation party afterwards was delightful. Days later, however, David decided to accept a job offer that would be five hours away in St. George, Utah. More miles would separate her from her grandchildren, this time beyond the Arizona border.

"Well, I guess it will give me and Larry another future vacation spot." She told her grandkids, but she knew **they** were very unhappy.

CHAPTER 58

ANOTHER CLOSE CALL-1993

Seeing some evidence of good counseling through Catholic Social Services was helpful for Larry's limited understanding. Carol and Norma were attending grieving classes as well.

The newest undertakings for her son were to attend the freshly opened reading and simple computer classes for the mentally disabled at the community college. There was still hope of Larry learning to read, even at 37 years of age. "Boy, we've come a long way baby!" Norma proclaimed.

On numerous occasions, and after his lesson, dial-a-ride picked him up and took him where he needed to go. He didn't have to ride his bike and certainly didn't need a family member driving him to college. Transportation was now available for the disabled and offered more independence. Larry loved the feeling, especially because he could make the arrangement himself and with very little assistance.

"I go to college now!" he said to listening ears. It was a sense of being a true grown up. Norma looked at his bulging smile and crinkled eyes that came with the statement. "I go to college like my bother and sisser," he boastfully stated!

The second encouragement was his job in the community working at Payless Cashways. His chores were to water all the plants outside. She hoped this new endeavor would truly work out for him and that he wouldn't blow it! For now, however, it was another uplifting accomplishment for her mature child.

"I have a, a, a different job, now!" were his words of important identity.

Filing taxes and managing his social security money was a continual headache. Norma worked with law offices to help her now that she was the "sole guardian and conservator of Larry Combs, an adult incapacitated and protected person." She was told he couldn't have money in a savings CD account and now much of her time was spent in talking to attorneys and the guardianship experts about his finances. Needing help she spoke to those who were recommended from other parents. If Norma was to be his payee and handle his money herself, then answering to state funding departments was a frequent requirement. Everything had to be documented, every penny accounted for and then relayed to authorities. Some parents were told to give up the guardianship, as the state would take care of the situation and it was less stressful for the family. Norma stated she would "take it under advisement," words she often heard her husband say.

Debbie's degree in education/special education found her teaching children with special needs through the public schools. Jeff's latest promotion with the sheriff's department was detective. Knowing Flagstaff would be the Drayton's home for many years to come, Norma was confident she would always have cool summers during her Flagstaff visits; and, now driving beyond Arizona borders and into southern Utah, she welcomed another option for rest and relaxation. Her and Larry could travel together.

Opportunities to explore expanded in the beautiful red-rock country and it was a joy to scout out more picnic grounds at Zion National Park. David found some bargain motel prices through his radio station. It gave the cousins lots of time to swim together and burn off energy in a cool pool. The adults regretted the day they ran a few errands in town and left all the cousins, including Larry, at the pool. When they returned they found 13 year old Kelsey in the motel room buried under the bed covers.

"What's wrong, Kels?" Debbie asked.

"Uncle Larry almost drowned me!" his voice quivered.

"What do you mean?"

"We were wrestling and he pushed my head under water and wouldn't let me up!" Kelsey pulled the covers back over his head and curled up in a ball.

Norma and Debbie's hands slapped their faces while sucking in a big gulp of air realizing what could have been his fate.

"Oh, dear God!" Debbie whispered and then scolded Larry for his senselessness. "Larry, you could of drowned Kelsey. He could have died."

"Oh, I not do that!" he responded

"You almost did!"

"No, I not! I just, I just play round." he grinned.

"Larry, it's not funny! That's not playing!"

"Forget it Mom, he doesn't understand!" was Kelsey's reply. Debbie sat next to her son on the bed and rubbed his back.

"You okay?"

"Yeah!" the words certainly weren't convincing.

"You just can't wrestle with him in the pool. He doesn't know his own strength. This is what he often did as a little boy when we would swim at the public pool." Debbie didn't know if she was helping or making matters worse for her already traumatized son.

"Oh, good niiight, Larry!" Norma snapped into his face. She pushed on his shoulders and made him sit down at the small table place near the TV.

"Listen to Debbie!"

"I am," he said flippantly and was beginning to work up an anger fit.

Everyone looked at Larry's scowling face and a silent judgment fell around the room.

The cousins knew he didn't understand boundaries but this was ridiculous!

"Get it into that thick skull of yours!" Norma was now beside herself and pacing.

"I can't believe he tried to pull that stunt again, He hasn't done that for a long time." She turned toward Debbie. "Sometimes I could just ring his neck. Ahhhhh!"

Norma, and everyone else for that matter, thought he was old enough to understand. It confirmed the unpredictable Larry they could never trust . . . no matter the age. Norma told herself she wouldn't allow such circumstances again.

"Thirty seven years old and you still have to have an adult watching you like a hawk!" She glared at him. "Next time I will leave you at the group home!"

He stomped out of the room, slamming the door.

They tried to move on with the events of the day realizing another day of God's overpowering protection and goodness! But in future events, Norma was quick to scold her grandchildren for teasing Larry too much! "You have to understand boundaries too!

CHAPTER 59

RENEWED-1994/95

Norma often wondered if she would ever get used to being alone. Actually, she was starting to enjoy parts of her quiet day. Her home was becoming a safe haven and she could call the shots of when to stop socializing by just going home. Maybe she could handle it after all. Her love for interaction with other widows grew, finding new friends or visiting and lunching with long-time relationships. But she had a short attention span and was ready to be by herself for an afternoon rest. Her energy certainly wasn't what it used to be. She had many choices of people she could talk to on the phone if she was too tired to go out: especially, in the unbearable heat. Often she desired to just lock her doors, dial a friend or family member, and converse with others, all while wearing her comfy pajamas and lying across her bed. During the hottest part of the day she rustled through papers in the cool bedroom, fans blowing, organizing Larry's stuff and putting together that promised time-line for the "Larry notebook."

The decision to finally leaving Redeemer Church was a tough one, but her mind was made up and she would never return. The church had brought her and her kids to higher levels of their Christian walk, and for that she was obliged, but things had changed and she just couldn't agree with the new pastor. When he spoke ill of her hero, Dr. Dobson, it made her sick. James Dobson was the constant in her life; she recorded his radio program everyday, read his books and often gleaned extra-ordinary motivation from this man of God. Now, this pastor said terrible things about him. No way! He was too "far out" for her and she was more than ready to move on. The past established relationships, however, would be missed. The memories of solid acceptance of her disabled son would always be imbedded in her mind as well as all the marvelous teachings over the years: inspiring her family to thirst after God and to study the Bible in depth.

Now, Grace Community Church in Tempe had vast opportunities appealing to her liking. She had already attended a few of their bigger-than-life events such as the singing Christmas tree during the holidays and then there were the well-known women retreats she had previously attended with her daughter. Membership was in the thousands, thus she had a variety of programs to choose from. It was the " Salt Shakers" where she found needed relationships with other widows and widowers and it seemed to be just what the doctor ordered.

The group planned trips and travels together: the next one, to the Holy Lands. This would be a dream come true; something she always wanted to do and she would feel no guilt in traveling without Larry. She decided there just couldn't be shame in doing the things **she** wanted to do! Norma remembered that many years ago, some friends had journeyed there and brought home a container of water from the Jordan River, which they used to baptize their youngest child. Even then, she had a burning desire to visit these places, and now, decades later, the chance was closer to reality than ever before. She wrote . . . "Thank you, Lord, for energy, money and health! The storm is beginning to pass and you have given me a new and refreshing hope! I'm ready for change in every aspect of my life

Another renewal . . . Norma decided to move! Moving from the home she grew to love and was showered with memories. Now ready to look out her front window and see an entirely different view, she reflected back to the time when she and Allen had come home from an all-day event to find the house broken into and robbed. The police investigation revealed the person who violated them was actually a drug addict and neighbor. She hadn't known exactly who it was but had wanted to leave and brought up the idea of moving at that time. "This is the second time this has happened; we need to get out of this neighborhood," she had said to her husband, but her request had fallen on deaf ears.

Today, she still had doubts and spoke to David about them. "It seems like it will be such a hassle and will it be worth it? Your dad and I have accumulated so much junk over the 36 years living here and it will be a huge undertaking."

Carol suggested a garage sale.

"I just hate to put you all through this, it's so much work!" Norma looked at her kids.

"Mom, we can do it, really. Everyone can pitch in." They encouraged her not to worry and assured her that with everyone's help they could make it happen.

The Pomeroy's, Drayton's, and Combs family all came to price items or box things up. Though Norma's near panic attacks surfaced, she finally conceded that it was not so bad after all. New people and old neighbors came by to look around. By now she just wanted to get rid of it all, so the public benefited from the swinging deals! The grandchildren talked about the memory that went with each item as they watched it leave in the hands of a stranger. Norma decided that the garage sale **was** a good idea and when she kept hearing two reoccurring words from the kids . . . "remember when," she understood that it was a good idea in more ways than one. One story produced another story and then another. The memories were now bringing laughter tunneled through the grief. Even Larry began to disarm and contributed his Allen jokes while adding his silly faces. Like hamburger and fries, Larry's jokes and goofy expressions just had to be together. This was good therapy for all and a rude awaking was taking place; although they greatly missed their dad and Tombez, they knew that they were better people to have known and loved him. Reminiscences of all the enjoyable times were what they could hold on to. It seemed to provide mental refreshment, healing and nourishment for the soul, especially for Larry

Norma had many conversations with her new friends at her new church. They were helping her by providing connections of possible affordable condos around the Tempe area. She was in high spirits, for many were giving her leads and assistance on selling the three-bedroom house, which was too big for one person. This old dwelling was completely paid for and now she could purchase a new one free and clear. Her days were spent scouting out some very popular gated communities, but she concluded they were just too expensive and settled for a small place near shopping and walking distance to her church home.

The sale of the Fifth Avenue house happened and her prior sleepless nights were once again uncalled for. When the actual big day was behind her, she would rest easy. Unloading the last box, she proclaimed, "Boy howdy, I'm weary to the bone for crying out loud!" She ran the back of her hand across her forehead, "I can actually hear myself think in this quiet neighborhood."

Settled, and loving the tranquil life, she looked out her screen door viewing a tiny area of grass. It was pleasing and she was more than happy to give up the yard work. Now it was time to focus on more important things, one being water aerobics in the swimming pool just a few feet away. She would certainly take advantage of the residents' community pool. Each day brought a renewed spirit and grateful attitude toward her Gracious Lord. Thrilled with her comfortable and quaint two-bedroom abode, church and new relationships close by, good health, and still- cancer free!

CHAPTER 60

GROWING PAINS.

Larry was also moving. He and Russell were placed in a newly opened home. It stood in a well-kept neighborhood and within walking distance to the Marc center. They would live under one roof again but this time having their own bedroom. Maybe Larry would keep better track of his belongings and she could buy added pieces of bedroom furniture with lots of drawers for organization. Each of the four male residents was promised plenty of space and closer supervision. Norma sat on pins and needles hoping these next assurances would have follow-through.

Larry's interest in Michelle was fading but Russell still going strong with his girlfriend. Mary Ellen spent numerous hours at the new place, just hanging out with the guys.

"Mom, do you think Larry could ever get married?" the kids asked. She had just told them of a new group home holding married, special-needs adults.

"I guess it's a possibility but difficult to even fathom. I mean think of all the aspects, even down to budgeting money. I just don't know if he could survive it."

"Don't want to think of all the aspects, too much information!" David chuckled.

The latest fury entering Norma's life and causing the famous Ahhhhh sound in her throat was the recent awareness of letting a GIRL live in Larry's house with the guys! She was a girlfriend to one of the other residents and would live in his room WITH him.

Norma felt another big battle a-brewing! She was not alone, other parents were mad!

Back at the home front was even more uneasiness and one she journaled frequently about: Rebecca and Michael's choice of friends and rebellious attitude toward authority. Making it a point to purposefully be involved, she hoped Carol wasn't repeating the same mistake her and Allen made… lack of awareness. She often picked the kids up and took them to various places but she couldn't keep them from arguing with each other and with her, while out in public. It was embarrassing!

Though the family had recently lost Rollie's mother due to cancer, another involved grandparent, she saw the peeling of teenage thinking not only with Carol's offspring but all her grandkids. Her Prayers were sounding different these days, for those she dearly loved. Beyond protection, she now begged God for good quality life- choices!

"The teens, oh how complicated they can be!!"

"Mom!" David's voice on the phone was low and mumbled. "Teona is gone!"

"What?" Norma said.

"She left this morning and there was a note! She moved out."

As soon as she hung up the phone, she called Debbie. Arrangements were quickly made for travel. She longed to be holding her hurting family and to do it as soon as possible!

The Combs kids were glad to see their Nana and their cousins. Great meals were going to be made, taxing to events and overall emotional help! Norma spent time discussing feelings with everyone involved. Her son was a wreck but now that they were together, they tried to spotlight on other things. It allowed for some temporary relief and at least some restoration.

Riding in the back seat going home, Norma tapped Larry on the shoulder in front of her. He was rocking with agitation. " Larry, turn that music down, it's too loud. Turn that thing down!" Norma pulled the head phones off his ears. She knew he was mad.

"Well, I don't like it! That's not right! I have feelings too! I don't like bavorce (divorce)! It's,umm not right! She, she, she ruin our family!"

This time the family decided to let him continue. He needed to spill his guts like anyone else. It sounded reasonable and realizing… he was feeling it just as strong as the rest of them!

"Teloynya, um my sistr-in-law. I have feelings too, ya know. That not right! She hurt me real bad."

"Larry, you remember what I always tell you?" She made for eye contact. "It takes two to fight. Like when you and Russell get into an argument. It's not just HIS fault. It takes two. You can't just blame Russell all the time you know. Well, it's the same thing, you can't just blame Teona."

"I know but, um, I just don't like it, that's all. I sad. I love Teloynya. She, um she, my sissr in laaaww," now accentuating the words and rotating his hand to spread his fingers.

"Larry, she will always be your sister-in-law . . . no matter what." she watched him put the headphones back over his ears and resumed rocking.

Upon returning home, Norma vowed to pray for this severe situation. She kept in contact daily on the phone with the Combs kids and prayed for her hurting son. Her pen moved along on paper, writing each full thought…

"I pray for David this day. He's suffered a lot of rejection, wounded-ness and guilt. Lord, may you reach out in comfort, love and grace. Give him clear direction in what he should say and do. Bless Gabe, Beckie and Amy in their hurts and confusion. Guide and direct as they try to find the meaning and yes, bless Teona. We don't understand, but may she find acceptance, direction and peace."

Since then, she learned of her daughter-in-law's pregnancy. Child number four, Norma's eighth grandchild. The couple was going to give it another try, at least if anything for the new little one. For now, Teona was spending time at her sister's house. She needed to clear her head and think things through.

The path Norma's prayers took, reflected on the new child in Teona's tummy and asking God to bring a healthy and stable pregnancy and birth.

It was time to plan her re-union trip to Kansas. Excited and nervous to visit with people she hadn't seen for 50 years, she sat down to write up her bio required by those in charge.

"Mom you need to go and not worry about Larry so much . . . he'll survive." her children reassured her after listening to the apprehensive words.

The chronicle of Larry's behaviors was still in place. She had no listening ears or sounding board at home to discuss his devious behaviors, and she missed it terribly. The phone call that came earlier saying Larry had gotten in trouble at the latest Marc swimming party cause he walked in the bedroom when the girls were taking off their swim suits... sent her to a scream!!

"Larry you make me so mad!! Why do you do things like that? You are so sneaky! If you think I'm going to come and rescue you, you gotta another thing coming."

"I sorry!!" He said. She had heard it too many times over the years and was tempted to hang up on him.

"Well, you are grounded again and I'm going on vacation. I'm going to be gone for a while. You better mind your peas and cues!"

"Where you gong?" his voice lowered but Norma determined not to let it bother her.

I will be going on many future trips without him, He mise well get used to it! I just can't feel guilty anymore. But then again... he misses his dad tremendously. He, himself, was subject to so many periods of loneliness. It was Allen who always helped him get through those dark times. A job he did so well.

She tried to explain her future travel plans as simply as possible. "Besides Larry, you got to go on a trip with Redeemer College and Career...two times and without me. Remember?"

"Well, I be okay, mom! I be, I be fine. I get, I get over it."

She smiled and said good-bye. Oh how she needed to believe this. At least he was thinking of her this time and not himself. Sometimes this difficult man had such maturity or was it that he knew exactly what to say, when to say it. Whether he meant it or not, she would let his words sooth her guilt-ridden soul.

CHAPTER 61

PUSHING INTO LIFE

When Norma returned from Kansas, she learned that Larry's Taco Bell job had dissolved. This was the third community employment in which Larry had been let go and had to return to the workshop.

"I got fired. Ala baawmer!" (What a bummer) Larry told his mother.

"Yeah, you didn't cut the tomatoes fast enough, Larry! Do you understand that? You have to work fast, not slow." An additional reason was his increased flirtation with employees. But this wasn't the time to bring it up; she could tell that he was already hurting.

"Well, course I do! But I um, get, I get a different job, anyway."

"I'm going to come and pick you up. We can go out to eat at Furrs restaurant. Don't forget to shave now and don't dillydally, I'm on my way."

"Oh, boy!" he said enthusiastically before hanging up.

Though she enjoyed the long break from the continued hassles, she missed her son; besides, his wounded self-esteem needed some maintenance. They discussed his weekly bowling activity and afterwards stopped at the sports store to purchase new bowling attire.

Her son also benefited from Grace Community Church services each Sunday. His mother's new set of friends were caring towards him, just as much as the Redeemer people had been, but the first thing Larry noticed was the elderly part.

"They are, umm, old, umm, old people. I young."

He still viewed himself as quite a youthful man, especially with his new mustache and permed hairstyle. Highly affected by movies, he wanted to look like the latest celebrity while scouting for another "gilfrien." *Happy Days* was his favorite re-run on TV and he hoped putting on the cool Fonz persona would attract women. However, a different kind of "re-run" persisted: his refusal to wear glasses. *His donkey stubbornness is kicking in again,* Norma thought.

"I don't like glasses, um it means handicap. I don't like handicap!" Handicap was a word spoken quietly or spelled when Larry was around. If Larry heard anyone say "that word", despite explanations, he would spin into an anger mode.

"Larry, lots of people need glasses. It's okay!"

"No thanks," he moved his hand back and forth, "not me. Umm, I not wear glasses."

Trying to get his point across, he hid them and hid them well. For weeks no one could find Larry's glasses.

"Once he has his mind set on something, you can't change it! What a pistol!" Norma told her friends. "He's also supposed to be wearing hearing aides, but I'm not even going there."

Norma began to plan more trips without her son. Friends and family often reminded her that she merited the time away. Her other children would be on call for "Larry duties" and they had to assure her of this over and over.

The next big trip and one that brought plenty of nervous anticipation, was the well-planned Holy Land excursion. She woke up feeling the jitters at 4:00 a.m. on the day of departure. It was a beautiful crisp February morning. She loaded her suitcase and bag onto the shuttle, met her travel partners at the airport and boarded the jet to Israel.

Writing every day in her newly purchased 1997 notebook and clearly describing the sites before her eyes, she had to continually checked to see if her camera was still around her arm and she didn't leave it lying anywhere (she was becoming more forgetful about her belongings). Clicking it over and over, she couldn't snap fast enough to get the perfect images of the numerous artifacts around her. The evening meal conversations with her travel partners centered on deep Bible theology. Discussions of the travels of Jesus, the people surrounding His life and the comparisons of current knowledge of history throughout the New and Old Testaments, continued far into the evening. She was getting heaps of information from the tour guides and the group discussions afterwards helped cement it all in her mind. Her brain hurt. Of course, Norma wouldn't be Norma if she didn't bring her newly purchased small Radio Shack gadget to make sure she had it all on tape. As always, she often talked to her Heavenly Father in prayer and had a much deeper appreciation of His purpose on earth. In turn, it gave her a strong foundation of understanding **her** purpose. History was laid out before her eyes. Seeing, smelling and touching the very parts of the earth she had never seen, but had spent years reading about, she was anxious to delve into the scriptures again— now with a renewed spirit, more knowledge and a desire for a fuller relationship with God.

When she returned home it took a while for her to feel "human" again. The jet lag and lack of sleep had taken a toll on her body but when she was up to it, would make trips to the store dropping off rolls of film to be developed. Then, taking advantage of her new VCR, she put in her favorite movies, got comfortable on her cozy couch, and chronologically organized the pictures into the photo album. The true satisfaction came when sitting down with her grandkids and sharing the day by-day sights of this unforgettable journey.

In between vacations Norma spent as much time as she could in more church activities. She was lucky to have the attractive building just two blocks away. She busied herself with a widening circle of friends; as well as, a growing list of restaurant choices. The Tempe, Mesa, and Chandler areas were expanding more than ever! She read in the newspaper that these cities were now the fastest growing in the nation. Days passed included trying recently built and delicious buffets. She scheduled time with new acquaintances but still fellowshipping with long-time buddies, all over fabulous meals.

Frequent engagements with other widows caused a longing in her heart towards Ouida. Teona's mother had recently moved on to God's eternal presence and was no longer suffering with Arthritis and Emphysema. Oh, how she missed her. Her heart was also heavy for Shari Little. Shari's son had leukemia and when Norma hung up the phone, after several conversations, she knelt down in prayer over this solemn situation. She repeatedly asked her friends at her new church to lift this family up in prayer.

Being a nanny for the Morrison family, dealing with Larry issues and stopping by the Pomeroy's were still on the top of her agenda. Though she tried desperately to remove herself from group home troubles, the issues had become a regular inner struggle. However, her gratitude was mounting. She had more down periods to speculate on her life and rethink the bridges she had burned in years past. She hoped to mellow herself and be more conscientious of hurtful words. Each journal entry was beefed up with thanksgiving:

"Lord thank you for a comfortable condo, wonderful friends, family close by, plenty of food to eat, strength and stamina, money to travel, travel safety and mercies." The more she wrote about strengths in her life, more blessings came to mind.

Her gratefulness also carried into another arena of relationships, this time out-of-state. It was through a friend that she heard about a weeklong retreat called Ravencrest: a get-a-way for women in the Colorado Mountains. Bonnie Barrows, daughter-in-law of Cliff Barrows, was one of the leaders. Bonnie's enduring heart for hurting women drew Norma to her. Norma often spoke to others of the heavy influence and the closeness of those many females attending. The annual trip punctuated her summers. Oh, how she longed for her two daughters to come with her one day. It seemed, however, their lives were just too busy! But she was able to involve her cousin, Donna, and the two met at the location for remarkable summer days together.

Because her home was also down the street from Arizona State University, she decided to take part in a foreign exchange mentor program and befriended two college students from China. It was her job to pick the girls up in her vehicle and take them for quick errands and grocery shopping. Norma went beyond her simple job description and invited them to church picnics and gatherings. She was impressed with their utter humility and thankfulness. She introduced Chow Shen and Lee Shin Young to as many friends as she could and spent time crossing cultural boarders by discussing customs and languages. Reflecting on the words of a wise friend . . . "Christ creates unity out of diversity."

Norma found opportunities everywhere. She didn't wait for them to come to her; she sought them out and knew how to grab life by the tail! Those who knew her and watched her from the sidelines were highly influenced and impressed. Her children were glad of her new-found friends at the University, travel opportunities, frequent gatherings at her new church, small paying jobs here and there and the opportunities to volunteer where needed. She was doing things that flowed from her heart's desires and it was all right in front of her. Everything was fresh, new and exhilarating. Opportunities were continually advancing. Her family and friends watched her attack the fullness of life. Finally, Norma was taking care of Norma, people shouted. "She deserves it!"

Kaysee Dawn was born. How delightful it felt to shop at the favorite second-hand stores for pink clothes. It had been a while since Norma had purchased baby toys.

Everyone longed to hold baby Kaysee, so more trips to St. George provided extra Vacation time. The difference would be . . . having to take turns with siblings and cousins to cuddle their new addition. "She will not lack for attention, that's for sure," Norma repeated with a chuckle.

So far, Norma and Larry had attended the high school graduations of Gabe, Kelsey, Rebecca and Becky. Amber was next. Gabe's theater college major at Cedar City gave chances to attend performances and learn about Shakespeare plays. Kelsey focused on percussion and music performance at Northern Arizona University. The Combs family had recently re-located to Page, Arizona so David could expand his radio career. Beckie was using her angel-sounding singing voice for some solo performances. Rebecca was still exploring careers; so, Norma was happy to take her to job fairs and hoped to give her confidence in future pursuits. Her granddaughter had won awards for her remarkable artwork. Amber was dedicated to learning sign language and studying the hearing impaired culture. Amy was showing interest in the business world and Michael was learning computer programming. Norma was proud of her grandchildren and loved each one individually and powerfully!

CHAPTER 62
IS THIS REALLY HAPPENING?

Marc Center had changed its name again to "Mesa Arc" and continued to increase services to up to 23 homes. Some were built after the purchase of land.[24] The organization needed to expand beyond the Mesa borders.[25] The Phoenix suburban cities blended together and were now called the East Valley with a population nearing 937,638 residents. Each new group home had its own focus and specific set-up for that particular population. Some served the elderly and others cared for medically at-risk individuals.[26] The organization had even added behavioral health services operating as a subsidiary corporation. Mesa ARC doubled the number of persons served in the vocational-related services, which was in excess of 1,000 individuals per day.[27] Public law 99-457 required "states to make available a free and appropriate education for children with disabilities ages 3-5."[28] It was correct now to refer to a handicapped person as a child or person with a disability. The language focused on the person first and the disability second.

Because of her previous mastectomy Norma made sure she kept up on the doctor visits. On this particular day she went for her regular female check-up. It was a brand new year and after all the Y2K-hype and the national scare subsided, Norma was ready to continue living her life full speed ahead.

But Dr. Long was concerned and made additional appointments with her to run further tests. "You have cancer. Cancer of the uterus, Norma, and it doesn't look good. People die from this kind of cancer."

She couldn't believe what she was hearing! "Surely this cancer is in the beginning stages, I have kept up on all my female visits. We surely found it early."

"No, Norma, it actually has moved along to later stages."

"How can this be?" Dumbstruck she couldn't breathe. As she wandered to the parking lot she was dazed, confused and couldn't remember where she had parked the car. "Is this really happening?" her words tumbled out.

By chance she noticed the yellow station wagon hidden between two trucks and as she swung the door open, she crumpled into the seat. Her body felt so feeble she couldn't pull the heavy door closed. She sat a minute with her head resetting on her age-spotted arm, which lay across the steering wheel. As the water burst from her eyes, she pulled a tissue from the box on the floor and placed it under her nose.

Maybe Dr. Long was being way too callous and maybe this news was not so bad. Maybe she could beat it; maybe God was putting her to the test, just maybe. How could he say such awful words? He was so straightforward and didn't hold anything back. How can doctors be so brutal sometimes? Her thoughts and body position seemed way too familiar. Her mind raced back in time to the familiar harsh words spoken to her many years ago by another doctor. She, again, desperately desired to get a second opinion: one that would be gentle and would encourage her to beat the odds. She sat in the silence and listened to her own labored breathing; thinking of the difficult task of sending the news to her children. How would she say the words? What would she say? She felt a powerful sting in her chest from the grief her kids would feel. Larry! What about Larry? I'm the mainstay in his life.

She bargained with God inside the stillness. "You surely aren't going to take me away from Larry! He won't understand. He won't cope! Lord, I want to live. I have so much more I want to do and need to do! I've got to take care of my son. You can't take away the most important person in his life! What about my grandchildren? They need their Nena." Is it really my time God? It just can't be. I'm not ready. Life is good. Please, please, please don't hand me this. I can't take it, I don't want it! Why God? Why? Why would you do this to me? I hate sickness. Cancer, I hate this disease!"

She immediately focused on heaven and remembered hearing a recent intense description from a speaker about the possible music, the beauty, the painlessness, the utter joy, and the unimaginable life beyond what our finite minds can fathom. Her thoughts came back to earth remembering her trip to the place where God's son walked; His purpose, His reason and His mission became so real. She thought about her thankful prayer when she got out of bed just hours earlier and how this day had come to, now, such a desperate moment.

Slowly turning the key, she let the motor run before putting it into drive. She eased out onto the street slowly and cautiously. She had to. Everything seemed a blur. What was she going to do? Jumpiness was taking over her body and she wondered if she should pull over, but she was just a few blocks from home and had only one more intersection to cross. A huge jerk set her back in her seat and she suddenly realized she had hit the car in front of her. Her legs felt like wet noodles when she stepped out onto the blacktop. The damage wasn't bad and no one was hurt. The driver in the other car, at least didn't yell at her but it was obvious he was irritated; oh, how she needed help from a friend. This was when she hated being alone. She struggled to focus on the officer's countless questions when he came to take the accident report. Upon releasing her, she told herself she would take care of the insurance part later. She just needed to get home.

Guardedly driving the short distance down the street, finally, she pulled into her personal covered parking spot. Her body was trembling so she concentrated on locking her knees as she unlocked the back door. I hope I don't bump into any neighbors; she looked around and pushed the door open. Dropping her purse and keys on the table she practically ran to her bed, buried herself under the blanket and cried into her pillow. The weeping was uncontrollable as the faces of her family played in her mind. Larry! What about Larry.

CHAPTER 63

SILENT THOUGHTS

The phone rang but she didn't answer it. She couldn't! She had never noticed the brash ticking of the clock in her room before. Time slowed down. It was several hours later and on her own timing, when she brought herself to make the dreaded phone calls. She thought through the exact words she wanted to say: replaying them over and over. Now barely able to describe the doctor's diagnosis, she also told her kids of the car accident while driving home. David spent the following days praying with her over the phone, Debbie wanted to beat this curse by fighting back, and Carol was at her doorstep to keep her company.

She welcomed the network of pray-ers now established via friends and family. As people spread the word, prayers were offered up to God, even in different parts of the country as prayer chains were starting at various churches. She was continually astounded as to how many people she knew and sensed their adoration while the phone continued to ring. Her brothers and sister called frequently, letting her know how much they cared about her well-being.

Her surgery was on schedule. Family and close friends made arrangements to come visit her; they also arranged for the care afterwards. Norma tried to grasp all the love now coming her way from others and this brought an extreme sensitivity toward life. The news of getting most of the cancer, but not all, was not hopeful. It was a waiting game. She hated that she still had disease eating away inside her body.

Weeks after the surgery she was able to finally keep up a slow pace of walking, but still everything took so much more time than she had patience for. Norma's strong desire for that blessed energy gave way to fear that it was gone forever. Bev Little stopped in often to take her to doctor appointments. Carol took her to her dentist appointments and picked up any needed medications. The Morrison family was available for transportation and several Grace Community members brought her groceries.

Understanding that his mom was sick, (but something she would get over)

Larry called a few times. "Mom, I want to, umm, want to help you," he would say. "I want to, um, to come over. I like to help. You know um, I like helping, that's all."

"Well, get Tina to drive you over here. You could vacuum for me."

"You betcha ya."

During the last few years she had become very close with some of Larry's group home managers.

She figured she needed to reach out to these people in a different way: making herself available more as a friend in assisting and educate, without judgment. She had previously spent hours talking with Donna (a group home employee) and even bought her furniture pieces to assist in furnishing her new apartment. Besides Donna, Tina and Doug were among Norma's favorite new Marc members. The problem was, however, that Tina was a beautiful and vibrant young lady. Larry often obsessed over her, always questioning where she was, even on her days off. He didn't want to go anywhere in the van unless Tina was driving. He had his favorites too!

Determined to travel to Flagstaff and be in attendance of Amber's high school graduation, Norma was able to climb the steps in the NAU dome and proudly listen to her granddaughter's small speech at the ceremony. But it was when she returned home that she could feel how much the trip had taken a toll on her body. Reality began to hit.

The next planned event was her 75th birthday. The entire crew, kids and grandkids, arrived to sit next to her in the pew at the Sunday morning church service. Proudly showcasing her offspring, she introduced her family to church friends and the camera rolled to capture the moment. Everyone gathered at the quaint and popular Landmark restaurant in Mesa, for lunch. This fancy place had to accommodate the large crowd. Gifts and cards were passed down the long table for all to see. Even unknown diners sitting nearby watched the festive party. But the thoughts on the young minds and those who loved her was . . . is this her last birthday? Smiles were forced while thinking of the worse.

For several nights she woke and slowly paced by her bed, her head pounding. She screamed out! The nights were the most severe part of the day and she dreaded the sun going down. Though she felt God's presence in the wee hours of the night, she listened to her tapes of worship music and grasped at anything for rest.

So many friends wanted to give advice and tell **their** stories, those who became cancer free from taking certain vitamins, drinking protein shakes and carrot juice, injecting vitamin C, and eating specific foods. Someone handed her videos of a knowledgeable doctor who beat her own sickness through healthy avenues. She and Debbie watched them together, listening for tips on what to do, but Norma wondered if it was too late. Her Flagstaff daughter was now taking several trips down the mountain to be with her mother on weekends and promised to be around most of the summer, once school was out. Carol was minutes away. Between her daughters and friends, Norma was able to run her normal errands and get to her frequently scheduled doctor appointments. Everything was becoming such a task, even the simple things like opening a jar of jam. Asking for help was against her nature. The helplessness was humbling.

Norma questioned again as to why all the years of healthy eating, exercising and faithful vitamin intake weren't paying off. She often negotiated with God and begged for more years. I want to do so much more on earth. She made a habit of giving friends, Christian or not, tapes of Bible scholars, teachers and encouraging speakers. It was her unique calling; she called it her "tape ministry." God had used these people in her life to mold her into a godly woman and yet even at the age of 75 knew she had so much more in her character to work on.

What about watching my grandchildren get married and have children! She questioned

God. She was getting angry and knew resentment and fear were taking root. That's why Dr. Long subscribed antidepressant and anti anxiety medications. They helped calm her fears but she also had to embrace many soothing words that came from friends. She wrote them in the corners of her well-worn Bible. "Iron crown of suffering precedes the golden crown of glory" and "We need not be victims because God is the victor." Large chunks of the day were dedicated to reading from Proverbs and the Psalms. "The spirit of man is the candle of the Lord." Proverbs 20:27. "Above all else, guard your heart, for it is the wellspring of life." Proverbs 2.

She opened her journal and read an entry from just a few months ago.

"Ten years ago today I had my mastectomy. Thank you, Lord, that you spared me from radiation, chemo, further suffering with cancer. Thank you for my health, ambition and energy to do so much during the day, the rhythm to rest and work, run errands, correspondence, movies, enjoy solitude, prayer and important programs on the radio."

These words were now returning to her void this day and she was helpless! What now? The pain, the medicine, the advice and conversations, the disturbed nights: it all produced tension and nervousness. Some days she had thoughts of just sleeping this nightmare away.

Debbie arrived and on the list of things to do was clean her mom's closet. Norma lay on her bed watching her daughter organize. Debbie pulled out one of her mom's outfits on a hanger, held it up and said, "Keep or save?"

Norma was in a self-absorbed slump. "I don't think I'll be alive to wear that one, it's my Christmas Eve church outfit. Toss it!

"Oh, Mom, don't talk like that. Of course you'll be around" was her daughter's reply.

Seconds of silence took over the room!

CHAPTER 64

NO WORDS- 2000

The children initiated discussions toward seeking extra help for their mother during daylight hours. They were on a mission to finding sufficient funds to cover in-home services. It was inevitable. Because of the many medications and medical attention she needed, her care was now reaching beyond the limited knowledge of her friends and family.

They had received information from the hospital people during her stay and the time had come to revisit the stack of papers. Now so grateful their mother was always thinking ahead, for she had purchased cancer insurance years prior. However, Norma was displeased with the services brought to her home and after she basically fired the third nurse, her children began the daunting task of finding an assistive living facility. It was not easy for her family to make such decisions while watching what used to be this go-getter woman weakens. Everyone could see that it was even more difficult for Norma to move from her independent self-sufficiency to a constant dependency on others.

On numerous occasions, David and Debbie traveled to connect with Carol in search for the best living situation for their mom, one that would make her happy. This took time, but once they found it, they organized another moving day. First, however, they had to convince their mother that it just had to be done. She settled again in a pleasant little set-up: her own apartment, just a few steps away from a dining hall and a hot meal. Those in charge would make sure she would get her meds on time and she could immediately push a button in case of an emergency. It was a relief to everyone. David offered to sleep on the couch the first night in her new place and to keep her company. All was glad he was present when they heard Norma fell while walking to her bathroom during the night hours.

Watching Larry trying to figure it all out was tough. He did not comprehend the necessity of the recent move but seemed to grasp the idea that his mother was not getting better. Not only was her physical being looking unlike the mom he knew but her personality was changing as well. Larry was using few words while spending time with her. Everyone attempted his or her own way of comforting him but he was not saying much or doing much. The long mourning process of this family was intricate and they desperately tried to keep things light for the sake of their brother, whose understanding was limited.

Norma's hands were shaking. She had already given up her writing and focused on only simple things she could do, most of it while laying on her bed. Visits from concerned and sorrowful friends were ongoing but Norma tired easily and she had to limit the length of her conversations.

Now only a few more months and already the last move had to take place, one to a hospice house. "We focus on comfort, not cure, and your mother will be heavily drugged but comfortable," the caring nurses told the kids.

"How long do you think she has?"

"We don't know. Could be months, weeks or days. It's hard to tell." The knowledgeable and merciful medical people went on to explain what to expect when visiting. "Her hearing, eyesight, and her voice will decline. And, she will be disoriented."

When Debbie and Jeff drove down from Flagstaff, they had to stop by her old apartment to pick up a few last items. Debbie opened the sliding glass door and ran into her mother's bedroom. She flung herself on the unmade bed, the outline and indention of Norma's body still fresh in the sheets. She wept out loud and could smell her mom's lotion. Crunching the blankets to her face, she screamed at God!

Visits happened every day at the hospice house. Friends came by to pay final last respects. Linda Little came holding a paper with words she wrote of the amazing influence Norma had made in her life. She began to read it but couldn't continue. Her brother sat next to her and took over to finish reading the heartfelt thoughts. It stated a thank you for being her second mom and showing what a loving mom looked like. "You always made me feel welcome in your home and some of my best childhood memories include you, always happy!" David L continued to read. "You were good at putting us kids to work, doing dishes or constructive play and of course included Larry in everything."

Larry viewed someone else feeding and taking care of his mother. Did he understand what was truly happening? It was November the 6th. Everyone knew when Larry's birthday was for he never held back giving this information to anyone.

"My birthday, um, Nobemeber the siss," he announced to the nurses when walking into the building.

(Over the years, since the time he was very young, Larry's memory of numerous birthday dates was unexplainable. He often reminded his family and others, weeks in advance of a certain someone's birthday coming up. The fact that he had an uncanny way of retaining this information year after year became his trademark. He could tell you the month and the day of birthdays from a long list of people. It was remarkable and often took friends and family by surprise. The best part was that it became a blessing to many for it was Larry's way of saying you're important to me).

"Well, Happy Birthday, Larry. You want to visit your mom?"

"You betcha!" he answered and hugged the pretty one.

Norma couldn't speak but motioned for Larry to come over to her bed. He walked over and stood by her head. She pulled on his shirt and he bent his ear toward her. She whispered as loud as she could, and in barely audible words sang "Haaaaapy Biiiiiirthday to you, Haaaapy Biiiiiirthday to you…"

"Thank you, Mom!" he looked into her eyes.

Tears flowed heavily from those watching in the room. This unique relationship was like no other. Their bond was out of this world and would never be replaced or replicated.

A few days' later a hospice nurse called the children to make preparations. Debbie had to keep her eyes closed while reclining in the passenger seat holding a pillow to her face while Jeff drove. The pain was cutting.

The cell phone rang. "Debbie, this is Rollie! Carol and I are here and . . . well, she's already gone." Debbie threw the phone across the car seat and burst into tears.

When they arrived, her mother's body had not yet been removed from the room. Debbie asked for time alone and lay next to her mother. David came shortly after. No one could speak. There were no words! Heads were low. Family members hugged in the hallway. Larry cried into the shoulder of his brother!

She was gone! She was really gone! This strong, astounding, remarkable and vivacious woman was gone. Feeling a deep sadness, yet honored (for they knew they were the lucky ones— privileged enough to call her mom). It just can't be! They said it over and over. Even knowing that this was inevitable, it was difficult for her children, standing outside her room, to truly fathom what just happened.

CHAPTER 65

AHEAD OF HER TIME

Phone calls once again permeated the phone lines. Everyone's question was the same, "How's Larry holding up?" He seemed to continue to take comfort in being with his siblings and visiting with friends . . . at least for the time being but often his face was long and sober and hugs from others were the only thing that could help, even if there was nothing to say.

It had only been ten short years since the last funeral was orchestrated, but this one would be conducted at Tempe's Grace Community. The children were appreciative for such a large auditorium because they knew they would need the space for their mother's many friends, ones they knew about and some they didn't. They split the task of phone calls to rally her favorite people. It would be important to have speakers representing each facet of her life.

A slew of pictures were gathered for the video and several meetings were planned at the funeral home to coordinate all aspects of the service, discuss finances and finalized arrangements. Everyone was grateful to see their two uncles and cousin travel miles as support for the children and could still hear the echo of their mother's voice referring to her youngest brother as 'little Donny.' She had often spoken endearing words of all her siblings and now those words were loud and clear. Larry hugged Uncle Don over and over.

Cards and flowers were coming quickly and by the bulk. Flowers lined the front stage and the piano was in place, microphones were available for those who wanted to use the opportunity, and the side screens were ready for the movie about Norma's life. Music played in the background. During the ceremony several people shared through their tears about the influence Norma had had on their lives. Her favorite songs were sung. All the children and grandchildren shared in the service; Kelsey played a song on the piano, church members spoke, along with neighbors, co-workers, and her Methodist group. Norma's life and influence had tapped into so many human beings and settings.

Randy Gray (still CEO of Marc), having searched the archives, gave a beautiful account of her involvement. "The contribution of time, blood, sweat and tears into the Marc organization which began with an idea and nine founding families way back in the fifties. Norma was ahead of her time. She petitioned and rallied and became a voice for those who couldn't articulate. She practically begged the public schools to allow disabled students to enter the same schools as the neighborhood children and siblings. Though she was rejected, she didn't give up." Randy continued by saying how "she rolled up her sleeves, tackled any task and gave of her time and energy when-ever and where-ever she saw the need."

(Larry always made it known that Randy was one of his favorites! "I, um, I known you a long time." he repeated)

A woman the family had never seen before stood up to the mic and said she was a truck driver. Norma had given her several tapes to listen to while on the road and because of Norma she was able to have church right in the cab of her truck. The tears began when it was confirmed once again that her influence was beyond their immediate family and friends.

There were some who came from the two Phoenix schools where she had been employed as social worker. A young lady told the family that Norma had changed her life when she made arrangements for the removal of a large and ugly mark on her face. "I had such a low self-esteem because of that birthmark and was teased continually by other kids, yet Mrs. Combs found the medical monies for surgery when I was just 12 years old. It truly transformed my life!" The children began to tear-up not knowing or ever hearing this story and realizing that there were probably many more out there like it. They reflected on the times she would tell them the perks of her job, one being the task of taking school kids who were shoe-less to buy brand new footwear before giving them a ride to school. She often expressed how she loved to see the smiles on their faces.

It was good to see all the Little family in attendance and even long time friend Nancy Little who was still viewed as that second mom the kids admired while growing up.

The children were reminded of the years and years of support from so many in this lovely setting.

The unique ways that this daughter, sister, wife of 47 years, mother of four and very involved grandmother to eight, organizer, prayer soldier, strong believer in Christ, brief cub scout leader, camp counselor, traveler, co-founder, board member, communicator and parent coordinator to a multi-million dollar non-profit organization, social worker to those in poverty for 18 years, activist for children, relief house-parent for Sunshine acres children's home, church member and historian, scrapbook and photograph arranger, nanny to other families, mentor to two foreign exchange students, traveler, coordinator of various groups and outings, teacher to children and adults but most of all an enduring advocate for her son with lots of unusual needs. . . ran deep. Her life was witnessed this day by the words spoken and heard from the masses of respectful people dressed in black. Numerous tears were shed as they tried to face the fact that her hard work on this earth was really finished!

Coach Carl Heath ended the service through spiritual words of wisdom: wrapping it all up and putting it into prospective as to our true purpose in this life. Norma's life was an excellent example of that.

Now . . . who would David talk to and pray with when circumstances were tough? Who would Carol call for an opinion or needed assistance? Who would Debbie talk to about the public schools, children and their behavior? Her grandchildren would miss the frequent discussions about life and people, the picnics, running errands and shopping, church activities, camps, dinners out and homemade meals, and relying on her photographs for life memories. What would Larry do with his time? He had no mother. He had no father. Who would rescue him when he needed a break from the flow of people in charge? He relied on her roots and stability in his fanatical life. She was his rock. It was going to be unbearable for all, but especially for Larry.

Thoughts and comments circulated throughout the building while everyone slowly exited. The lack of understanding and depression that Larry would most likely experience was on everyone's mind. It was hard enough losing his best friend and dad but now the person who had always been there to listen, knew every aspect of his life **and** was involved in every detail . . .was also gone. Her listening forced action, the actions caused change and the change benefited the son God had given her. But, beyond her own flesh and blood, so many others in this community were affected by the enormous efforts of this steadfast and unwavering woman.

The race was finished only with her physical body but would continue with the clear legacy she was leaving. For now the petitions to God would be for the large dose of emotional stability and support that Larry would need for the rest of **his** time on this earth.

CHAPTER 66

REALITY

Now the four children were faced with the overwhelming task of filing through their mother's belongings . . . piece by piece. This work was too much for Larry, so they tried to get him back to his daily schedule. Maybe his regular routine would help retain some normalcy in his life. The phone calls and visits were still coming but it was time to refocus, think rationally and attend to her estate. They needed to find Larry's guardianship papers among the boxes of organized files, diaries and photo albums. Norma had assured the children that they would be Larry's guardians upon her passing and that it was all in writing.

It seemed they knew about "healthy mourning" from previous experience and Carol remembered the many tips she had received from the grieving class she and her mother attended after Allen passed. They tried to get Larry to remember the good things about his mother and to talk about it without focusing too much on the sad fact that he would not see her again.

"I'm afraid, I'm afraid to die. It's dark in there." Larry's head was down.

"What do you mean, Larry?" Debbie said.

"I don't like dark! I,um, I,um afraid of dark." Debbie looked into his serious blue eyes trying to fathom his perception of death.

"He thinks you spend the rest of your life in a dark coffin and are aware of it." She said to David and Carol.

They attempted to explain that their mother was peacefully sleeping and that her spirit is in heaven. They found the explanation was needed over and over. But to how much he was getting, no one knew.

"I afraid! I don't like dark. I don't like die!" He tried to share his feelings. The depression was profound and talk of antidepressant medication, at least for a short time, was discussed.

His siblings saw him teetering on the edge and began to make plans for who and when they would pick him up from the group home. "We need to be close by. He's going to need us more than ever now!" They agreed.

Because Carol lived in the same town, she could easily drive over and get him on Sundays for church and then out for dinner afterwards. "That's what mom always did! Lets keep that routine in place!"

"He can visit Flagstaff every month for a 3 to 4 day vacation, and the group home people could even put him on a bus to make the trip," Debbie explained. "I will be right there to get him off the bus on my end. We can make sure the bus driver knows that he is to sit in the seat directly behind him so the driver can keep an eye on him. The trick would be to make sure he has all his belongings even down to his C-pap machine. The need to do a lot of communicating with Marc employees, just like mom did, will be critical. It would tragic if he lost some of his expensive and needed stuff that mom worked hard to get for him.

"Or, it would be bad if he got off the bus at the wrong stop." Carol added.

David lived the furthest away but since the family now lived in Page, Arizona, he would only be four hours in distance and could be available to help with holidays. Everyone agreed that it should be mandatory that they all attend the six-month review meetings, share in the decision-making and be constantly involved in Larry's life. Norma had given each of her kids, a few years back, the tedious and promised Larry-history folder that she spent hours to comply. This will now be exactly what is needed in order to help collaborate with others and to assist in making the same tough decisions they often watched their mom "stew over." Debbie would handle all the paper work by becoming Larry's authorized payee and take care of his finances. (Norma had previously trained her on this process). Everyone would call him at the group home as much as possible.

"It will help him understand that we are still here for him, and always will be. He needs that assurance." They conversed.

No guardianship paper was found among her belongings, but they did stumble upon a beautiful prayer written in 1998. The children read . . .

Larry is 45 years old today. Thank you, God, for his life, his determination and frustrations to _not_ be handicapped. For his love and loyalty to his family, for the many adjustments he's had to make in so many different living situations, for the hundreds of staff personnel that he's had to get used and submit to. For the loss of his dad, for the two worlds he lives in, disabled and normal. Not being able to marry and have children and to accept that he can't be independent, drive or live where he wants, for his frustration over the opposite sex. For all the things he has taught us: compassion, sensitivity, patience and learning to sacrifice, stretching ourselves on his behalf, and to help him find the best quality of life! May God Bless Larry!

Carol drove to the group home to get her brother for the arranged church and lunch engagement. Afterwards, they stopped to place flowers at the gravesite. Larry walked directly to the two headstones after exiting the car. Standing on the ground between his mom and dad's graves, he bowed his head and fell to his knees. Carol watched him pound the ground with his fist and cry uncontrollably!

CHAPTER 67

VISUAL DEPRESSION

"I just got a phone call from Marc Center " Carol was concerned as she spoke to David and Debbie, "Larry walked over there last evening and threw rocks at the windows of the Marc building. He broke several!"

Debbie quickly called and made arrangements to repair the broken windows out of Larry's money. But, this would be mild compared to the next act; a few days later another phone call came.

"We can't find Larry. He was working at the workshop and walked away during the lunch break! No one can find him. We've called the police and they're now checking the streets."

Debbie was in the middle of teaching her class and swiftly called for a substitute. Time was of the essence. She had to get down to the valley ASAP. David made phone calls from his destination and was getting ready to do the same. Hours went by and still no Larry.

"Debbie, I have channel 10 news here and they're ready to set up a satellite in the yard of the group home." It was Shari Little on the phone and she was doing everything she could for the hunt. "Getting his picture on TV could definitely help. Someone might spot him." She expressed through a calming voice.

"I'm on my way and thanks so much, Shari." Debbie hung up. Knots were tightening in her stomach. She and Carol were talking to Marc staff every few minutes. Everyone felt a common helplessness. Larry was capable of anything and now holding of breath and preparing quick actions was all one could do.

"Please, God, let nothing terrible or serious come out of this." Was the prayer on many lips.

"I just don't understand how he could have gotten very far. He walks so slowly. We can't find him anywhere! There are lots of people out looking for him now. The police have scanned every major street in Mesa. Nothing!" was the reply of employees.

Then it happened!

"A policeman spotted him inside Sky Harbor airport in Phoenix. Larry told him he was hungry and the officer was buying him a hamburger when he heard the description on his radio."

"What?" everyone said. "How in the world did he get to the airport? He's sitting there eating a hamburger and French fries while we run around frantic? Carol said.

"Don't forget the diet soda. . . so he can get skinny!" David laughed. "He got on a bus, said he was going to Flagstaff and Page, said 'He wanted to be with his family- that's all!' David imitated his brother. "Apparently he had enough change on him for the shuttle bus. He knew what he was doing, alright!"

"But the airport, really? I don't get that!" Debbie questioned.

"He said he could fly to Page or Flagstaff- I don't know. He had it in his poody-brain that he could get on a plane to get there."

"I just wanta be with my family." Larry said over and over and cocked his head stressing the word **family**.

"Whew!" the masses of frantic people involved in this endeavor, let out a sigh of relief. However, this episode confirmed the necessity of acting upon the anti-depressants idea or other similar situations might take place without such a happy ending.

"I'll come and get him after his doctor appointment and bring him to Flagstaff. He can hang out here for a while." Debbie said.

Carol vowed to take him to the weekly grief support group held at her church. "He might just get something out of it. Who knows? It's worth a try." She said.

238

CHAPTER 68

ACTOR

The three siblings mulled over the missing guardianship papers mystery. Several three-way calling sessions in search of an attorney started events down a new path. They were blessed to find Mr. Causey. He said he would help in any way and cautioned them that a court session was inevitable. They did find papers of guardianship but there was an indication the state would be taking over Larry's affairs! It was perplexing to all.

"This is not right. Something is not right!" David, Debbie and Carol brought the paper work to Mr. Causey's office. "We know our mother wanted all of us to be his guardian for she told us that many times, and yet the last several months of her life she appeared confused about a lot of things, so we don't know what this is about. We have gone through everything and this is all we have."

Mr. Causey's assurance of the next several steps was calming. He stayed with the family every inch of the way and brought them through the system. All three would be Larry's guardians. The final part would be the court hearing.

"We are going to court, Larry. You like court!"

"I like, ummm, I like court," he said.

Larry was game to be a part of anything that looked like Hollywood's court cases on TV. He watched those shows frequently and couldn't wait to play the part, just like a movie star. Everyone would meet at the courthouse in downtown Phoenix.

"Boy, if mom saw how Larry was dressed, she'd be furious!" Debbie said when looking at her brother walking down the long hallway towards them.

They were in a prestigious downtown skyscraper. This soon to be up-coming event was highly significant. A group home employee they had never seen before walked beside Larry. It was obvious he didn't care much about Larry's appearance. Larry's hair was a mess; he was unshaved, had on tattered jeans and wore an over-sized t-shirt.

"Some things never change," Carol said.

"Mom would be saying 'goooood night!' right about now." David imitated the Norma-look and swatted the air with his hand.

"She also would be saying that he looks like he just rolled out of bed." Debbie squawked.

"That's because he does." Carol laughed.

"We are going to court, Larry, you should be dressed up!" Debbie told him.

Jeff quickly took him in the bathroom and tried his best at wetting down the pieces of hair sticking straight up. David hurriedly re-looped his brother's belt and tucked in his shirt. They were due inside the high-status room in a matter of minutes.

The judge called Larry up to the front. Larry's face remained serious as she talked to him.

"Larry, do you realize how much your brother and two sisters love you?"

"Yes, I do!" he answered like a paid actor.

"Do you realize how lucky you are, Larry? They want to be your guardians and help take care of you?"

"I understand." The answer, spoken clearly and concisely, came as if scripted.

His siblings watched him while cracking a smile. They knew he was walking on clouds and soaking in every bit of attention while looking out at the audience. In his mind, by being on TV, he was getting 5 minutes of fame. The only thing missing were the TV cameras; but, then again, who noticed?

It was a done deal! Guardianship was now sealed on paper! Each guardian was given a small card to keep for easy access. In celebration, afterwards they all went out for lunch at a nice Phoenix restaurant. This very out-of-the-ordinary celebration deserved an out-of-the-ordinary reward.

"Look, Lar! I have a guardianship card." David pulled it from his wallet. "You don't listen to me, then I'll whip out this guardianship card and you'll HAVE to listen!" He slapped Larry's shoulder with the flick of the wrist, added a chuckle and gave him the Combs' family sign. David didn't take the place of his dad's funny teasing but was in second place in Larry's eyes.

"Yeah riiiight! Some, umm some guardian, you are!" Larry hit his brother back and returned the look"

"Yeah, well I know you like a book, so you better yisten." David responded. Everyone laughed.

Still, it was the same humor—the glue that had held this family together since 1953. It felt good to laugh and finally see a smile on Larry's face!

CHAPTER 69

ENDING....

The Combs children and grandchildren continued to hear about the astonishing influence Norma had on others for months and even years to come. Several family members looked forward to and traveled miles on a Saturday afternoon to the dedication of a brand new Marc Center (Mesa ARC) building. This cutting edge and beautiful three-story architectural structure was constructed and standing on the Country Club Street. The goals and vision of the nine founding families were articulated from various speakers. Then, many other heroes' were named who contributed and continued the legacy; ones who had given to the cause, either through time, money or both, and helped make it what it stood for in the present.

A well-known Arizona politician was the guest speaker that day and a choir of children sang like angels. Food was provided as the public strolled through the large rooms, examining the brand new furniture, painted walls, statues, tiled floors and high-class elevator.

Marc Center completed its greatest growth spurt in history, expanding Behavioral Health programs in the areas of adolescent services, community living, vocational training/placement and an outpatient clinic. Since 1980, Marc Center had increased its operating budget from $1 million to $18.2 million to accommodate the increased number of people served from 145 to 2,100.[29]

Pictures were taken of Carol and Debbie in front of the Norma and Allen Combs plaque in a downstairs room. An anonymous donation of ten thousand dollars was given in Norma's name and a room was dedicated in her honor, as was all nine families.

The Comb's kids were indebted!

Norma Lee Harrold Combs . . . A trailblazer!
She embodied self-discipline, assertiveness and a tender heart. She was a true campaigner for her son and took her mission seriously. She didn't stop there for she widened the path for many others. She lived life with passion and the world stepped aside for this vivacious woman of God and of heavy conviction. She stood for change!
Sometimes she didn't go about it in the smoothest of ways but many times did! Either way she was

able to get others to listen and could accomplish more than most in a lifetime. God certainly knew what he was doing when she was handed that tightly wrapped hospital blanket bundle holding Larry Allen Combs on November 6, 1953. It was in a small Cheyenne, Wyoming hospital that Norma Combs' life would change forever! This was God's plan. She influenced many in various capacities and all would be affected!

Norma Lee....
Normally, most wouldn't conquer life in such an extraordinary way!!

ENDNOTES

1. Satterfield, Rick. "Temples of The Church of Jesus Christ of Latter-Day Saints." Mesa Arizona Temple. 1998-2017. www.ldschurchtemples.com

2. "History of Mesa." Mesa Historical Museum, accessed June 2017, www.valleyhistoryinc.com

3. "Traditional and Ecumenical," Apostles Creed, accessed May 2017. http://www.umc.org

4. "History of Mesa," Mesa Historical Museum, accessed May 2, 2017, http://www.valleyhistoryinc.com

5. "Marc's Founding Families," Marc Community Resources, Marc Cr Timeline. Accessed, May 2017, http://wwwmarccr.com/about/marc-cr-history-timeline

6. "Brown vs. Board of Education," access May 2017, https://en.wikipedia.org/wiki/Brown v Board of Education

7. "First Permanent Location," Marc Community Resources, Marc Cr Timeline. accessed May 2017, http://wwwmarccr.com/about/marc-cr-history-timeline

8. "Headstart Program-History," access May 2017, http:sites.google.com

9. "Our Story," Valleylife.org/index.php/about_us, access May 2017

10. "Beauty Salon Massacre," Mara Bovsun by Special to the News, accessed May 2017,

11. "Mesa Public Schools Provides Educational Training," Marc Community Resources Inc., Marc Cr Timeline, accessed May, 2017, http:// www marccr.com/about/marc-cr-history-timeline/

12. "What is Down Syndrome? History, Causes and Characteristics," accessed May 2017, http://www. downsydrome.about.com

13. "Mongoloid," from Wikipedia, the free encyclopedia, accessed May 2017, https://en.wikipedia.org/wiki/mongoloid.

14. Norman, Larry. "Why Should the Devil Have all the Good Music?" *Only Visiting This Planet.*

15. "Name Changed to Marc School for the Handicapped," Marc Community Resources Inc., Marc Cr Timeline, accessed May, 2017, http:// www marccr.com/about/marc-cr-history-timeline/

16. "Vocational Program Established for Adults," Marc Community Resources, Marc Cr Timeline, accessed May 2017, http://wwwmarccr.com/about/marc-cr-history-timeline

17. "Major Reorganization, "Marc Community Resources, Marc Cr Timeline, accessed May 2017, http://wwwmarccr.com/about/marc-cr-history-timeline.

18. "Education for All Handicapped Children Act," accessed May 2017, http://wikipedia.org/wiki/Education_for_All_Handicapped_Children_Act.

19. "First Residential Group home Opened," Marc Community Resources, Marc Cr Timeline. accessed May 2017, http://wwwmarccr.com/about/marc-cr-history-timeline

20. "Name Change," Marc Community Resources, Marc Cr Timeline. accessed May 2017, http://wwwmarccr.com/about/marc-cr-history-timeline

21. "Marc Center and Mesa Arc focus on a Dual Role" Marc Community Resources, Marc Cr Timeline. accessed May 2017, http://wwwmarccr.com/about/marc-cr-history-timeline

22. "Marc Center Awarded Three-year Accreditation by CARF" Marc Community Resources, Marc Cr Timeline, accessed May 2017, http://wwwmarccr.com/about/marc-cr-history-timeline

23   "Marc Center Purchases New Properties." Marc Community Resources, Marc Cr Timeline. accessed May 2017, http://wwwmarccr.com/about/marc-cr-history-timeline

24   Mesa ARC officially changed it's name to "Mesa Arc," Marc Community Resources, Marc Cr Timeline, accessed June 2017, http://wwwmarccr.com/about/marc-cr-history-timeline

25   Satellite Vocational Program Opened, Marc Community Resources, Marc Cr Timeline, accessed June 2017, http://wwwmarccr.com/about/marc-cr-history-timeline

26   Marc Behavioral Health Services Began Operation Subsidiary Corporation, Marc Community Resources, Marc Cr Timeline, accessed June 2017, http://wwwmarccr.com/about/marc-cr-history

27   Marc Center Doubles Number of Persons Served, Marc Community Resources, Marc Cr Timeline, accessed June 2017, http://wwwmarccer.com/about/marc-cr-history-timeline

28   "Public Law 99-457, from Wikipedia, the free encyclopedia, accessed May 2107 https en.wikipedia.org/wiki/Mongoloid

29   "Marc Center completes its Greatest Growth Spurt in History." Marc Community Resources, Marc Cr Timeline, accessed June 2017, http://wwwmarccr.com/about/marc-cr-history-timeline

CPSIA information can be obtained
at www.ICGtesting.com
Printed in the USA
LVHW01s1527041018
592373LV00001B/1/P

9 781489 7183